W9-ANH-881

Sunset WESTERN GARDEN BOOK OF LANDSCAPING

THE COMPLETE GUIDE TO DESIGNING

BEAUTIFUL PATHS, PATIOS, PLANTINGS & MORE

Edited by **Kathleen Norris Brenzel**

CONTENTS

Living Outdoors

"YOUR GARDEN should seduce you to the outdoors," says Jamie Durie, the Australian-born landscape designer, environmentalist, author, and TV star. "It should be comfortable—as though you'd lifted up several rooms in the house and moved them outside." A dash of decadence, luxury, and resort-style glamour doesn't hurt, either, he says.

I think about this whenever I receive emails from *Sunset* readers, sharing details of their own backyards. One of my favorites starts out: "My boyfriend plays the cello. He wanted a tranquil garden to view from his deck while he plays." The photo attached to the email showed a barefoot, jeans-and-shirt-clad guy perched on a deck chair off the back of the house, playing his cello to a verdant patch of green, lost in a moment of pure bliss. Other readers share different triumphs: The mom and daughter who turned a patio into a cantina, with a striped serape for a tablecloth, softly glowing lanterns, and a blazing chiminea. Newlyweds who built a bamboo tiki bar on their patio, then strung up lights so they could dance there "under the stars." A DIY dad who built his own pizza oven just for the fun of it. And a lucky few, living on the edge of wildland, who chose to forgo a garden altogether and let nature lap at the back door. Clearly, gardens around the West are as different as their owners—each innovative in its own way. But no matter what the style, "connection to nature is key," says landscape architect Jeffrey Gordon Smith, whose work appears in this book. "A garden is the Zen place that feeds your soul."

It's also a place to entertain friends, play, dine, nap, or celebrate the beauty of a community of plants. On the following pages, you'll find inspiring ideas from gardens around the West. You'll also find tips for sustainable gardening—a loose thread that runs throughout this book—because the need for it has never been greater. (Find more about earth-friendly gardening on the next two pages.)

My own garden is mostly a wildlife crash pad, filled with native plants. Seductive? Sure. Late in the day when the sun bathes the tops of tall redwoods in a rosy glow and hummingbirds dart through the penstemons, I can almost hear a cello play.

—Kathleen Norris Brenzel, *Sunset* Garden Editor

Tomorrow's Garden

BACK IN THE 1940s, before the postwar boom ignited the West's population growth and ushered in everything from surf songs to space shuttles, an article in *Sunset* magazine unveiled a new, revolutionary kind of garden that pushed aside the "lawn-and-hedge" model of previous generations. Pioneering landscape architect Thomas Church led the charge; the article showed one of his gardens, with places for dining and for play. A growing group of homeowners, the article said, "are not only willing to forget tradition but anxious for new values."

Today, Westerners continue to add the latest features for outdoor living, from wood-burning ovens and lap pools to yoga decks and skateboard ramps. At the same time, we are addressing some pretty steep challenges. Lots are smaller, yet bigger houses are crowding whatever outdoor living space remains. Our water supplies are limited, while a growing population is outpacing those supplies. Housing developments continue to creep into wildlands where fire danger is high. And resources are dwindling worldwide.

Surprisingly, these new challenges have not put a lid on the beauty and pleasures of our gardens. Instead, they have sparked a new golden age of landscape design, centered around sustainability. The Sustainable Sites Initiative, created by the American Society of Landscape Architects, along with the Lady Bird Johnson Wildflower Center at the University of Texas and the United States Botanic Garden, now provides guidelines for mindful use of water, soil, and other limited resources that apply to landscapes of all sizes, from home gardens to parks and public spaces.

The evolving garden A 1950s-era garden *(inset, far left)* in Southern California, designed by landscape architect Frederick M. Lang. A garden in Sunnyvale, California *(center)*, with permeable paving and a fringe of kangaroo paws. **DESIGN:** Bernard Trainor. A native sedge lawn *(Carex praegracilis)* and a fountain made from a jet engine cowling *(above)* soften the courtyard at the Wing House in Malibu, California, built entirely of recycled parts from a 747 jetliner. **ARCHITECT:** David Hertz. **GARDEN DESIGN:** Aaron Landworth.

How will Western gardens reflect this shift in landscape priorities toward sustainability? They already do. Modern gardens are filled with eye-catching plantings and family activity areas that take full advantage of the West's benign climates. Many are also models of sustainable landscape design, helping to protect the environment for future generations by thoughtful use of resources.

Water-consuming lawns are being replaced by drought-resistant plants and more efficient irrigation systems. Small fountains and shallow reflecting ponds create a sense of coolness and calm, while using water sparingly.

Tough plants that need little water, fertilizer, or pest control are becoming more popular. Native flora is gaining in popularity as well, with improved varieties that are better suited to garden conditions now more available. Less than a generation ago, you'd likely encounter California fuchsia *(Zauschneria californica)* only in High Sierra passes, its vivid scarlet patches glowing against gray granite. Now, at your neighborhood nursery, you can shop for improved varieties such as 'Ghostly Red', an easy-care landscape stalwart.

Sustainable gardens are making smart use of Earth-friendly materials. Instead of lumber from our diminishing forests, we can choose from sustainably harvested woods, recycled woods, or composite wood products for decks and other landscape projects. And there's local stone for paving and walls, as well as mulches made from recycled materials. Smaller lots are using shrinking spaces more efficiently, with edibles in the front yard or on the rooftop, or flowers on walls.

What this sustainable design revolution shows us, more than anything else, is that regionally appropriate gardens can be both beautiful and livable. Which makes us wonder why we ever tried to force rhododendrons or acres of lawn into inland Southern California in the first place!

A while back, I replaced water-guzzling roses with *Ceanothus* 'Ray Hartman'. A few springs later, every bee within five miles—dozens of different species desperate for their native diet—started showing up among the cloud of blue blossoms. This, just a few feet from my pizza oven and outdoor grill. It's another example of what *Sunset* talked about in the 1940s—creating a garden to suit your family's interests, while making the most of the West's climate, topography, and natural world.

—William R. Marken
Fellow, American Society of Landscape Architects

GARDENS

A garden reflects your interests as well as your needs. No matter where in the West you live, you'll want one that fits your lifestyle—whether it's a place to relax, party, catch up with friends, connect with nature, or simply celebrate the beauty of plants in beds and borders. Perhaps you love to cook and want a steady supply of fresh greens for the salad bowl, or homegrown veggies to toss on the outdoor grill. Maybe you have an active family, with children who like to romp on lawns, eat barbecue fare, and jump into a pool in summer. Maybe you're not a gardener at all and prefer a tranquil patio with a water feature and tough, easy-care plants. Whatever you're seeking, you'll find ideas and inspiration on the following pages. Use them to help you envision your own outdoor space.

HILL VIEW A bridge of ipe wood and a path of poured concrete pavers lead from the poolside decks to the house in this Berkeley, California, garden. Mexican beach stones and Japanese rush edge the pool, while *Calamagrostis* 'Karl Foerster' grows behind. A glass fence separates a play lawn from the pool. DESIGN: Bernard Trainor + Associates.

Small but Smart

A SMALL GARDEN can feel cramped and claustrophobic—or cozy and comforting. The difference boils down to how the space is arranged. The Venice, California, garden shown here is petite (16 by 24 feet), but vital to the success of this home. Since the house itself is only 750 square feet, the garden needs to function as an additional room for dining, relaxing beside a cozy fire, or soaking in a tucked-out-of-sight hot tub.

Homeowner Steven Shortridge, who is an architect, fit a firepit, a generous sectional sofa, and a dining set into this compact garden and still managed to let the room breathe. To accomplish this, he moved the furniture to the edges of the deck, leaving the center open, and designed his own space-saving furniture. Plants, chosen primarily for screening, grow mostly upward, not intruding onto the deck. Color is provided by the house itself—its orange tones repeat in the mahogany furniture—and by the bright green chairs and the dash of burgundy foliage.

As small as it is, this garden holds a big surprise. The step by the sofa leads to a tiny alcove just large enough for a hot tub. **DESIGN:** Steven Shortridge, Shortridge Architects.

Space-savers *(opposite page)* The mahogany dining table, designed by the homeowner, has a built-in slot for the sun-shade pole. The sofa, also his design, is equally efficient. It wraps around the lip of the firepit, making that ledge available as a side table. The bench between the two cushioned areas folds out when more table surface is needed.

Slim firepit *(top left)* The steel firewall creates the fourth wall of the garden's outdoor space. It also provides privacy for the hot tub area behind the fireplace.

Secret corner *(top right)* An old-fashioned hot tub is hidden behind the firewall. The Australian brushwood backing on the wall dampens sounds, making the tiny space seem even more intimate. The seating bench houses storage drawers for towels.

Optical illusions *(bottom left)* A lightly screened window offers a glimpse into a well-lit indoor room, visually extending the small patio, while the outward thrust of the horizontal beams above, capped with translucent plastic, add to the illusion of depth. Mexican weeping bamboo *(Otatea acuminata aztecorum)* at right is held upright by the branches of an ornamental plum. Slender queen palms *(Syagrus romanzoffiana)* grow near the fence at left.

City Sanctuary

A SMALL URBAN BACKYARD can be a big retreat, even on a tight budget, as Ross Wehner and his wife, architect Renée del Gaudio, discovered when they renovated their newly purchased home and yard on a narrow, derelict lot in Denver's historic Central Park West neighborhood. "We were nervous to buy in such an urban area," says del Gaudio, "because we are—at heart—more mountain than city people. The only way we could justify living in town was to create an outdoor room that felt really private."

After hiring workers for preliminary work in the backyard—removing concrete paving and building walls to screen out a back alley and neighboring houses—the couple plunged in and completed much of the redesign themselves, with help from family and friends. Inside the walls, they planted aspens, golden raintree *(Koelreuteria paniculata)*, and honey locust *(Gleditsia triacanthos)* to form a leafy canopy that "makes you forget you're living in the city." They built a dramatic three-level deck—hugging the house—for lounging and entertaining. To further the retreat theme, they created a small satellite patio just big enough for a picnic table. **DESIGN:** Renée del Gaudio Architecture.

“We located the patio as far from the house as possible, so it feels like we’re really eating out in the garden.”
—RENÉE DEL GAUDIO

Tiered deck *(left)* A series of ipe wood platforms, set at different heights, make up the graceful decking that leads visitors from the house into the garden. A river of maiden grass (*Miscanthus sinensis* 'Gracillimus') separates the top tier—which functions as a long narrow boardwalk—from the rest of the deck. It helps soften the hardscape and mimics the effect of a pier above water.

Shadow gate *(right)* A family friend made this gate, which incorporates translucent panels, framed by vertical-grain fir, to allow light and shadows to pass. “It doesn’t feel like we’re trying to block everyone out,” says del Gaudio, “but we still get all the privacy we need.”

Picnic patio *(below)* The small brick patio is perfect for informal meals outdoors. “We located the patio as far from the house as possible,” explains del Gaudio, “so it feels like we’re really eating out in the garden.” To build it, the couple brought out bricks that they found in the basement of their turn-of-the-20th-century home. Using recycled materials helped lower the cost of this do-it-yourself remodel.

Light-Touch Garden

MAKING SUSTAINABILITY a design priority produces better gardens, easier on the planet. But that's not the only benefit; the thinking that goes into them creates landscapes that look more at home with their natural surroundings. The Santa Barbara, California, home of architect Ken Radtkey and landscape architect Susan Van Atta is a good example.

The planted roofs over the main structure and garage insulate the house, harvest precious rainfall, and provide a fire-resistant surface that's especially important in Santa Barbara's fire-prone hills. But their planted surfaces also help the house blend seamlessly into the foothills behind it.

The tiers of plantings in front of the house aren't just pretty; they're hardworking. Most provide food—both for the family and for birds, butterflies, and bees. Harvested rainfall and gray water fill all the irrigation requirements. The neat rows also lend an agricultural flavor, emphasizing its rural location. Even the compost piles are well thought out. For convenience, Van Atta wanted to set them up close to the kitchen. But in such a visible spot, they needed to be attractive. From the outside, her solution looks like a handsome fence; within, it's producing compost quickly. The design is as efficient as it is elegant. **DESIGN:** Susan Van Atta, Van Atta Associates.

"Guilt-free abundance is what our home is all about. Because everything was planned to be regenerative, we live well at no great expense to ourselves or the environment."

—SUSAN VAN ATTA

Ordered planting *(left)* Each tier of the front landscape has its function. Nearest the house are ornamental edibles. Next is a nonthirsty lawn of native buffalo grass *(Buchloe dactyloides)* for family games, then a band of natives, followed by a row of raised vegetable beds, a water-catchment basin covered by *Dymondia,* a bocce ball court, and, finally, a citrus orchard. Stone-fruit trees and natives grow along the driveway.

Roof meadow *(below)* The *Carex praegracilis* lawn that covers the garage roof (visible at right in large photo) absorbs rain as well as provides living space. Small succulents dot the foreground.

THE DETAILS

This Santa Barbara, California, house and garden make thoughtful use of materials, both inside and out. They're designed to save energy, water, and other resources, to respect the surrounding natural landscape, invite pollinators, and provide food for the owners. Here's an at-a-glance summary of their many Earth-friendly features.

PLAY LAWN. The native grass lawn is just large enough to use as a play surface. It's watered by a subsurface distributed cistern. Broken concrete slabs from a previous demolition support the edge.

EDIBLE GARDENS. The orchard, along with terraced vegetable and herb gardens, are irrigated with filtered gray water and harvested rainwater.

NATIVE PLANTS. Throughout the property, plants native to Southern California echo the surrounding habitats and help restore woodlands, grasslands, and chaparral.

LIVING ROOF. Succulents hold water in their leaves, which helps to cool the home in summer and warm it in winter, and they provide a fire-resistant surface.

PERMEABLE PAVING. It reduces runoff in the driveway and covers the bocce court.

WATER-SAVERS. A detention basin collects and filters rainwater runoff from the roof and other sources, while low precipitation-rate sprayers provide any needed irrigation.

Green ideas *(above)* A solar panel shades the roof viewing area; the structure at the top of the meadow is also a solar panel. The steps alongside the garage are recycled stone; the nearby green area is an artificial-grass slide. Eucalyptus that was harvested from the site makes a handsome covering for the garage.

View roof *(left)* Sedums in two colors (*S. album* and *S. spurium* 'Dragon's Blood') connect the roof to the surrounding trees, making the space seem more like a park than a roof. The plants act as insulation, cooling the house in summer, warming it in winter. And much like sponges, they soak up rainfall and moisture in the air.

"When we shower, our water is heated by the sun, and gets reused to irrigate our fruit trees. Nothing is wasted."

—SUSAN VAN ATTA

Classy composting *(right)* The three-bin composting system, based on a design by legendary landscape architect Thomas Church, is as handsome as it is effective. A beehive is nearby.

Safe hens *(below)* A wire enclosure and a border of spiky agaves protect Buff Orpington and Golden Laced Wyandotte hens from coyotes, bobcats, and hawks. The flock provides eggs for the table and manure for the compost.

White on White

GARDENS WITH WHITE WALLS, furnishings, and accents can look sterile and austere. But they can also look welcoming with the addition of texture, which can warm up the frostiest hues. In the Laguna Beach, California, patio of Tami Topol, the color scheme is very limited. Hardscape and furnishings are white, blond, or gray warmed with beige. And the plants are primarily variations in green. Furniture is minimal as well—just a pair of lounge chairs pulled up to the fireplace and a few deck chairs and a table tucked up next to built-in wall benches to create an efficient dining alcove.

But the garden is filled with earthy textures. The floor is made up of a full range of bluestone—the mix of colors and sizes chosen to appear as organic and warming as wood. The fountain is of weathered sandstone. And the wood and faux leather furniture, the piece of coral used as a centerpiece, and the straw frame on the mirror add their own subtle palette. As the final touch, a shade sail bisects the patio. Besides softening the light, it adds a bit of dynamic tension, just enough to keep things lively. **DESIGN:** Molly Wood Garden Design and Erin Curci Design.

"I wanted both the serenity of a luxury spa and the energy of a sunny hilltop terrace on Santorini, and I got it."

—TAMI TOPOL

Multipurpose patio *(left)* With its cozy fireplace seating area and dining corner, the patio is the owner's primary entertaining space. Aeoniums surround a bubbling fountain in the foreground, while exposed beams serve as mantels over the fireplace—perfect perches for portable lanterns.

Built-in banco *(below)* It provides lots of seating without taking up much space. The table, an Indonesian import, marries a teak base with a bleached elm top. Chairs combine three textures: wood, metal, and synthetic leather.

GREAT IDEA

Create a sea scene in seconds for the outdoor table. Start with the dramatic air plant, *Tillandsia xerographica*. Then, to complete the vignette, add an assortment of faux coral or starfish (made of resin) to suggest a tidepool environment. Mist the *Tillandsia* once a week to keep it healthy.

Northwest Natural

SOMETIMES A GARDEN LIABILITY—wind, in this case—can be among its most important assets. That was designer Susan Calhoun's thinking when Bev and Dan Wick asked her to design their hilltop garden on Bainbridge Island, Washington.

Their property had much in its favor: a stunning view of Puget Sound, native trees, and plenty of light. So Calhoun started by building on existing vegetation, planting native-compatible exotics among the site's Douglas firs, snowberries, and maples, then lacing the meadowlike landscape with crushed-gravel paths. Ornamental grasses and sedges give the garden its billowy structure, moving gracefully with every passing breeze, but staying low enough to preserve the view.

Carefully chosen groundcovers keep the landscape interesting at every step, while evergreen lingonberry plants fit well with native red and evergreen huckleberries.

Nearly all plants here are deer-resistant, making the garden's other liability, Columbian black-tailed deer, more ornament than adversary. **DESIGN:** Susan Calhoun, Plantswoman Design.

Preserve the view *(above)* A collection of low plants borders an all-weather, crushed gravel path that is durable, informal, and as natural-looking as a meadow trail. Plants are allowed to encroach on the path just enough to soften the edges.

Set the tone with foliage *(left)* Brilliant, translucent red Japanese blood grass (*Imperata cylindrica* 'Rubra'), cinnamon New Zealand hair sedge (*Carex tenuiculmis* 'Cappuccino'), and pink-flowered Japanese silver grass (*Miscanthus sinensis* 'Flamingo') give this garden a warm ambience, especially in summer and fall.

FOREST BACKDROP
Native Douglas firs inspired this meadow garden. Gold-tinged bigleaf maples—perfect conifer companions—grow just across the path. Both frame views of distant Puget Sound.

MIX TEXTURES

Grasses and greenery establish the garden's color palette. Above, chartreuse Scotch moss rambles around a mounding dwarf conifer and soft green *Veronica umbrosa* 'Georgia Blue', while a mounding, coppery-colored New Zealand hair sedge fans out behind.

SETTLE THE STONES

At top right, a carpet of golden green Scotch moss and deep green Irish moss rambles around gray boulders, helping them look settled in the soil. Native bunchberry grows in front; it blooms in late spring.

ADD ACCENT PLANTS

Little surprises tucked among boulders along the path invite stopping for a closer look. Calhoun uses them to extend the season; good examples include the candy-colored winter-flowering cyclamen (bottom right), *Narcissus* 'Tête-à-tête' (early spring), and Canadian dogwood (late spring, early summer).

Zen and Now

THIS COURTYARD GARDEN in Corona del Mar, California, was designed to promote tranquility. Homeowner Blythe Fair is a practitioner of Jin Shin Jyutsu, an ancient Japanese method of harmonizing energy in the body through gentle touch, and her two home workrooms look out on this space. She asked the landscape designer to create a mood that would complement her practice.

The result is a streamlined version of a Japanese Zen garden. But instead of the usual simulated river currents, visitors here are greeted with a calm sea of smooth gravel. Wide concrete pavers create a bridge across the sea, and chunky boulders act as landing docks for stepping into the practice rooms. A raised planter, a fountain that spills into a small koi pond, and a few carefully placed plants are the only other details.

The serene space isn't just for viewing. Blythe and husband Jerry sunbathe and stargaze here. Friends gather for musical evenings around the firepit, and grandchildren love watching outdoor movies and fixing s'mores. "The calmness appeals to everyone," says Blythe. **DESIGN:** Margaret Carole McElwee Landscape Design.

Keep it simple *(above)* A concrete fire bowl in the same blond tones as the Del Rio gravel provides a focal point for client and family activities in the courtyard.

Slow-down stone *(top right)* A chunky boulder at the office entry causes visitors to pause and shift focus before entering.

Focus on foliage *(bottom right)* A nearly all-green plant palette adds to the tranquility of this garden. Big, heart-shaped *Ligularia* contrasts with the fine needles of a juniper and the grassy leaves of water iris.

Paradise Found

WHEN GUESTS ARRIVE at this home in Kailua, Hawaii, a block from the beach on windward Oahu, they pass through a tropical garden paradise to get to the front door. That wasn't always the case. "The front yard was a jungle of fishtail palms, planted by the previous residents for privacy," says owner Chris Beddow. "I wanted simplicity." Undaunted by the task ahead, he and his wife, Mary, removed some of the palms to open up the garden to sunlight. They visited nurseries in nearby Waimanalo to get ideas for what might grow well here. Then, with the help of friends, they filled in the bare spots with low, colorful foliage plants such as croton, along with smaller palms and Hawaiian tree ferns *(Cibotium glaucum)*. They added miniature gardenias for fragrance and built a wide, welcoming deck near the front door.

Finishing touches include a small fountain—which the couple made from a ceramic bowl and pump—and turquoise containers—filled with low, jungly plants such as philodendron and zamia.

"Mary and I look out sometimes and wonder: Have we created a monster? It's a lot to keep up," says Chris. "But at the same time, it's satisfying to have such beautiful plants around us, and to savor the results of our labor." Now the garden feels more like a true Hawaiian paradise. "I think we've captured the essence of the Islands."

Tiered deck *(left)* A three-level deck steps up to the front door of this traditional (raised) Hawaiian post-and-pier house. Built of ironwood, the deck uses Tiger Deck construction (which involves hammering the boards into metal "tiger claws" instead of securing them in place with nails). The owners keep it looking new with occasional applications of a hardwood oil called Penofin.

Jungly screen *(top left)* A trio of stately Manila palms helps to create a lush green screen beside the deck, along with assorted ferns, *Sansevieria*, and bromeliads.

Recycled lighting *(bottom left)* Left behind by the property's previous owner, rusted iron lanterns from Asia sit atop concrete pillars near the deck, adding a sculptural accent by day and soft lighting at night. (For similar lanterns, check import stores. Or substitute more contemporary lanterns of perforated powder-coated steel.)

Easy seating *(bottom right)* The owners painted unfinished Adirondack chairs and matching footrests soft gray-green to match the house's roof. The chairs set the stage for relaxing by the front door—the coolest part of the house in the afternoon. A 19-inch-high glazed container with a 20-inch-diameter tempered glass top forms the table; small silicone pads cushion the glass.

Hot plants *(below)* "The vibrant jungle backdrop turns our deck into Shangri-La," says Chris Beddow, who chose most of the plants for this garden. One key element: ti plants *(Cordyline fruticosa)* in various colors, which glow like torches in sunlight, waking up the mostly green palette. In cooler climates, substitute *Canna* 'Tropicanna' or 'Tropicanna Black', or *Cordyline* 'Festival Grass'.

Gate to paradise *(above)* The side-yard gate gives a nod to tropical plants growing nearby. To create the leaf motif insets, builders Charlie Castro and Randy Hixon used foliage from the garden's red ginger plants as templates. They traced the outline of the leaflets on plywood, cut around it with a saw, then enclosed the wood leaves in frames made of 2-by-4s. The gate is painted soft gray-green to match the deck chairs and roof.

Seaside Harmony

WITH A VIEW as stunning as this—it's Los Osos Back Bay along California's Central Coast—the homeowners wanted a view deck that offers as many opportunities to be outdoors as possible. The lower portion of the large ipe wood deck, for dining and entertaining, has a concrete table with a built-in firepit as its focal point. Evenings are usually cool, so gas lines run up through the table legs to the trough, keeping diners comfortable. The upper deck contains a spa, hidden from view by a wooden sectional sofa and a screen of reeds.

The deck's outside walls mimic the S curve of the bay. The steel and cable railing, which doubles as a backrest for the wall bench, further emphasizes the sinuous line. The materials include steel, cable, and wood—the same used for boats. The polished concrete tops of the table and benches repeat the sheen of the bay's still waters. Finally, the warm tint of the concrete echoes the golden flagstone paths in the garden below. **DESIGN:** Jeffrey Gordon Smith Landscape Architecture.

MULTIPLE VISTAS
A concrete seat wall wraps the deck's dining area. Small firepits built into the wall encourage guests to settle in and enjoy the view.

GREAT IDEA

Succulent plants add interest around the dining deck. Planted in square, custom-built concrete containers, they resemble mini tidepools. A tall *Aloe plicatilis* rises like kelp above silvery gray *Dudleya* and small sedums. A fine blue-gray stone mulch covers the soil.

Pool View

A LONG, NARROW LOT isn't a liability. It's an opportunity to put in a lap pool with enough length for real exercise. It also creates the chance to achieve high drama, as this Phoenix example clearly demonstrates.

When visitors walk into Patti Reiter's living room and look out her French doors, the first thing they notice is that slim sliver of turquoise that seems to go on forever. "It creates a 'wow' moment," says Reiter. Orienting the pool in this direction versus crosswise also leaves room near the house for outdoor dining and other activities.

Landscape architect Christy Ten Eyck complemented the bold rectangle of the turquoise pool with other strong geometric blocks of color—the cocoa of the concrete patio, the green of a small patch of turf, and the dark red of two perimeter walls. The result is a design as balanced as a Mondrian painting. **DESIGN:** Ten Eyck Landscape Architects.

Multitasking *(above)* The low concrete wall separating the outdoor dining area from the grassy play area culminates in a fountain that spills into the pool. It also provides additional seating when needed. The red wall behind the dining area and the one at the far end of the pool counterbalance the bold blue of the pool, as well as echo the warm hues of the large orange sectional sofa indoors.

"Balancing the big blocks of color so that no single one dominates is the key to this garden's success."
—CHRISTY TEN EYCK

GREAT IDEA

An opening was left in the block wall shown below for a steel ledge, which supports a long row of votive candles that illuminate evening dinner parties.

Deliberately retro *(above)* The white plaster finish of the pool gives the water the vivid turquoise color that the designer wanted for this garden. This type of finish—as well as the center stripe to designate swimming lanes—was characteristic of pools in the 1960s, the era when the house was built. The aluminum arbor that shades the long passage next to the pool has a second function. Its outer edge lines up with the middle of the pool so swimmers doing the backstroke can use it as a guidepost to stay centered.

Aesthetic camouflage *(right)* The dark red wall that provides a backdrop to the dining area hides a gravel pathway leading to the front yard. The wall defines the perimeter of the outdoor room and keeps attention focused inward.

Savoring Oaks

"EVERYTHING ABOUT THIS GARDEN is magical," says landscape architect Vera Gates of Liz and Chris Dressel's pastoral hillside hideaway in Woodside, California. "The light is magical. So are the plantings around the sculptural native oak." And those blue Adirondack chairs around a portable firepit? "Guests just want to recline in them, relax, and enjoy the view of the garden. No one ever wants to leave." Perhaps that's because the aim of the design is to celebrate the wild oak tree habitat that surrounds this terraced garden. Its unthirsty plants stay low, framing the views of gnarly oak trunks, and its decomposed granite paths feel rustic and natural underfoot. This late-summer mood can be re-created in any garden corner, even one without rolling hills, by using a few well-chosen plants and accessories. **DESIGN:** Vera Gates and Scott Yarnell, Arterra Landscape Architects.

> "These existing oaks are magnificent. We wanted to celebrate them in every aspect of the design."
>
> —VERA GATES

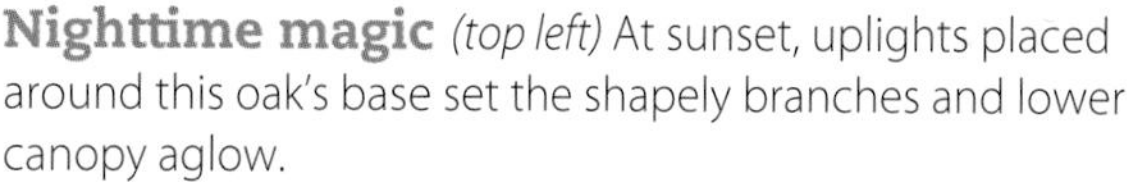

Nighttime magic *(top left)* At sunset, uplights placed around this oak's base set the shapely branches and lower canopy aglow.

Pool area *(top right)* Just a few steps down from the firepit area, the pool is edged with a rustic stone wall. Penstemons, lavender, and other low unthirsty plantings soften the paving.

View *(bottom left)* The negative-edge pool acts like a mirror that reflects the native oaks' spreading canopies. A fringe of low golden grasses just below it appears to blend with the wild green grasses downslope.

Firepit area *(opposite page)* Grasses such as *Carex tumulicola* catch the late afternoon light as they mingle with perennials that bloom into fall, including Santa Barbara daisy *(Erigeron karvinskianus)*, beard tongue *(Penstemon)*, catmint *(Nepeta × faassenii)*, and salvias. Spiky phormiums add accents; French lavender fills the air with fragrance.

Sea Creature Succulents

"Late in the day, while the tide is still out, those tidepools reflect the sunset sky. They show the same colors as these plants."
—JOE STEAD

SUCCULENTS are terra firma's answer to sea creatures, as jewel-toned as shells, as sculptural as seastars, or as fluttery as sea anemones. This garden, in California's Corona del Mar, shows off succulents' wilder, more colorful side. The plantings create a spot-on connection between land and sea, as though they sprung from the waves—like Venus on the half-shell—to their perch atop the bluff.

When succulents expert and horticulturist Joe Stead saw Anton and Jennifer Segerstrom's patio, he wanted to set it off from the Pacific below, but with appropriate edging. "As a kid, I explored tidepools down there," Stead says of the rocky coastline. "I marveled at the starfish and sea anemones. I wanted to bring that sense of wonder to this garden."

In beds around the patio, Stead planted purple echeverias, orange *Euphorbia tirucalli* 'Sticks on Fire', and cool blue aloes. All thrive on little water and stay low enough to frame the Segerstroms' coastal view without blocking it. In fact, the garden's faux ocean sometimes seems to merge with the real one. **DESIGN:** Joe Stead.

Tidepool star *(left)* A striped tuxedo agave (*Agave americana* 'Mediopicta Alba') is the star among orange *Euphorbia tirucalli* 'Sticks on Fire' and smaller succulents in this Southern California coastal garden.

The "crab" *(top left)* Spikes of deep orange flowers emerge like crab claws from this echeveria's large (12 to 16 inch), loose rosette in summer. Leaves are powdery and normally pinkish lavender with brighter pink edges. But when stressed by sun and sea air, they turn the vibrant hue pictured here. Plant in sun or light shade.

The "seastar" *(bottom left)* Leaves of *Echeveria subrigida* 'Fire and Ice', with red edges and a nearly iridescent sheen, make this succulent appear to glow like a seastar in a sunlit tidepool. Echeverias tend to stretch with too little light, so give this large (18 inches wide) echeveria sun or bright shade. A colony of ghost plants *(Graptopetalum paraguayense)* surrounds it.

The "kelp" *(bottom right)* As though swaying in ocean eddies, this yellow-green *Senecio vitalis* has semi-prostrate stems and narrow, upward-reaching leaves. Its shrubby (to 2 feet tall) nature makes it an excellent backdrop for a dry garden. In front are *Kalanchoe luciae* 'Fantastic' and spiky *Crassula capitella thyrsiflora* 'Campfire', a chameleon that's green in part sun, vermilion in full sun.

DESIGN TIPS

ADD A SHOWSTOPPER

Every garden needs a plant—one that's bigger or more colorful than the rest. The star-shaped *Agave lophantha* 'Quadricolor' (top left) draws attention with its green stripes. The delicate chartreuse *Sedum rupestre* 'Angelina' that rambles around the agave sets off its star shape.

MIX LACY WITH BOLD

Keep your planting lively and interesting by clustering more textured, delicate succulents—like the trio of ruffle-edged echeveria hybrids above—around bolder, more muscular ones. On page 37, *Euphorbia tirucalli* 'Sticks on Fire' has the same effect behind a whopper agave.

FILL IN WITH TINY MATS

The little guys make the big ones stand out. Thanks to bands of star-like *Crassula corymbulosa* 'Shark's Tooth', knobby blue *Senecio serpens*, and lime green *Sedum rupestre* 'Angelina', the three echeverias and the *Aeonium* 'Sunburst' (far left) really pop.

Summer Colors

LIVING ON A HILL overlooking Washington's Puget Sound and Olympic Mountains, Randi Fattizzi wanted a sustainable, chemical-free, low-maintenance, low-water-use garden—and a lot of color—instead of a boring lawn. Taking on the challenge, Seattle designer Stacie Crooks created the vibrant landscape pictured here. "The house is the jewel, and the garden is a garland around it," Crooks says.

"All the furniture, fabric, everything goes with the house," she adds. "I used reds and blues and coppers, and a lot of fall color." Plants were mostly selected for drought tolerance and easy maintenance. "Everything is indestructible; there's very little pruning, there's no deadheading. It's very easy."

Because Crooks wanted the garden's plants to take hold fast with minimal water, she planted them in organic-rich topsoil and installed the landscape in fall. Everything was well established before the next summer and is now watered only in hot weather. It's a front yard to linger in as the sun sets over the Sound. **DESIGN:** Stacie Crooks, Crooks Garden Design.

Primary colors *(above)* Red *Crocosmia* 'Lucifer', blue lavender 'Hidcote', and green turf set the color scheme. Burgundy barberry, purple sage, and straw-colored blue oat grass fill in nicely.

Fire lookout *(top right)* Low perimeter plantings (the tallest is a 4-foot *Crocosmia*) preserve the western view. The chairs around the firepit are made from recycled materials.

Soft screen *(bottom right)* Feathery heaths, heathers, Bosnian and mugo pines, and Japanese maples screen the house.

Cool Courtyard

A GARDEN THAT HAS A FEW SECRETS is intriguing, and this one has several. Take the way the sandstone paving is broken up, for instance. When landscape architect James Lord renovated the interior courtyard at his parents' Palos Verdes, California, home, he replaced the existing concrete with a more permeable surface of sandstone pavers set in sand. He tucked in long ribbons of thyme plus larger planting pockets meant to suggest cracks from seismic shifts. "My father, brother, and sister are all structural seismic civil engineers," he explains. "It's an homage to the family."

Because his mother is from New Zealand, Lord included many "Kiwi" plants, such as the dramatic grass tree planted in a large saucer next to the spa. Even the color of the sandstone has meaning. "Sunsets are gorgeous here," says Lord. "I wanted my parents to enjoy that warm pink cast all day long." **DESIGN:** James Lord, Surfacedesign.

Sense of enclosure *(left)* The addition of large planters at two corners and the veiling effect of an Australian grass tree *(Xanthorrhoea quadrangulata)* in a container at a third give this spa an intimate, desert oasis feel.

Geometric but unpredictable *(opposite page)* Ribbons of creeping thyme begin a straight path, only to be interrupted by ribbons of sedum traveling in the opposite direction—but the succulents, in turn, stop, setting up a pleasing staccato rhythm.

GREAT IDEA

Strips of creeping thyme between pavers create a tidy look, but are they perhaps a bit predictable? Shake things up by breaking out larger sections of hardscape roomy enough for a substantial plant that doesn't need a lot of root space. This *Agave parryi*, for instance, is perfect. Fill in the pocket with groundcover to unite it with the rest of the design.

Movie-Lover's Garden

WHEN BRIAN TEN AND RIKA HOUSTON turned their spacious but largely unused West L.A. front yard into an outdoor living room, they went a step further, adding all the features for screening movies outdoors.

Working with landscape architect Mark Tessier, they installed an ipe wood fence in front to screen out the street, planted a hedge of clumping bamboo along the side to block views of neighboring houses, and replaced the former lawn with a patio of permeable decomposed granite, edged with concrete pavers. Then they furnished the new outdoor room with a cushioned teak sectional large enough for their family of five plus a slew of friends, and mounted a screen to the garage wall.

Now neighbors and other guests pass through an inviting garden filled with water-wise plants. Once inside the gate, they sink into the cushy sofa or mod Adirondack chairs with lanterns lit overhead, watch *The Birds* or *The Sound of Music* on a large screen, then, afterward, catch up with one another around the warming firepit. "In summer, every Friday is movie night," says Houston. "With this outdoor theater, we've gotten to know our neighbors much better." **DESIGN:** Mark Tessier Landscape Architecture.

"Screening" room *(above)* Seating for up to 12 and a firepit with room for plates and glasses encourage lounging. (For extra seating, Houston puts cushions on the lid of their daughter's old sandbox.)

Movie wall *(right)* The garage supports a 14-by-8-foot screen for watching movies and television. When not in use, it retracts into a protective metal box tucked under the eaves. An underground conduit carries HDMI and audio cables, which connect an indoor television and DVD player to an LCD projector and speakers outdoors.

Welcoming garden *(opposite page)* The 20-foot setback between the sidewalk and the fence contains unthirsty plants, including California fuchsia, Jerusalem sage, and red yucca. Windows let light through the fence, while a small fountain continues to the inside of the fence.

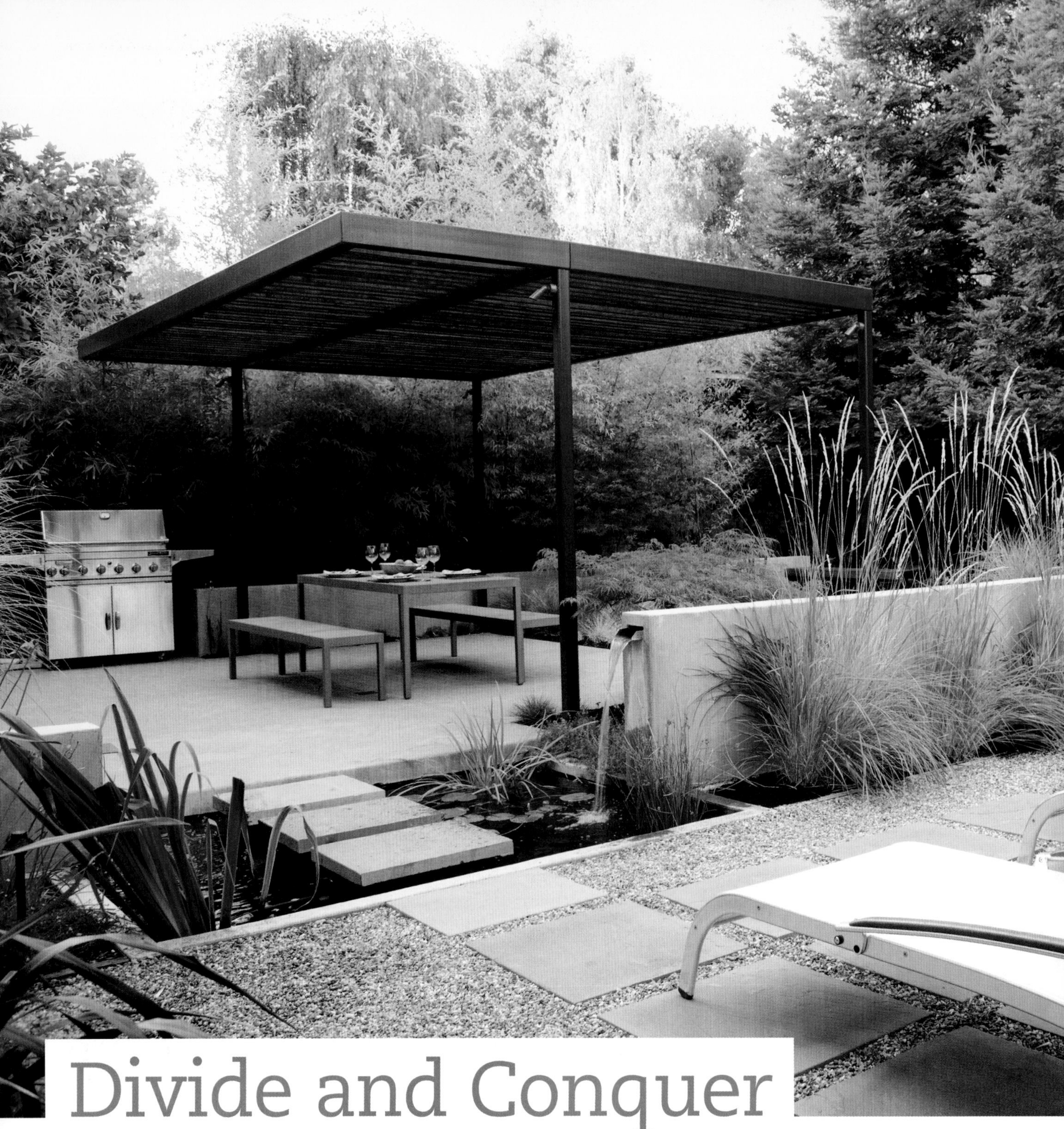

Divide and Conquer

ONCE GOPHERS GOT HOLD of this backyard in Pleasant Hill, California, all that remained was a scruffy plot. To reclaim the space, the owners transformed the small garden into four rooms. It is now the ultimate outdoor living space.

Evelyn Huang and Jack Mangan had a wish list: areas for dining, reading, and growing edibles, all using easy-care, low-water plants. They turned to landscape architect Joseph Huettl, who gave them that and much more, including a patio for sunning. In the dining area, a steel-and-redwood arbor shades the table and benches. Between this main gathering spot and the reading corner is another patio, defined by square pavers, which provides additional space for entertaining. In the corner devoted to edibles, raised beds keep the area looking tidy. A low rosemary hedge screens the beds from the sunning patio.

Now the couple spend much of their time in the garden. And for some mysterious reason, says Huang, "the gophers haven't come back!" **DESIGN:** Huettl Landscape Architecture.

GARDEN ROOM BASICS

CREATE FLOW. Outdoor rooms may have separate functions; to connect them, use stepping-stones and paths.

KEEP WALLS LOW. When walls are no higher than 30 inches, the entire garden is visible all at once, and the rooms don't feel cramped.

CHANGE PAVING. Different paving helps define each room. For visual continuity, repeat the same material in some parts of the garden.

Separate but connected patios *(left)* Square bluestone pavers define the sunning patio and blend with the ones that cross the pool and lead to the dining area. A see-through screening of feather reed grass *(Calamagrostis × acutiflora)* softens the low wall.

Reading nook *(top right)* This serene retreat in the corner farthest from the house is bordered by redwoods. Relaxing here feels like being in the forest. A built-in bench of ipe wood appears to float above a bed of crushed rock.

Veggie garden *(bottom right)* Tomatoes and chard thrive in raised beds of rusted steel beyond the rosemary hedge.

Alfresco Lounge

TO ENJOY A GARDEN IN ARIZONA, some kind of shade structure is essential. Without a way to escape the area's brutal sun, no one stays outdoors for long. Dominique Lunt had a large patio with gorgeous mountain and desert views at her Tucson home but, except for a mesquite tree at one end, no shaded place to sit and take it all in. Now, at the opposite end of the patio, there's a Turkish-inspired pavilion—luxurious enough to make a pasha proud.

Instead of adding outdoor furniture, landscape designer Elizabeth Przygoda wrapped a concrete banco around three sides of the 12-by-20-foot space and topped it with comfy cushions and a plethora of pillows. The cozy built-in is roomy enough for a host of friends or for two people to curl up for an afternoon nap. A mosaic toe kick reinforces the casbah effect, as do Moroccan lamps, antique olive jars, and other accessories.

A fringe of native and other drought-tolerant plants hugs the edge of the lounge, adding fragrance (Cleveland sage), movement (ornamental grasses), and butterfly visitors (lantana) to the pleasures of the space. The same palette of plants is repeated beside the steps leading down into the garden. **DESIGN:** Elizabeth Przygoda, Boxhill Design.

BLEND ***(opposite page and this page)*** **Barrel cactus and red-flowered lantana soften the edge of the lounge patio, where ethnic textiles add coziness. Some of the same plants, along with golden grasses and agaves, edge the path and the stairs leading to the rest of the garden, to unite the two spaces.**

> "There's something about built-ins—maybe their stability—that encourages people to burrow in and hang around."
> —ELIZABETH PRZYGODA

Soft lighting *(right)* Tabletops built into the concrete bank make a good display area for lanterns and garden accents. Perforated metal stars overhead *(boxhill.com)* add to the ambience.

Covered lounge *(bottom left)* Just steps away from the outdoor dining patio, the cozy lounge has all the comforts of an indoor living room—soft cushions, twin coffee tables for parking drinks and appetizers—and a view of the garden.

Bold graphics *(bottom right)* The striking pattern on a single round cushion adds an eye-catching finishing touch among the many solid-colored pillows on the built-in banco.

NATURAL SHADE
The dining area adjacent to the pavilion has its own shade source, the graceful native mesquite tree *(Prosopis velutina)*.

Coastal Hideaway

WHAT CAN BE DONE if the only logical space for outdoor living is a sliver-thin 13 feet wide? And to make matters worse, the two-story house next door is almost an arm's length away. That's the dilemma Jeanne and Jim Carmack faced at their home in Newport Beach, California, and presented to landscape designer Molly Wood.

To address the privacy issue, Wood constructed a pavilion out of powder-coated steel posts and vinyl cross-beams—steel because it can be used in thinner pieces that take up less room than wood, and vinyl for ease of maintenance. A vertical screen behind the central area has panes of frosted blue glass for more privacy. Even more important was to make the most of every inch of the space, as if designing the cabin of a boat (after all, the garden has a marine theme). A small but stunning fountain adds interest near the front door and soothing sounds that buffer out noise.

There's a surprising amount of seating—most of it built-in—and the wide stairsteps absorb any overflow. And remarkably, the pavilion still had room for a small wet bar and the barbecue behind it. **DESIGN:** Molly Wood Garden Design.

GREAT IDEA

Shell fragments pressed into the limestone integral-colored concrete hardscape reinforce the marine theme. To re-create this texture, nearly bury the shells in wet concrete. Then use a broom to brush away some of the surface concrete to expose the shells along with some of the aggregate.

Tidepool pot *(above)* A planting in a turquoise container echoes the beachy feel of the garden. Gray-green sedum and jade green echeveria share the container. A glass fishing float completes the picture.

Galley *(left)* Though small, this narrow outdoor room contains plenty of amenities—barbecue, wet bar, ample seating, and soothing fountain. A muted color scheme of white, sandy beige, and sky blue and simple vegetation—dark green leaves and a few white flowers—keep the space from feeling busy.

Splash pool *(opposite page)* A slender pool (7 feet wide, 13 feet long) and a concrete pad just large enough for twin deck chairs and a sun umbrella provide an intimate private retreat. The beach ball sculpture is made from the straps of old wine barrels.

Pack in the Veggies

EVEN A POSTAGE-STAMP KITCHEN GARDEN can produce big results—and look great too. This one in Palo Alto, California, is like a front-yard grocery store. Although small, the space gets lots of sun, which is why Elaine Uang and her husband, Mike Greenfield, chose to grow edibles alongside their driveway. They harvest more fruits and veggies here than they imagined possible. The keys to their success are good design, raised beds, and espaliers.

When they got started, Greenfield, a longtime gardener, focused on planting as many crops as possible; Uang, an architect, wanted to make sure everything looked good. Uang came up with an overall plan, then brought in collaborators to complete the vision. Now the couple harvest something whenever they're hungry, whether peppers for lunchtime salads or melon for dessert. And by placing edibles in front, they've inspired neighbors to grow food too—and now they swap crops. "Every season is a learning experience," Uang says. "It doesn't matter what you grow as long as you give it a try." **DESIGN:** BaDesign (metalwork, planting plan); Star Apple Edible + Fine Gardening (planting).

"I call it my front-yard grocery store. Picking lunch is easy. I just go see what's ripe."
—ELAINE UANG

Blueberry hedge *(above)* An informal hedge of blueberry plants, growing beneath the front window, produces lots of luscious berries in summer.

Fruiting "sculpture" *(left)* A shapely pineapple guava shrub presides over the ornamental planting across the front entry path. In the evening, its branches are lit from below. Around it are low, mounding blue fescues and white-flowered groundcover.

Space-savers *(opposite page)* A rusted metal framework for espaliering fruit trees serves as a fence between this property and the neighbors' driveway. River rock mulch at the base neatens the space.

> "Every season is a learning experience. It doesn't matter what you grow, as long as you give it a try."
> —ELAINE UANG

Ornamentals *(top left)* To keep the entry garden looking its best, the designers planted mounding blue fescue in front of the beds, then filled in behind them with yellow-flowered yarrow. Both are easy-care and look good without much water.

Tidy fruits *(bottom left)* A ripening pear, flushed with red, dangles from a rusted metal support along the couple's espalier fence. "My husband loves fruit—he wanted to put in as much as possible," Elaine Uang says.

Billowy herbs *(bottom right)* Thyme, golden sage, and other low, mounding herbs are planted near the bed edges, where they spill over the sides, softening the rusted metal.

DESIGN TIPS

KEEP THE SPACE TIDY
Unless they're tended regularly, veggie gardens can give a front yard a disheveled look. But in this garden, river rock edging, along with paths of decomposed granite and concrete pavers, keep the space tidy and easily accessible for tending.

RAISE THE BEDS
Densely planted rusted steel beds are good-looking, high enough for easy access, and productive. The harvest, from May to October: eggplant (40 pounds), lemon cucumbers (30 pounds), peppers (7 pounds), squash (70 pounds), plus three cantaloupes and twenty onions. Steel trellises keep crops tidy.

ESPALIER THE FRUIT
Serving as a low fence along the property line, a 30-foot-long steel espalier supports six fruit trees: Asian pear, 'Bearss' lime, blood orange, cherry, European pear, and 'Pixie' mandarin. The fruiting branches are trained along wires that run through holes in the steel posts.

FOOD·SCAPING

EDIBLES ARE THE ROCK STARS of Western gardens. Planted with panache and mingled with ornamentals, they are stealing spotlights everywhere, and not just because you can eat their leaves or fruits, but because they are beautiful to look at. Many make outstanding landscape plants—citrus and other fruit trees as accents, for example, or fig trees as espaliers along fences, or rainbow chard or bok choy in containers. Basil, carrots, or parsley create delicate, if temporary, low edgings; strawberry plants can thrive for years as groundcovers. You can mix veggies and herbs with flowers in beds and borders, pairing them for leaf color and textures. Or stage herbs, veggies, and berries like flower arrangements in shapely raised beds located near an outdoor dining table. That way, you can graze on the bounty while taking a break from gardening chores.

Celebrating citrus *(above)* A small grove of lemon trees presides over this Mediterranean-style garden in California. Purple iris bloom among them. DESIGN: Molly Wood Garden Design.

Grazing garden *(above)* Scarlet runner beans grow on trellises against the fence, while artichokes, herbs, peppers, squash, and chard fill rock-lined beds around it. The raised bed at left contains herbs, along with golden coreopsis, white feverfew, and tall sunflowers that attract pollinators. **DESIGN:** Lauren Dunec, Johanna Silver.

Edible tapestry *(right)* A creative use of vegetables makes this garden at Stone Edge Farm in Sonoma, California, as striking as any flower bed. Deep purple basil and golden *Bidens* bloom in a colorful border. Yellow 'Gypsy' peppers add a pop of color. Sturdy branches tied together give a casual sense of structure. **DESIGN:** Roger Warner.

Playing with Scale

THIS SMALL GARDEN in Laguna Beach, California, is as clean and serene as the sand and sea nearby. But a few carefully chosen accents make it a standout, even with the garden's mostly neutral color palette. A pair of oversize (4-foot tall) Vas-One planters, chosen by homeowner Andy Wolf and architect Warren Hutcherson, create an Alice in Wonderland effect that contrasts dramatically with the simple dining set on the patio. Made of molded, recyclable polyethylene, they're lightweight and easy to move. A striped awning over the patio provides a bit of vivid, beachy color, while detailing adds interest to the garden's back wall.
DESIGN: Warren Hutcherson.

Bold wall *(above)* From the patio, the view is just as stunning. The yard's rear retaining wall shows off its own drama, with geometric cutouts that let in light and give the wall an airy look. There's also a built-in bench to accommodate a crowd, and art panels that, at night, can be lit from above.

Giant plants *(left)* Clumping bamboo grows in the large containers that frame the patio. The plants get groomed every month to stay within the city's regulation height because, as the owner says, "views are respected in Laguna Beach."

Growing Forward

SHARING A GARDEN with a few kindred spirits may be the new formula for sustainable urban living. Or so hopes Dennis Allen, the developer of the Santa Barbara, California, experiment in shared green living shown here. (He also owns and lives in one of the units.) Allen and his wife are one of three couples, all friends, who purchased a 50-foot-wide, 225-foot-deep lot near downtown Santa Barbara. They refurbished an existing Victorian house up front where one of the couples lives, constructed a three-unit building in back, and created a communal garden in between. "We're so close to downtown now, more often than not we just walk," Allen says.

The residents' communal garden is large enough to feel like a minipark. There's space enough for fruit trees, a beehive, a vegetable plot, wildlife habitats, an outdoor dining area for the whole group, and quiet corners for relaxing or reading. Rain feeds directly from the roof to a 14,000-gallon storage bladder in the basement via copper guttering. That's enough water to satisfy the landscape's irrigation needs for the entire year. The process of planning a project like this brought the families closer, and the shared garden helps them maintain that bond. "We look out for each other," Allen says. "We're a community."

Thanks to the home's many features, such as solar photovoltaic panels, the energy needs of the buildings on the property are nearly carbon neutral (the project was certified Platinum by the U.S. Green Building Council's LEED for Homes). The garden is just as sustainable. This is the first residence among 155 projects worldwide selected to participate in the Sustainable Sites Initiative pilot project (find more at *sustainablesites.org*; also *asla.org/sites*). **DESIGN:** Margie Grace, Grace Design Associates.

Double duty *(above and right)* The seat wall around the vegetable plot provides extra seating during parties to supplement the garden's more intimate spaces.

Edible arbor *(opposite page)* Fig plants are beginning to trail across a series of steel arches built to support them. Eventually they will form a green tunnel.

THE DETAILS

PERMEABLE PAVING. Paths and patios are of gravel or decomposed granite. Both allow rainwater to pass through to plant roots.

STORM WATER INFILTRATORS. Rainfall not absorbed by the soil recharges the groundwater table; none flows off-site.

SUBSURFACE IRRIGATION. This feature eliminates surface evaporation and overspray.

AUTOMATED PLANT FEEDING. An injector pump provides organic nutrients through the irrigation system.

RAINWATER COLLECTION. A 14,000-gallon cistern collects roof runoff for watering plants.

HABITAT PLANTS. Most of the plants attract pollinators and tolerate drought. They include catmint, grasses, penstemons, and salvias.

WATERWISE LAWN. 'UC Verde' buffalo grass fronts the property.

RECYCLED MATERIALS. Seventy-one percent of the materials generated from the original structure were reused in the remodel or recycled.

Communal dining *(above)* A large table, conveniently close to the vegetable garden, accommodates everyone who lives in the complex. The long water feature behind it is low enough to draw wildlife.

Garden gallery *(opposite page)* The walkway leading to the alley and garages is designated the Art Walk because of its wall hangings. Like the rest of the garden, this path was designed to be wide enough for wheelchairs.

"This is a *Big Love* project. These people like each other. They jumped in together to live closer to the land, and to each other."
—MARGIE GRACE

Backyard Meadow

IN THE BRIGHT SPRING SUNSHINE, this backyard in Palo Alto, California, looks every bit as vibrant as wildflower fields in, say, the state's Antelope Valley after a rainy winter. California poppies blaze in shades of orange; splashes of yellow and white meadowfoam and pink checkerbloom fringe the paths. Bees are buzzing; butterflies dance among the petals.

As natural as the planting might look, owner Melanie Cross ditched a lawn to create this wildflower fantasia. (She covered the grass with cardboard and plastic to kill it, then let it decompose in place.) In late summer, she planted seeds and seedlings from nurseries. A labyrinth of steppingstones wiggles through the meadow, allowing her to walk among the blooms, tend them, and enjoy them close-up.

Following peak bloom time, "the garden looks messy for a while in summer," Cross admits. But she refreshes the meadow each fall with a light topping of soil amendment and a layer of oak leaf mulch.

"I love native plants," says Cross, who found inspiration for her garden in the fields around her childhood home in rural Southern California. "Wildflowers have evolved in California. They belong here. They're important to birds, butterflies—the web of life. We humans take away from the natural habitat. I wanted to give back."

Star of the show *(opposite page)* Mounds of poppies carry the show in spring, followed by buttercups, then clarkia and other species as the garden evolves through the seasons. Magenta-flowered *Salvia spathacea* grows near the pond. To expand the meadow, Cross pulls up spent plants to use as haylike mulch. In late summer, she tosses them where she wants new poppies to grow, then lets them drop their seed.

Supporting cast *(this page, from top)* Blue-eyed grass *(Sisyrinchium bellum)*, white meadowfoam *(Limnanthes alba)*, and California poppies *(Eschscholzia californica)* mingle in this meadow.

"The garden is unpredictable, surprising, exciting. There's no boredom with natives."

—MELANIE CROSS

Garden Gallery

AN ENTRY COURTYARD can serve as the perfect place to linger a moment and focus, before setting out to face the world. In the same way, it's a welcome haven for decompressing at the end of the day. That is the best use of an entry, believes Los Angeles artist and garden designer Ketti Kupper—and that is what inspired the design of her own courtyard.

Kupper enclosed the space with patinated steel panels, then hung art against the beautifully mottled surfaces. The pictures are segments from her paintings, blown up and then printed on aluminum. They often contain a few cryptic words. She explains, "I surround myself with images that stimulate the kind of thoughts I want to have."

The rest of the garden follows the example of the walls. Areas rich in details, especially the koi pond surrounded by a lush assortment of plants in one corner, are meant to encourage longer contemplation, just as Kupper's prints do. But there are open spaces in between to quiet the mind as well. "The garden is about balance," she says. **DESIGN:** Ketti Kupper, Conscious Living Landscapes.

Driveway entrance *(far left)* Twisted and curved brass columns, designed by the artist, suggest reeds growing on a riverbank. The grassy plants at its base—blue oat grass and fescue—further the illusion. Similarly, fishhook senecio *(S. radicans)*, spilling out of planters on the far wall, complements a marine-mood print.

Interior pond *(left)* This koi pond is pretty traditional—except for its unexpected zigzag front edge. The ribbon of grass planted in the zigzag emphasizes the feature.

Viewing bench *(below)* Like a Victorian love seat, this modern concrete version allows two people to sit near each other but face in opposite directions, which, in this case, also means enjoying different works of art.

Front-Row Seating

FRINGED WITH CONIFERS and aspen trees on the edge of a vast meadow, this tiered patio is designed to echo its natural surroundings, near Sisters, Oregon. Yet it provides plenty of opportunities for the homeowners to gather and relax near a firepit, or soak in a tub while taking in the views. Paved with soothing Connecticut bluestone, accented with rugged lava rocks, and softened with plants—many native to the region—it creates a nearly seamless transition to wildland. **DESIGN:** Karen Ford Landscape Architect.

Mini meadow *(above)* Lava rock, excavated on-site during house construction, edges the intimate firepit area on the patio's lower level and defines a small planting bed on the upper level. The tufted hair grass *(Deschampsia cespitosa)* in the bed echoes the open meadow beyond, while red-flowered penstemon *(P. barbatus)*, bluish-purple *P. fruticosus*, and white-flowered native yarrow *(Achillea millefolium)* add pops of color. Wild strawberry *(Fragaria virginiana)* rambles over the ground between the taller plants.

Soak in the view *(right)* A heated spa is perfectly positioned to allow soakers to enjoy the view of volcanic Mount Jefferson through a grove of native aspen trees. When not in use, its mirror-smooth water reflects the views. Nearby, the bark of existing ponderosa pines, which resembles "the top of a really good brownie," says the designer, adds visual interest. The retaining wall of lava rock (foreground) doubles as a seating area.

Hiking home *(below)* A broad, meandering Connecticut bluestone path leads to the front door; at 6 feet across, it's wide enough for a small crowd to saunter, as through a meadow, to get to the front door. The tufted hair grass *(Deschampsia cespitosa)* flanking each side of the path gets mowed once a year. This simple trick keeps the plants the same height as the surrounding meadow, but looking fresher and fuller than those on wildland.

GREAT IDEA

Scarlet bugler *(Penstemon barbatus)* is one of the best penstemons for areas where summers are humid and winters somewhat chilly. With loose spikes of red flowers to 3 feet tall or more, it makes a striking accent with golden grasses. For a meadow effect in warmer climates, try firecracker penstemon *(P. eatonii)* with grasses.

Beachfront Getaway

PEOPLE LIKE TO LIVE NEAR THE OCEAN; plants, not so much. Subjected to salt spray and stiff winds, many plants along the coast fail to thrive. Fortunately, the ones that do survive these conditions have sterling characters. Rather than depending on ephemeral flowers for interest, they rely on sculptural shapes, bold foliage colors, and interesting leaf textures, so they're good-looking year-round. And not only are they salt-proof—most are also drought-tolerant. Plants don't get any easier.

For this Malibu, California, deck garden, landscape designer Heather Lenkin made the most of these resilient wonders: *Euphorbia (E. characias wulfenii)*, flax (*Phormium* 'Maori Queen'), melaleuca *(M. quinquenervia)*, Mexican blue palm *(Brahea armata)*, and queen's wreath vine *(Petrea volubilis)* fill in the border between the ipe deck and the enclosing walls. And now that the plants are established, the drip irrigation is rarely turned on—they mostly get by from the moisture in the air.

Even tougher are the aeonium and maidenhair fern *(Adiantum)* in the vertical garden that provides privacy for the dining deck. They rely solely on humidity, with no supplemental irrigation. **DESIGN:** Heather Lenkin, Lenkin Design.

Resort style *(far left)* Edging the entry deck at the front of the house, potted citrus, aeoniums, and orange kangaroo paws pick up the warm hues of the nearby cushions. Most need only occasional watering and yearly trimming, leaving plenty of time to relax on a lounge chair and enjoy the sun.

Secret path *(left)* Pavers trace a path through agaves, blue *Senecio*, and chartreuse *Euphorbia characias wulfenii* along the wall.

Weathered deck *(below)* The deck is made of sustainable ipe wood that has weathered to a soft gray. Beachy accents in this corner include striped cushions, a colorful umbrella, and low bowls filled with succulent rosettes that mimic tidepool life.

"Sitting on this deck feels like having a private balcony on a cruise ship."
—HEATHER LENKIN

Cool accent *(above)* 'Alphonse Karr' bamboo grows in an aqua container, along with snake plant and *Senecio rowleyanus*. Beyond the gate at right, a boardwalk leads to the home's second deck, which overlooks the ocean.

Tidepool wall *(right)* This freestanding living wall consists of two iron frames, covered by brown indoor/outdoor carpeting on the front and by moss-stuffed chicken wire on the back. Dark burgundy *Aeonium arboreum* 'Zwartkop' rosettes and small maidenhair ferns were inserted into the carpet through small slits.

GREAT IDEA

Floral foam attached to a steel cutout with floral tape forms the base of this starfish-shaped centerpiece. Tiny circular cactus—*Astrophytum aster*—grow around the center, while pinkish gray *Lithops* stud the arms and cluster in the center. The succulents are set into the floral foam and get misted occasionally.

Urban Elegance

HILLTOP GARDENS usually have splendid views, but they're also likely to have scary drop-offs. That was the case with Bob Gain and Gene Ogden's garden in San Francisco. As a safety measure, the previous owner had planted a barrier of hedges at the rear of the property. Over time, the shrubs dominated the small garden, hogging way too much space and, worse, blocking the city skyline.

Landscape designer Beth Mullins removed the hedges and replaced them with a less obtrusive retaining wall. Then, to draw the eye to the newly revealed vista, she left the center of the garden nearly bare—just a long, slim reflecting pool framed by a path of blond gravel. The low retaining walls on either side of the pool meet at a step that leads up to the view deck. The walls form a rectangle that mirrors the shape of the pool, reinforcing its command to look out toward the stunning skyline.

The retaining walls double as seating during parties, eliminating the need for extra furniture. Elevating the plantings protects them from the owners' two active dogs, which stay out of the beds and now race around the gravel.

To contrast with the elegant minimalism of the garden's center, the planters display a rich layered tapestry of ajuga, azaleas, cypress, flax, and maples. The borders soften the garden without competing with the grand city view. **DESIGN:** Beth Mullins, Growsgreen Landscape Design.

Green walls *(above)* Adding texture to a wall near the garden's second patio nearest the house, Boston ivy *(Parthenocissus tricuspidata)* turns yellow, orange, and red in fall before dropping its leaves in winter.

View framers *(left)* The garden's long center pond and low border of easy-care plants confined to the perimeter frame rather than block the fantastic view. A pair of Adirondack chairs are set to drink in the San Francisco cityscape.

Destinations

WHERE A POOL IS PLACED determines the whole mood of a garden. Its usual position, close to the house, makes the pool the focal point of the entire space and creates a resort-like ambience. But at this Pacific Palisades, California, property, designer Rob Steiner took the opposite approach. He placed the pool as far back as it could go and obscured the pool with lush plantings that hide it until it is almost in sight. "I wanted getting there to feel like a garden experience," Steiner says.

To encourage lingering, the raised walkway to the pool zigzags to extend the journey. "It's a classic Japanese technique forcing you to slow down," he says. Stops along the way—at a tiny kitchen and a warming firepit—also serve to relax the pace. Tall billowy ornamental grasses all around and a bamboo hedge that screens out neighboring homes concentrate the focus on the garden.

Past the zigzag comes the first glimpse of water, and only at the end of the walkway is the full extent of the pool revealed. The leisurely pace of the journey suggests strolling through a meadow, rounding a bend, and discovering the delightful surprise of a cool, refreshing pond. **DESIGN:** Rob Steiner, Rob Steiner Gardens.

Gentle textures *(far left)* Autumn moor grass *(Sesleria autumnalis)* and *Miscanthus sinensis* 'Morning Light' spill softly onto the walkway. The branches of an Indian laurel fig *(Ficus microcarpa)* arch above the path, creating interest overhead.

Hidden amenities *(left)* A sideboard housing a sink and refrigerator is conveniently located near the firepit seating area. Thanks to its low-key ipe wood facing, it almost seems more plant than furnishing.

Calm colors *(below)* Twin sofas tuck against a stone wall and nestle up to a concrete fire table. The quiet neutral tones add to the garden's serene aura.

"The best destination in any garden is a place of repose...where you can experience a sense of peace and refreshment. This daybed is large enough for the whole family. It feels very luxurious."

—ROB STEINER

ROOM FOR A CROWD
A giant daybed provides a fun place to lounge after swimming laps or extra seating at parties. The steps and seating ledge at this end of the pool offer a spot to sit and stay cool.

Lake-View Terrace

HUGGING THE SUNNY, WEST-FACING SHORE of Lake Washington, this garden takes full advantage of its sloping terrain and sweeping views. Just outside the home's main living spaces, crisp terraces of colored, saw-cut concrete are fringed with Japanese maple trees that frame lake views. From the terrace, stairs and paths lead downslope to a waters-edge garden area that includes a wood-enclosed hot tub, horseshoe pit, dock, beach, and firepit.

Natives and other compatible plants, suitable for Washington's Puget Sound region and chosen for easy maintenance, echo the natural waterfront habitat. They include native wild strawberry and purple osier willow *(Salix purpurea)* and ornamental grasses that interact with the changing patterns of light and wind. **DESIGN:** Randy Allworth, Allworth Design.

Firepit *(above)* Rugged and natural-looking, the sunken firepit is hard-edged and geometric on the patio side, but gently curving on the beach half, where natural granite boulders pack its sides. Feathery grasses blend with the shoreline habitat beyond. A boulder seat is just right for extra guests.

Zigzag edging *(left)* Like the lake's rocky shore nearby, the garden's top terrace has a jagged edge, enhanced by low, green groundcovers.

Sun catchers *(below)* Framed by vibrant Japanese maples, ornamental grasses such as maiden grass, giant feather grass *(Stipa gigantea)*, feather reed grass (*Calamagrostis × acutiflora* 'Karl Foerster'), and fountain grass *(Pennisetum alopecuroides)* glow in the late afternoon sunlight and shimmer in breezes that blow in off the lake. Like other plantings in this garden, they mimic the natural vegetation growing nearby.

Slope Solution

HOW DO YOU CREATE a garden on land that stair-steps downhill, its terraces edged by concrete retaining walls? That was the dilemma faced by landscape architect Jarrod Baumann and his client, a passionate plant lover. But working together, the two turned the difficult site in Los Gatos, California, into a series of outdoor rooms, each with its own spectacular personality. To mask the concrete block walls, Baumann created "wave walls" of embossed steel by propping sheets of plywood, end to end, against the concrete retaining walls, sketching the "waves," taking the numbered panels to a metal fabricator, and then mounting the finished metal panels to the front of the concrete walls.

Paths at the ends provide access to all terraces, while a series of rills and fountains down the center connect them visually. "We started with harsh, hard lines," says Baumann, "then layered the garden on top. Now the billowy plants have taken over and softened everything." **DESIGN:** Jarrod Baumann, Zeterre Landscape Architecture.

Patterns in grass *(top left)* Edging the second terrace from the top, soft mounds of blue fescue, silver puya (*Puya coerulea* 'Coerulea'), and *Phormium* 'Amazing Red' fringe the embossed steel wave wall. Lavenders and *Erysimum* 'Bowles Mauve' bring cool-colored flowers to the party.

Fence detail *(top right)* Two stairways connect all the terraces. This one is edged with a narrow bed filled with heucheras. The same embossed steel used in the wall repeats on the stair risers, allowing natural light to reflect onto the steps. Elephant's ear *(Colocasia)* spreads its big fanlike leaves behind.

Bocce garden *(bottom left)* The same blue fescue, silver puya, and phormium edge the third terrace (in front is a bocce court). But here, thread-leaf nandina adds soft-textured, vibrant green foliage. Rich purple 'Ebb Tide' roses and blue-flowered catmint accent the bed behind the wall.

"Spring" walk *(opposite page)* Edging a path near the house, goldenchain trees *(Laburnum)* dangle their hanging clusters of yellow, sweet-pea-shaped flowers above candy-pink rhododendron blooms in mid- to late spring. The trees' flexible branches are easy to espalier to make beautiful allées (tunnels). Lavender perfumes the air in the distance.

A Surfer's Haven

MANY NEW HOMEOWNERS share the same problem: They're left with a small, bare-bones backyard and—after down payments, furniture, and other expenditures—a nearly empty wallet. Professional surfer Timmy Reyes faced that situation at his new residence in Costa Mesa, California.

An affordable hardscape now covers most of the space, forming an outdoor entertainment center. A poured concrete patio just outside the living room provides one conversation center and, just a few steps up, a deck made of Trex offers a second gathering spot. The changes in level and materials create interest and encourage circulation during parties.

For needed privacy, bamboo fencing hides the existing back wall—two rows of concrete block topped by metal bars. This thrifty solution gives the space a tropical ambience, embellished by the addition of a few palms and papyrus around a small fountain. The rest of the planting is mostly bulletproof succulents. All are on drip irrigation.

Furniture costs were shaved too. The teak sofa, a knockoff of a designer's line, was built by a carpenter for a fraction of the price. The remaining furniture comes from Pier 1 and Ikea. **DESIGN:** Brooke Dietrich, Green Landscapes to Envy.

A small row of echeveria tucked between the upper and lower patio reminds visitors to step up. Similarly, larger succulents—three kinds of aeonium—signal that the upper patio drops off. These are also ways to tuck a little more greenery in a landscape with limited planting opportunities.

Investment plants *(above)* The bulk of the plants in this garden are inexpensive succulents. But a few larger specimen plants, such as the green *Cordyline* shown here, are worth their higher price for their instant impact.

Bargain lights *(left)* Candles in Moroccan lanterns are an inexpensive and romantic way to illuminate a garden.

Thrifty fountain *(opposite page)* A tall ceramic urn, found at a discount garden center and reconfigured as a fountain, adds a dramatic focal point. Its narrow shape doesn't take up much real estate, which is another plus in this small garden.

Keeping It Simple

IT'S POSSIBLE TO BANISH CLUTTER and chaos from one's life—and from the backyard as well. Just ask landscape designer and horticulturist Brian Kissinger, who hates clutter, having grown up in a house full of knickknacks collected by his antique-dealer parents. That's one reason he was attracted to this 1960s modern house in Paradise Valley, Arizona. The home's clean lines inspired the garden renovations.

Kissinger's mantra: Provide enough detail to make the garden feel like a relaxing retreat, but not an iota more. Less clutter, he believes, leads to less stress. Accordingly, Kissinger chose plants with repetitive shapes, giving the major players in each bed enough room to show off, while restricting the supporting cast to a few plants that complement the stars. "This garden is so clean and spare, the natural landscape jumps out at you," he says. **DESIGN:** Brian Kissinger.

Reclaim *(above)* When the frosted glass panels of the front gates slide together, the space behind them becomes an intimate outdoor room shaded by a canopy of date palms.

PATH AS PARK Thyme grows between wide steps made of concrete aggregate. Boulders, cactus, and rosemary fringe the edges. The entry path offers a nature walk that encourages guests to slow down and enjoy the journey.

"I wanted to create the feeling of a David Hockney pool painting. A simple rectangle of blue."

—BRIAN KISSINGER

Repeat *(above)* One plant, and one plant only, is stunning when it has as dramatic a shape and color as barrel cactus *(Ferocactus cylindraceus).*

Create an oasis *(right)* Date *(Phoenix)* and Bismarck palms *(Bismarckia nobilis)* flank a pool inspired by the paintings of David Hockney.

Borrowed Scenery

THE WILDFLOWERS AND GRASSES surrounding this Ketchum, Idaho, property look as if they traveled downhill, jumped the paths, and snuggled in next to the sleek, contemporary home. And that's just the effect the landscape architect was after.

The pristine land around this home inspired the landscape design. Plants found in the nearby natural setting are arranged more formally in the garden, but just slightly so. For example, in a series of shallow terraces in front, native species were planted en masse to create a more ordered look and to emphasize their individual forms. As you edge away from the house, the grasses and flowers merge together again, the way they naturally grow on the hill.

The hardscape and soil blend together almost as seamlessly. Because the local earth is distinctly red, the designer chose crushed red stone for the pathways and a pinkish stone for the hardscape.

The trees reflected in the front window are also part of the merger. Their images in the glass make sections of the house look more like landscape than structure. **DESIGN:** Ron Lutsko Jr., Lutsko Associates.

Vary textures *(above)* A small rectangle of cool lawn looks twice as plush next to an expanse of concrete deck. Native wildflowers add a lacy fringe.

Use horizontal lines *(opposite page)* Bands of steel create a strong pattern—the risers of the steps continue as the edge of the planting beds. The way the plants are arranged en masse—unexpected with native species—also emphasizes the geometry of the parallel lines. The plants used, back to front, are wild rye *(Elymus cinereus)*, goldenrod *(Solidago canadensis)*, and yarrow *(Achillea)*.

The same native plants growing on the hillside above this home were used on either side of the path behind it to connect the house with its wild surroundings. Planting loosely and casually reinforces the illusion that the grasses, penstemon, and flax just blew in and seeded themselves.

Tough Love

WINTERS ARE FROSTY and summers are sizzling in New Mexico, but there are xeric (drought-tolerant) plants that thrive under these challenging conditions, and many of them are as showy as they are gutsy. At this Santa Fe garden, landscape designer Donna Bone concentrated these stellar performers near the house, where their colorful blooms would be best appreciated. She put flowers with saturated colors in the hottest exposures because their hues stand up best to the bright sun, and saved the pastels for the shade. Moving away from the house, Bone gradually decreased the floriferous perennials and added natives that needed even less water. The landscape ends in a native grass meadow that looks like the wildlands around it.

The garden's cultivated portion is watered from rainfall harvested off the roof, collected in drain boxes below, and piped to a 32,000-gallon underground cistern. The meadow, like the native landscape, survives on natural irrigation alone. **DESIGN:** Donna Bone, Design with Nature.

"Lush greenery is a comforting sight in our challenging arid climate, so concentrating its use near the house feels very welcoming."
—DONNA BONE

Cheerful native *(top left)* Well-named Perky Sue *(Tetraneuris argentea)*, a New Mexico perennial, enjoys a long bloom period.

Blocks of color *(top right)* Red and blue provide a big punch in this seating area. The red comes from a New Mexico native, *Penstemon pinifolius*; the blue, from 'Walker's Low' catmint *(Nepeta racemosa)*.

Fall splendor *(bottom left)* The lavender-blue of aster (*A.* × *frikartii* 'Mönch') is perfectly complemented late in the year by the changing color of New Mexican privet *(Forestiera neomexicana)* leaves.

Wave a welcome *(opposite page)* An intermittent ribbon of catmint *(Nepeta)* leads visitors toward the entry garden.

Wall of Light

THE ULTIMATE BACKDROP for garden gatherings, this multilayered wall edges a long, shallow lawn behind a mid-century ranch house in Los Altos Hills, California. Framing views of golden grasses and other plants on the slope behind, it modernizes the entire garden and visually connects (and defines) two outdoor living spaces: a kids' play area and lounge area at one end and an outdoor kitchen, dining area, and fireplace at the other. The wall also visually breaks up the long, narrow backyard and contains a built-in bench.

"Layered walls are like sculpture," says Gretchen Whittier, of Arterra Landscape Architects, about the wall's overlapping panels of wood and stucco. "They are focal points from every room of a house and yard." When the sun goes down, uplights bathe the wall in a soft glow. With a fire blazing in the stone fireplace, there's no place the owners would rather be. That's when their garden is pure drama. **DESIGN:** Kate Stickley and Natasha Libina, Arterra Landscape Architects.

Nestled among existing fruit trees, a play area balances the yard's entertaining area on one end by providing a quiet and contemplative space for relaxing with the kids on the opposite end. Colored concrete stepping stones lead to a large, circular sandbox, which can be converted into a firepit once the children have outgrown it.

Glow wall *(above)* Thoughtful repetition and layering of stone, ipe wood, and concrete create a bold, contemporary context for the garden. At the foot of the wall, a path of concrete pavers leads from the lounge patio at one end of the garden to the fireplace, kitchen, and dining area at the other.

Outdoor kitchen *(right)* Adjacent to the fireplace-lounge area, an outdoor kitchen has a built-in grill, sink, and bar area for entertaining. The patio in the foreground is where the family dines on summer evenings.

Beach Bliss

WHEN THE SUN SETS over the Pacific and waves wash softly on the sand nearby, this garden's owners sit back and savor their beachfront view. Nothing else can disturb the serenity, because there are no fussy plants to announce—by their presence—"weed me, feed me, mow, please!" Formerly covered with lawn grass, it never felt quite right to Gordon and Julia Held: It guzzled water and looked out of place against sand and surf. So, the couple hired Jeffrey Gordon Smith. His solution: turn the 20-by-60-foot yard into a "soft hardscape," combining pavers with a wind-whipped plant palette.

With their Mediterranean colors, the water-wise plants blend naturally into the landscape and require less attention than lawn. "Now we spend less time looking down at weeds that need pulling and more time looking at the ocean," says Gordon Held. "We feel more a part of the beach scene."

DESIGN: Jeffrey Gordon Smith Landscape Architecture.

Patio *(far left)* Poured-in-place concrete pavers top a 6-inch sand base; spaces between them keep water from running off. Acid-washed to add texture, "they feel like sand underfoot," says Smith. Mexican pebbles in mixed sizes fill the spaces between the pavers in the foreground, giving way to silvery blue *Dymondia margaretae* in the background, for a visual change of pace. Lyme grass (*Leymus condensatus* 'Canyon Prince'), native to Southern California and the Channel Islands, edges the patio, forming a low privacy hedge in summer. It flows with the wind and has more of a feeling of a dune. *Juniperus rigida conferta* 'Blue Pacific' laps at pavers nearest the house.

Living screen *(left)* Big, mounding pride of Madeira *(Echium candicans)* shrubs are well placed to provide privacy from the neighboring houses; their tall candles of lavender-blue flowers bloom in spring.

Focal point *(below)* Driftwood from elsewhere on site ("a poetic piece," Smith calls it) doubles as bench and sculpture. Tufts of blue moor grass *(Sesleria caerulea)* fan out in front, while succulents—made for close-up viewing—grow behind.

THE SPONGE EFFECT

Coastal cities from San Diego and Santa Monica to Portland are encouraging ocean-friendly gardens for all residents, not just for those living near the beach.

The key elements: porous soil, climate-appropriate plants, and permeable paving to soak up or channel rainfall directly into the soil. Unlike heavily watered and hard-paved landscapes that can send pollutants into storm drains and, ultimately, the ocean, spongelike gardens prevent runoff. Find guidelines at *surfriderfoundation.org.*

SAND•SCAPING

GARDENERS LUCKY ENOUGH to live where beach sand laps at the back patio need tough plants to make a garden. Native grasses, for example, or low, mounding shrubs that have evolved with deep tap roots, succulent or downy leaves, or other traits that help them to withstand drought, wind, salt spray, and porous, somewhat shifting soil. In other words, plants that resemble those growing naturally in dune habitats along the West Coast, such as artemesias, buckwheats, beach aster *(Erigeron glaucus)*, and sea thrift *(Armeria maritima)*.

But even if you don't live on the beach, you can create a beachy corner in your own backyard, similar to the "barefoot" path shown opposite. Just dig a channel 6 inches deep in the soil, pour in sand from a building supply yard, then plant some grasses on either side to catch the wind.

Dune tapestry *(above)* A boardwalk of weathered wood winds past silvery artemesia, clusters of blue lupine, and a carpet of pink-flowered iceplant in this beachfront garden in Carpinteria, California. **DESIGN:** Isabelle Greene & Associates.

Barefoot path *(above)* This 6-inch-deep ribbon of sand meanders through a Malibu garden. Varying from 3 to 12 feet wide, it has no hard edging—the sand drifts, beachlike, into the plantings. Beachy grasses (including *Sesleria* and *Muhlenbergia*) shimmer in sunlight on either side. *Arbutus* 'Marina' spreads its shading canopy behind. **DESIGN:** Pamela Burton & Company Landscape Architecture.

Sea-foam blooms *(right)* Dotted with white flowers, snow-in-summer *(Cerastium tomentosum)* appears to spill through buff-colored boulders and wash like sea foam across sand in this Carpinteria, California, garden fringing a coastal wetland. **DESIGN:** Isabelle Greene & Associates.

Gardens-at-a-Glance

"IN AN URBAN SETTING, one of the biggest criteria is that the garden can be viewed as a composition from above," says landscape architect Roderick Wyllie of San Francisco–based Surfacedesign and creator of the garden above. Indeed, compact city lots are most often either long and narrow, or postage-stamp-size. This bird's-eye perspective is an opportunity to create two gardens at once—one to be enjoyed from above and another to experience from below.

What works well when viewed from up above? Strong geometric lines, muted plantings, and simple hardscaping. All can make the tiniest outdoor spaces feel larger, while accommodating outdoor living, play, and more.

The three gardens here are designed to make small gardens look and live larger. Each employs clever techniques so that even the smallest of spaces pops from above and feels welcoming from below.

Change levels *(far left)* Long Cor-Ten steel walls divide this sloping city backyard into a raised dining room and a play area down below. Viewed from above, the garden reads as a geometric work of art. **DESIGN:** Roderick Wyllie, Surfacedesign.

Go bold *(left)* Set in deep shade, this urban garden is packed with elements that brighten it. Black concrete walls, honed to a polish, turn shiny when wet. The walls frame beds, planted with white-flowering perennials that seem to glow at dusk. Stainless steel bands extend the graphic, glossy look, and cobalt blue LED track lights brighten up the space at night. **DESIGN:** Andrea Cochran Landscape Architecture.

Create rooms *(below)* Clever repurposing transformed a narrow San Francisco yard into terraced outdoor rooms, including a dining patio built from old bricks found on the property, a raised deck for casual gatherings, and a small patch of lawn. **DESIGN:** Beth Mullins, Growsgreen Landscape Design.

Front Yards

A FRONT YARD is the most visible part of any property; like a business card, it tells passersby something about you. Ideally, it should balance a feeling of welcome with a bit of privacy. And it should echo the home's architectural style and reflect the garden's personality. Most of all, a front yard should be inviting to your guests. The walkway should be wide enough for two people to walk side by side as they come and go, and it should visually separate from the driveway; lighting should direct guests at night. The best plantings for a front yard are easy to care for—increasingly in the arid West, that means unthirsty groundcovers instead of thirsty lawns whose only purpose is to be seen.

Sculptural *(above)* Elm trees frame this lush entry garden in Palo Alto, California. Clusters of yellowish *Liriope* edge the walk, while a green Japanese maple (*Acer palmatum* 'Sango Kaku'), ferns *(Woodwardia fimbriata)*, and plum-colored *Loropetalum chinense* 'Majestic Red' grow on either side. An L-shaped bench near the door invites lingering. **DESIGN:** Jarrod Baumann, Zeterre Landscape Architecture.

Tailored *(above)* Stripes of red, "wheat," and blue add color and motion to this Los Angeles front yard. Blue *Senecio mandraliscae* (foreground) echoes the hue of the front door, while Mexican feather grass, 'Big Red' kangaroo paws, and a 'Bloodgood' Japanese maple grow behind. **DESIGN:** Greg Sanchez, GDS Designs.

Rounded *(right)* Like a framed painting, this circular garden shows off agaves, lantana, yuccas, and other desert plants, all settled among boulders and a rock mulch in Palm Springs, California. Tall ocotillo, topped with vibrant red blooms, rises in the center. **DESIGN:** Steve Martino Landscape Architect.

Side Yards

MANY SIDE YARDS, especially in the West's crowded urban areas, are narrow and often shady. But with a little careful planning, it's possible to make them interesting; there's almost always space for at least a few compact plants that like shade, or to tuck in a hidden retreat. Try interplanting steppingstones with low-growing, shade-tolerant groundcovers, or tucking a few potted plants at the curves of a winding path. If unattractive block walls separate the yard from the neighbors', a curtain of greenery tumbling from flower boxes placed atop the wall can provide camouflage.

Northwest green *(above)* Long and skinny, this paved side yard looked like a bowling alley. That was before someone took a jackhammer to it. With the concrete gone, the designer used foliage to give the space a warm, lush feel. Rich goldenrod walls now set the mood, and drifts of gold-tinted perennials—Japanese forest grass, autumn fern, and 'Bowles Golden' sedge—reinforce it. Blue hosta 'Halcyon' adds contrasting color, and Japanese maple gives a sense of volume. **DESIGN:** Darcy Daniels.

CALIFORNIA ZEN

A clean-lined path skirts the north side of a home in Newport Beach, California, where it connects a series of courtyards for dining and lounging. A bridge crosses a pond beside the spilling fountain, while a piece of art amid the greenery at the end provides a focal point. DESIGN: Glen Brouwer, with the owners.

Driveways

ONE OF A PROPERTY'S most visible features, the long stretch of paving where you usually park your car is often overlooked as a potential area for landscaping with plants for privacy or for a patio for outdoor living. If your garden space is limited and you have access to parking elsewhere, a driveway can provide a narrow plot for training espaliered fruit trees along a fence or for growing herbs, strawberries, or succulents. Add a dining table, a few chairs, a colorful umbrella, and a cluster of colorful potted plants, and you have an outdoor living room. If your driveway is long enough, you can install a gate across the front half, park in front, and turn the back half into an outdoor living area complete with a trickling fountain and a firepit.

Sitting area *(above)* The owners of this driveway chose to rethink it without permanently blocking the garage. They added a built-in bench, topped it with colorful cushions, then freshened the cinder block wall behind with evenly spaced redwood strips. DESIGN: Katherine Spitz Associates.

Planting beds *(left)* After converting their 1927 garage into a garden shed and cabana, the owners of this garden removed the rear half of the driveway and put in a path of curved concrete pavers. Then they added beds of astilbe, bear's breech, hellebore, and hosta. DESIGN: Mary Baum.

Outdoor dining *(opposite page)* A teak table and chairs, along with an assortment of container plants, turned this back portion of driveway into a private outdoor dining patio. DESIGN: Brent Green.

Rooftops

NOT EVERY GARDENER has a plot of land for a garden—especially in the West's urban areas. But even a balcony or rooftop can hold a beautiful display, whether potted grasses or metal troughs filled with lettuce and herbs. Add a couple of chairs and a small table, and you've got a little piece of paradise perched on high. Rooftop gardening does take some planning, though.

Choose plastic or resin containers that are lightweight and moisture retentive. Make sure they have good drainage, and use liners or saucers to protect the roof or floor. Safe distribution of weight is an important concern. Your contractor or homeowners' association can advise you about weight limits for recently built structures. If you live in an older building or plan to amass heavy pots and furniture, it's worth the cost to get advice from a structural engineer.

Beach "boardwalk" *(top left)* This rooftop aerie, atop the guest house of a Shell Beach, California, property, offers sweeping views of the Pacific Ocean. Wild rye, native to the Channel Islands, edges the deck, which has a sunken firepit at its center. **DESIGN:** Jeffrey Gordon Smith Landscape Architecture with architect Richard Blair LeGros.

Roof lounge *(top right)* An outdoor bed and cozy lounges brighten this roof deck in San Francisco. Yarrows echo the furnishings' cheerful hues. **DESIGN:** Surfacedesign.

Island in the sky *(bottom left)* Planters filled with grasses, 'Sunburst' aeonium, and perennials border this San Francisco rooftop. **DESIGN:** Loretta Gargan Landscape + Design.

ROOM·SCAPING

EVEN WHERE GARDEN SPACE IS TIGHT, it's possible to tuck in an outdoor room that feels like a destination from your back door, for instance, a partially enclosed outdoor room like the cozy and private hideaway pictured here. Designed for *Sunset's* Menlo Park, California, test garden by Eric and Leslie McKenna (a father-daughter design team), it has homelike comfort, yet is open to warming sun and cooling breezes. "We envisioned an enclosed outdoor living room for entertaining guests and relaxing with family," says Leslie. To build the structure, the McKennas used recycled wood and window frames, giving new life to materials that would otherwise end up in landfill. "Whether old wood or a mature tree, there's something very appealing about materials that already have been well loved," says Leslie. "Maturity feels comforting. Yet this enclosure feels incredibly fresh." **DESIGN:** McKenna Landscape.

Theme *(above)* Against a plant palette of mostly greens and gold, pillows add pops of vivid lime green and orange to a couch built of recycled wood. Reed grass *(Calamagrostis)*, chosen for its tall, slender plumes that wave in the wind, catches the light behind the window.

Finishing touches *(left)* For the flooring, rebar bent into circles top ⅜-inch taffy gravel. An akebia vine climbs up through an old glassless window frame behind a pair of chairs, made of recycled wood. Orange canvas panels from Sunbrella add a cheerful note overhead and provide some shade.

Structure *(opposite page)* Framed with recycled wood posts, it's 18 feet long, 8 feet wide, and 8 feet tall. Planter boxes, made of recycled wood fencing in various shades of cinnamon and tan to gray-brown, flank the entry, while dry-stacked Connecticut bluestone edges the beds along the entry and inside. Thyme and dwarf New Zealand flax grow around potted citrus.

STRUCTURES

Structures give your garden its shape and dimension—fences, by dividing the space into rooms; arbors and trellises by adding shelter, privacy, and support for vining plants. Walls can double as seating and backdrops for garden art. Decks, patios, and outdoor kitchens bring livability outdoors for parties and family dinners, while warming firepits and cooling water features set the stage for relaxation. Unless you choose recycled materials such as broken concrete for paths, wooden planks salvaged from an old barn for fencing, or vintage manhole covers to make a patio, you'll find that all structures and hardscaping are a garden's costliest features. But by paying attention to the materials you use, you'll end up with arbors, walls, paths, and patios that are durable, functional, and richly textured.

DECKED OUT Wood on wood unifies this backyard in Menlo Park, California. A floating deck is the perfect setting for a rough-hewn custom dining table, and the simple board fence offers privacy and visual warmth. DESIGN: Arterra Landscape Architects.

Arbors and Trellises

ALTHOUGH AN ARBOR IS REALLY JUST an "outdoor roof," it has a magnetic effect in the garden. People tend to congregate beneath it, whether mingling at a garden party or just relaxing with a good book. It's also a major structure that can dramatically reconfigure your outdoor space, tying together different areas or architectural elements of the garden, directing foot traffic, and providing privacy or screening.

The most natural adornment for an arbor is a climbing vine—favorites include clematis, grapes, honeysuckle, jasmine, kiwi, roses, trumpet vine, and wisteria. Many of these are hefty, long-lived plants, so be sure your arbor is strong enough to support the weight of foliage and fruit.

A trellis—a smaller version of the arbor—is generally a more delicate structure whose primary purpose is to support plants. But a trellis can also add screening and vertical interest and serve as a divider in the garden. If attaching the trellis to a wall or fence, use wooden spacers to improve the air circulation between them.

SHADE STRATEGIES

The way you position the rafters of an arbor allows you to control the degree of shade. Rafters that run east–west provide the most shade, especially at midday; those running north–south cast less shade. Setting 1-by-2s or 1-by-3s on edge offers more shade when the sun is at an angle in the morning and late afternoon. Arranging them with their greatest width flat provides more midday shade when the sun is directly overhead. Depending on how much shade you want, you can leave the rafters bare or cover them with vines or a material such as bamboo or lattice.

Hillside haven *(above)* Perched halfway up the slope in Healdsburg, California, this modern arbor of metal and wood shelters a sitting area while adding a light, shapely element to the landscape. **DESIGN:** Blasen Landscape Architecture.

Patio cover *(left)* An elegant lath arbor, edged with vines, shades comfortable lounge chairs and a fountain made from a massive boulder. **DESIGN:** Blasen Landscape Architecture.

Citrus tunnel *(opposite page)* Lemons and oranges stay within easy reach as they dangle from metal arches that form this backyard tunnel—a fragrant, shady place to stand while harvesting—in Los Altos, California.

"Scarlet runner beans are double-duty beauties. Their flowers attract hummingbirds, and their young edible pods develop into tasty shellable beans."

—JOHANNA SILVER, *Associate Garden Editor, Sunset*

"Moongate" trellis *(opposite page)* This circular trellis from TerraTrellis *(terratrellis.com)* is made of rustproof steel. Vine-covered or bare, it is a sculpture you can walk through. Here, it supports scarlet runner beans.

"Eyebrow" trellis *(right)* Framing an inviting entry gate in Southern California, this sturdy trellis supports a sky flower *(Thunbergia grandiflora)*. **DESIGN:** Mark Tessier Landscape Architecture.

Santa Fe flair *(bottom left)* Rustic log beams add Southwest flavor to a patio alcove dressed up with a coat of brilliant blue paint. **DESIGN:** Donna Bone, Design with Nature.

Tuck-in trellis *(bottom right)* Nestled between walls in a stylish rooftop garden in San Francisco, this ladder-style, painted wrought-iron trellis gives just enough support for delicate vines. **DESIGN:** Lutsko Associates.

> "With the right balance of privacy and openness, you can create an inviting entry that gets used for outdoor living."
>
> —RUSS CLETTA, *landscape architect*

Decks

A DECK, LIKE A PATIO, is an extension of your house that provides space for dining, entertaining, and just hanging out. A raised deck can create new space in the garden, and it can easily overcome the challenge of a sloping, bumpy, or poorly drained site. Also, a wood deck doesn't store heat the way a stone, brick, or concrete patio does.

Decks can lie alongside the house or be tucked into a remote corner of the garden. A wraparound deck can link interior spaces with a series of outdoor boardwalks or landings, following the shape of the house or playing off it with angular or curved extensions.

Detached decks form quiet retreats, whether sited in the dappled shade beneath trees or elevated to catch the afternoon sun. To enhance the sense of a hideaway, consider adding an overhead arbor, water feature, or spa.

Entry deck *(left)* A tiny front porch in Pacific Palisades, California, got a bold update with this contemporary deck made from sustainably harvested ipe wood and outfitted with a recirculating fountain. Tinted concrete pavers lead to the sidewalk. **DESIGN:** Russ Cletta Design Studio.

Pool deck *(above)* A spacious L-shaped deck hugs this stunning vanishing-edge pool in the hills of Berkeley, California. Maintaining the elegant mood are comfortable, oversize deck chairs in complementary wood tones. **DESIGN:** Bernard Trainor + Associates.

Rooftop deck *(left)* The simple patterns of the deck and furniture, along with their muted tones, keep the focus on the San Francisco skyline view. A chimney echoes the skyscraper theme. **DESIGN:** Blasen Landscape Architecture.

Serene circle *(opposite page)* A perfectly round deck tucked beneath an old cypress is the ideal spot for viewing a scenic stretch of the Santa Barbara, California, coast. Ocean-toned accessories add just the right touch of color. **DESIGN:** Derrik Eichelberger, Arcadia Studio.

For 26 deck ideas, see sunset.com/decks

ECO-SMART WOOD

Shrinking forests and dwindling supplies of quality lumber have encouraged the development of both environmentally sensible wood products and engineered materials suitable for decks and other garden structures. To protect Western forests, consider woods other than the best grades of redwood and cedar, which generally come from the oldest trees. Instead, seek out plantation-grown woods like ipe, or look for suppliers of salvaged lumber from demolished buildings.

Some manufacturers combine landfill-bound wood or bamboo with plastic to make wood-polymer composites. These weatherproof products are suitable for decking and railings—but not for structural members. Available in several colors, they can be painted or stained, and then cut, drilled, and shaped just like standard lumber. For families with young children, these synthetic boards have the additional advantage of being splinter-free.

Fences and Gates

IN THE GARDEN, you can have fun with fences and gates depending on the materials you choose and how you use them. A fence can be anything from a functional combination of boards and posts to a vine-covered lattice or a whimsical screen of woven twigs. Whatever the material, a fence represents a boundary between different areas of the garden, or between public and private spaces.

While fences are often considered functional dividers or backdrops, gates are more likely candidates for making into a showpiece—whether painted a high-contrast color or constructed of unexpected materials. A gate signifies a transition, both an entry and an exit, so make it interesting. Also think carefully about whether your gate needs to be locked. Keyless combination lock kits make it easy to enhance security.

Fences

A good-looking fence helps foster a sense of a secure, private retreat from the outside world. Aside from marking a property line, it can divide the garden into separate rooms, filter the sun, moderate strong winds, and mute the sounds of street traffic.

Most fences are built of wood, whether split rails, bent twigs, grape stakes, lumber, poles, plywood, or bamboo. Alternative materials run from chain-link to custom metalwork panels that become works of garden art. Whatever your choice of fencing, make sure it coordinates with the style and materials of your house.

Most communities have regulations restricting fence height—generally 4 feet high in the front yard and 6 to 8 feet in the backyard. Check with your local building department or community planning office.

Fences along boundary lines are often owned and maintained by both neighbors. Make every effort to come to a friendly agreement with your neighbor on the location, design, and construction of the fence. But if you can't agree, just build the fence entirely on your land, a few inches inside your boundary.

Friendly fence *(above)* More a suggestion of private space behind than a barrier, this fence's horizontal boards, open design, and dark color add modern curb appeal to a Redwood City, California, house. **DESIGN:** Jared Vermeil Landscape Design.

Industrial slats *(left)* Cor-Ten steel slats, allowed to rust naturally, give this fence the look of a sculptural installation. Because the slats are arranged vertically and set apart by several inches, the fence practically disappears when viewed straight on. **DESIGN:** Randy Thueme Design.

Salvaged planks *(opposite page)* Boards from an old horse corral and from a railroad station give this fence in Santa Monica Canyon in California its modern lines. Both sets of boards are screwed to a fabricated and powder-coated metal frame, whose posts are sunk in concrete footings. **DESIGN:** Eric Brandon Gomez.

Bold panels *(above)* Raised above stone-filled gabions, these oversize panels are arranged with views in mind. One board doubles as a bench atop a gabion wall. **DESIGN:** Laura Crockett, Garden Diva Designs.

Metallic weave *(right)* Aluminum flashing weaves like a ribbon through standing sections of rebar in a Phoenix garden. The result is a contemporary art piece that also provides complete privacy and blends with the metallic patio furnishings nearby. **DESIGN:** Steve Martino Landscape Architect.

GREAT IDEA

Looking for a way to dress up a plain wood fence? Try painting it white and using it as a backdrop for decorative metal panels with cutout circles or other shapes. The effect is especially delightful at night, when uplights give the impression of a projected image. DESIGN: Shades of Green Landscape Architecture.

Get twiggy *(above)* This enchanting twig-and-branch fence suggests a cottage garden from simpler times. Constructing it atop a stone wall helps keep the wood from rotting through contact with moist soil. **DESIGN:** Roger Warner.

Rotate the gate *(left)* This innovative gate is hidden when closed, appearing as just another panel in the sturdy wooden fence. Light-colored gravel within the courtyard coordinates nicely with the concrete walkway outside. **DESIGN:** Surfacedesign.

Gates

Gates are functional necessities—but that doesn't mean they can't be interesting. A walk-through gate should be large enough to provide clearance for moving sizable items in and out—36 inches wide is the minimum. For a wider entry (a driveway, for example), a common solution is a gate that opens from the middle or moves on rollers. Entry and boundary gates usually swing in toward the house or garden, but a gate within the property can swing in the direction of the greater traffic flow.

Your gate can be inconspicuous—seeming to blend in with the materials used for the fence—or it can be a contrasting element that reflects your personality. A solid gate provides total privacy, while one with a window frames a view. Open-style gates are more of a visual statement, communicating to the visitor a sense of passage from one garden area to the next. Whichever style you choose, make sure the gate is solidly constructed and easily operated.

Gated carrots *(above)* To spice up an entryway, the veggie-loving owner, JJ De Sousa, designed a metal gate with cutouts of giant carrots.

Open transition *(left)* There is no functional need for a gate along this path, but placing it here practically guarantees that visitors will pause and take note of what's ahead. Decorative spheres crown the metal gateposts. **DESIGN:** Chandler & Chandler Landscape Architects.

Geometry out front *(opposite page)* Simplicity is key in this Tucson entryway, where a rusted metal gate provides a modernist accent against the home's soft curves and subtle colors, and a shapely ocotillo.

Fireplaces

> "The crepe myrtles create a feeling of a natural canopy, while the fireplace provides warmth and intimacy."
> —STEFAN THUILOT, *landscape designer*

AN OUTDOOR FIREPLACE transforms a patio into a true open-air room—one that is warm, welcoming, and comfortable in all but the most wintry weather.

You can install a fireplace in a sheltered entry courtyard, along the rear wall of the house, at the boundary between paved and planted areas, even in a wooden deck—anywhere you want to create a gathering spot. And it can fit into almost any landscape design, with chimneys and hearth surrounds made of stone, stucco, slate, or tile. To customize your fireplace, add a fancy mantel or a hearth that doubles as seating.

If you'd rather not burn wood, a natural gas–fueled fireplace is a great alternative. These may contain "logs" made of a ceramic material, or the flame may arise directly from a bed of lava rock or crushed glass. Gas fireplaces don't require a chimney because the exhaust is released through slots in the frame.

Check with your local building inspector to find out code requirements for both setback and chimney height. In most municipalities, a freestanding fireplace is considered a separate structure that requires a building permit.

Poolside hearth *(left)* A tall chimney points to the hillside of this Northern California garden, while a built-in bench provides a warm place to sit. The "rug" is an inset of ipe wood. **DESIGN:** Stefan Thuilot, Thuilot Associates.

FIRE BASICS

Common sense dictates that you take extra care when dealing with fire. Here are important fire-safety guidelines.

- Situate fire features away from combustible materials such as dry grasses and other highly flammable plants.
- Burn dry, well-seasoned firewood only. Generally, hardwoods (ash, hickory, madrone, maple, and oak) burn cleaner than softwoods (cedar, fir, and pine). Or switch to wood substitutes when fire danger is high in your area. And don't overfill the fireplace or firepit.
- Use a spark arrester—a screen that prevents large embers from escaping—on the chimney.
- Observe fire ordinances and don't use your fireplace on no-burn days or when it's smoggy or windy.
- Never leave a fire unattended, and keep a fire extinguisher or a garden hose with a sprayer nearby.
- Get your fireplace cleaned regularly by a professional.

Hot lava *(above)* This open fireplace design situates natural-gas flames between a row of large lava rocks and a rusted metal backdrop. Variegated agaves and New Zealand flax grow behind. **DESIGN:** Nicole Lopez Landscape Design.

Open flame *(left)* This stylish gas fireplace in Beverly Hills, California, is simply a niche in the retaining wall that has been lined with fireproof panels. **DESIGN:** Ecocentrix Landscape Architecture.

Low slung, high style *(opposite page)* To preserve the view of the vibrant 'Barbara Karst' bougainvillea and gorgeous Camelback Mountain beyond, the owners opted for a long, low fireplace. Its neutral, natural tones help it blend right in with the Arizona landscape. **DESIGN:** Michael Dollin and Sunni Jackson, Urban Earth Design.

Firepits

IF A FIREPLACE DOESN'T SEEM RIGHT for your garden, consider a firepit. Permanent types burn wood, propane supplied by a tank, or natural gas. These built-in pits often include a bench where you can sit and enjoy the warmth and glow of the fire.

As an alternative, almost any patio can accommodate a small, portable firepit, which can be easily moved for parties or with the changing seasons. Or for more enclosed flames, try a chimenea (Spanish for "chimney"), a small freestanding fireplace with an open front for loading wood and a chimney for venting smoke. Make sure your portable fire feature is completely level and stable, and set it up on a patio of stone, concrete, or gravel (patio bark is flammable).

FLOATING FIRE A pair of side-by-side square firepits form a Phoenix garden's focal point, especially after dark. Elevated on uneven pedestals, they appear to hover above the golden decomposed granite. DESIGN: Troy Bankord Design.

Mod campfire *(above)* Edged by a deck made of Trex and lit by lanterns, this sunken firepit and seat wall accommodate life at Stinson Beach, California, complete with sandy feet, wet kids, and dogs. "The design is like a well-organized campsite," says architect Peter Pfau. **DESIGN:** Pfau Architecture.

Fire, water, spheres *(left)* Industrial chic meets pure whimsy when a rectangular concrete pool is fitted with a beam bench on one side, a row of gas jets on the other, and two painted spheres. **DESIGN:** Katherine Spitz Associates.

Rebar rising *(opposite page)* In this Phoenix garden, rebar is used in an unexpected way: it juts randomly from the circular firepit. Rebar holds up well to the desert climate, and its rugged aesthetic looks at home amid bristly plants and jagged cliffs. **DESIGN:** Steve Martino Landscape Architect.

"Everyone is drawn to a campfire—even a mod one. The flames in this firepit dance around in the slightest breeze. It's mesmerizing."

—JEFFREY GORDON SMITH, *landscape architect*

GREAT IDEA

A built-in firepit mimics a campfire in this garden. Sandstone cobbles edge the 5-foot-diameter lava rock–topped pit, which blazes with gas-fed flames. A sandstone wall, scattered with cushions, serves as seating. Thyme and other herbs grow around the firepit and between the seat wall's stones. DESIGN: Margie Grace, Grace Design Associates.

Balls of fire *(above)* A collection of spheres appears to float on a sea of black lava in this concrete fire bowl. It looks stylish whether lit or not. **DESIGN:** Russ Cletta Design Studio.

Water trough *(left)* Flames leap from the water in this prehistoric-looking fountain fitted with gas jets. Water spills over the edge and is recirculated through a buried collecting basin. **DESIGN:** Matt Randolph, KornRandolph Landscape Architects.

Bold geometry *(opposite page)* Framed in charcoal gray concrete, this gas-fed firepit warms the lower patio of a hillside garden in Shell Beach, California. Vivid red tumbled glass mulch inside adds to the drama. Benches nearby are of ipe wood. **DESIGN:** Jeffrey Gordon Smith Landscape Architecture.

Kitchens

COOKING AND DINING OUTSIDE for much of the year is one of the great traditions of living in the West. The centerpiece of family cookouts and entertaining has long been the barbecue, and its familiar kettle shape still graces many patios and decks. But you can also customize your outdoor kitchen to suit pretty much any kind of cuisine and your own entertainment site.

As with an indoor kitchen remodel, an outdoor kitchen project can quickly grow in size and scope, so do a little research before you call in the contractor. If you live in a cold-winter area and cook outside for only part of the year, a simple grill and some counter space may be enough. More elaborate facilities might include food preparation and serving areas, storage cabinets, a refrigerator, a vent hood if the grill is under a roof, a sink, and a place to eat.

An outdoor kitchen is subject to local building, electrical, and plumbing codes and will require permits from the appropriate inspectors. If you're planning an extensive kitchen addition outside, it's best to consult a landscape architect or contractor familiar with such projects.

For 21 outdoor dining room ideas, see sunset.com/outdoordining

KITCHEN BASICS

LOCATION. Most often, the best place for an outdoor kitchen is adjacent to the house, so you can tap into plumbing and electrical lines. Another favorite spot is near the pool.
SHELTER. For protection from the elements, cooking and eating areas should be at least partially sheltered.
LIGHTING. Downlighting illuminates preparation areas; more diffuse fixtures create ambience.
GRILL. The grill should not touch a combustible surface; allow a clearance of at least 36 inches. Connect a built-in grill to a permanent gas line.
SINK. Decide whether you need hot and cold water or just cold. Stainless steel is sleek and highly weatherproof; stone and ceramic are more expensive but more easily damaged.
FLOORING. The surface should be durable and easy to sweep or hose down.
REFRIGERATOR. This is most often placed under the counter; buy a model specified for outdoor use.
COUNTERS. Choose a durable, noncombustible material such as granite, tile, slate, or fabricated stone. Counters should be at least 30 inches deep and 36 inches high.

Deck kitchen *(above)* Wooden stairs and deck, a plank bench, and wood-faced cabinets repeat the cohesive theme for this outdoor kitchen. Exposed metal bench supports echo the stainless steel fixtures. **DESIGN:** Arterra Landscape Architects.

Hide-away kitchen *(left)* To conceal the grill and pizza oven when not in use, this design features Cor-Ten panels that slide to either side. To keep it fun, one panel is shaped like a pizza paddle. **DESIGN:** Hood Studio.

View kitchen *(opposite page)* LED lights shine through cutouts in the wooden deck, and irregular panels of glass in the railings make for a dazzling display in this rooftop kitchen. Sleek stainless steel cabinets intensify the effect. **DESIGN:** Topher Delaney, SEAM Studio.

Ideas from *Sunset*'s Outdoor Kitchen

YES, IT'S BIG. But because the outdoor kitchen at *Sunset* headquarters, in Menlo Park, California, takes home entertaining way beyond the grill (and we develop recipes here), it's filled with ideas from which you can choose.

1. WORKSPACE Stain- and acid-proof sealed concrete tops the two islands in the main prep and grilling zone. Deep stainless sinks ease cleanup of large pots and serving dishes.

2. GRILLS Two 42-inch grills ensure efficiency in our multichef kitchen. While one cook rotisseries a Thanksgiving turkey at one station, another can sear flavor into an everyday entrée at the other.

3. PIZZA OVEN The versatility of the Mugnaini Prima 120 won our hearts. You can fire it up once, flash-bake a pizza at 750°F, then slow-roast a leg of lamb in the fallen heat.

4. STONEWORK Saltillo tiles connect indoors and out. Their terra-cotta color complements the Eldorado Stone veneer on the islands and Belgard pavers elsewhere.

5. WINE BAR A 20-foot-long island includes chillers, glass storage, a sink, and a two-burner grill.

6. FIREPIT Ringed with concrete, it's lined with crushed glass and warmed by a gas flame.

THE KITCHEN GARDEN

Fruit trees, a berry patch, herb beds, and an all-in-pots veggie garden keep ripening crops close enough to pick for garnishes, seasonings, and quick stir-fries. Strawberries form an edible groundcover **[A]**, while figs are espaliered against the fence **[B]**. Peppers, tomatoes, mint, and 'Japanese Long' eggplant **[C]** grow in large containers near a sink and work counter. Beds around the patio are filled with pineapple guava **[D]**; easy-care herbs such as chives, fennel, marjoram, sage, and thyme **[E]**; and lemon trees **[F]**.

Paths

A PATH DOES A LOT MORE THAN get you from here to there. It defines the way your garden is viewed. It calls attention to lush plantings, offers surprises, or presents itself as art underfoot. A path can even become an experience—arranged in a spiral to form a labyrinth, or widening to allow for seating before narrowing to invite further strolling.

Determine the width of your path based on how you'll use it. If the path will wind discreetly through the garden and serve only as a walking surface, 2 feet is adequate. To allow room for lawn mowers and other equipment, make it at least 3 feet wide. For two people to walk abreast, as on an entry path, it should be 5 feet wide.

Tailor your choice of material to your garden's style. Major access walks should provide easy traffic flow and an even, nonslip surface such as brick, pavers, concrete, unglazed tile, or uniform stone slabs.

Well-defined edgings can keep plantings at bay. In more casual areas, a rustic path of gravel or bark chips blends into the surroundings with its uneven texture and natural colors.

Rustic *(top left)* In this rambling, country-style garden in Santa Cruz, California, an unassuming steppingstone path is all that's needed. These pavers were set flush to the ground to allow for occasional mowing.

Mod *(top right)* As functional as a sidewalk, but way more stylish, this metal-edged concrete path was crafted with contrasting aggregates in a random pattern of circles.

Playful *(bottom)* Why settle for just one paving material? In Ketzel Levine's front-yard garden in Portland, bricks, circular pavers, concrete sections, and two kinds of gravel keep the ground level interesting.

GREAT IDEA

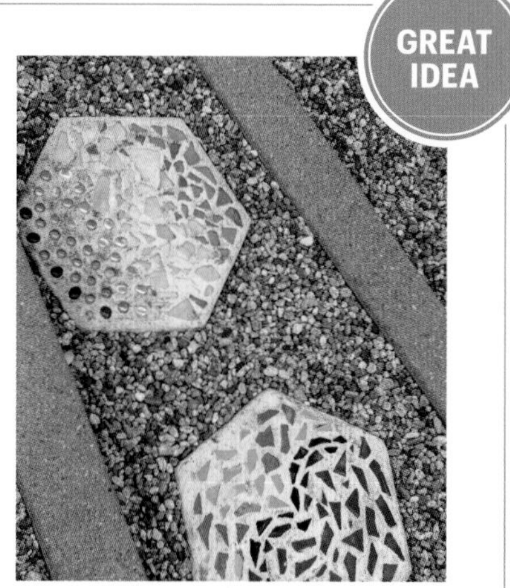

Here's a fun weekend project that the kids will love. To bring new life to a gravel walkway, add concrete steppingstones with whimsical inlays. Here, hexagonal forms were filled with concrete and embedded with bits of colorful glazed pottery that would otherwise have gone into the trash bin. Kits are widely available online and in garden centers.

Casual *(above)* A simple flagstone-in-gravel path curves through a sea of mounding blue fescue accented with blue agaves, taller ornamental grasses, and cactus.

Natural *(left)* An informal gravel path leads through Mediterranean and California native plants, providing a permeable surface for rainwater to pass through.

Whimsical *(opposite page)* Beautiful but dangerous, Western diamondback rattlesnakes are not uncommon in the foothills of Southern California. This concrete homage to the critter makes an artful garden path from veggie garden to greenhouse. **DESIGN:** Richard Krumwiede, Architerra Design Group.

Hard edging *(above)* The plantings are informal, as are the path materials (irregular flagstones set among beach pebbles), but a crisp edging of brick keeps wood-chip mulch where it belongs. **DESIGN:** Kelly Marshall Garden Design.

Soft edging *(left)* Flagstones seem randomly scattered among low-growing blue-green *Dymondia*, but they suggest a straight line toward the exquisite tile fountain. Tree aloes frame the scene from either side. **DESIGN:** Brandon Tyson.

Transition zone *(right)* You can change up your path materials to signal a switch from one mood to another. Here, close-set pavers near the main path give way to casually placed flagstones. **DESIGN:** Lane Goodkind Landscape Architect.

PATH ENHANCERS

A path is more than a "stroll-road" through the garden; it's part of the landscape. Here are ways to settle it among the greenery and make it more interesting.

SOFTEN THE EDGES. Plant low grasses or groundcovers along the path to soften its edges. 'Tom Thumb' cotoneaster, shown above, is a perfect plant for this use, as is the yellow Japanese forest grass *(Hakonechloa macra),* which fans out over a self-sown baby gunnera.

ADD EYE CANDY. A path is more interesting when there's something to stop and look at along the way—such as the stone bowl, above. Other eye-catching options: shapely boulders, a piece of garden art.

HAVE A GOAL. Every path needs a destination, whether it's a garden shed, a tree-shaded seat, or a patio with a vista. If your path ends at a fence, set a colorful solid gate in front to suggest that the journey might continue. If the path leads through an arching arbor, put a glazed urn, birdbath, or garden bench at the end.

For 41 gorgeous garden paths, see sunset.com/gardenpaths

Patios

WHETHER COVERED BY AN ARBOR or open to the sun, a patio is quite likely to be the most-used part of a garden. The usual spot for a patio is immediately outside the house, but if room allows, there's no reason to limit the possibilities. Consider a series of interrelated patios connected by steps, or a detached, protected patio in a secluded corner of your property. A neglected side yard may be just the spot for a private, screened sitting area. Or convert an unneeded driveway into a piazza. Enclosed by a wall and accented with plantings, a boring front lawn is transformed into a charming entry courtyard.

The material you select for your patio needs to be weatherproof and should harmonize with your house and the other landscaping materials in your garden. Pavement choices include brick, flagstone, cut stone, tile, pavers, and poured concrete. Loose materials like gravel and crushed rock work well too, but be sure to include edging to keep the materials out of beds and lawns.

For 40 patio ideas, see sunset.com/patios

Tropical mood *(left)* Surrounded by tropical-looking plants such as angel's trumpet and colocasia, this sunken gravel patio—complete with a firepit and lightweight but comfortable chairs—makes an inviting gathering spot in a Pacific Northwest garden. The "rug" is actually a tile mosaic. **DESIGN:** Laura Crockett, Garden Diva Designs.

Flexible space *(right)* A corner of a Palo Alto, California, patio furnished with a metal cafe table and chairs offers an intimate setting for a tête-à-tête. When it's time for a party, this otherwise unfurnished entertainment patio has plenty of room for a larger table and more seating. **DESIGN:** Bernard Trainor + Associates.

Elegance squared *(below)* Black-and-white-striped chairs face off within a square of darker gravel on this tasteful patio.

GREAT IDEA

The owners of this rooftop garden wanted to retain their skyline view, but they needed some protection from wind and wanted to block less attractive parts of the vista. The design team at Lutsko Associates came up with a splendid solution: a metal-framed screen with three out of four panels filled by frosted glass.

"Away went the water-intensive lawn. In came playful geometry—traditional, but with a modern twist."

—MATHEW HENNING, *landscape architect*

Fireproof and lawnless *(opposite page)* This modern patio of bluestone pavers, crushed rock, and low groundcovers is edged with a sinuous concrete seat wall. The contained fire burns in a custom firepit of Cor-Ten steel. Patches of Irish moss, creeping thyme, and chamomile soften the rock. **DESIGN:** Mathew Henning and Heather Anderson.

Natural patio *(top left)* Tucked into a small corner of the garden, this little dining area feels intimate but not crowded. Decomposed granite makes a smooth, permeable surface underfoot. **DESIGN:** Joseph Marek Landscape Architecture.

Raised patio *(top right)* Gray stone steps lead past a Japanese maple onto a raised patio beneath blooming cherry trees. Contemporary takes on Japanese themes are clear in the stylized fence and squared-off water feature. **DESIGN:** Surfacedesign.

Fresh-air lounge *(bottom)* With a view like this, you might want to keep your patio elements simple: gravel flooring, a raised rusted-metal bed for a few cactus, and comfortably low-slung Adirondack chairs. **DESIGN:** Ten Eyck Landscape Architects.

LET IT FLOW

There was a time when "patio" meant "concrete slab." Turns out it can also mean rainy season problems, when water tends to pool on the solid surface, or storm-water runoff carries pollutants into local water supplies. An environmentally sound alternative is to use permeable paving materials instead, which allow rainwater to drain into a deep gravel layer, where it slowly percolates into the soil. For a casual patio surface, consider a loose material like gravel or crushed rock—use small pieces for easy walking—or decomposed granite. Or go more formal with a cut-stone, brick, or cobblestone patio constructed with joints wide enough to let the water through. Some paving systems have open cells that can be filled with soil and planted with grass or other low groundcovers, creating a sort of living pavement. Another benefit of permeable paving: It absorbs much less heat than solid surfaces.

Recycled patio *(right)* When this Los Angeles backyard got a makeover, the first things to go were an old hot tub and half of the driveway. But rather than going to a landfill, materials from both were reused. The bench seats are fashioned from broken concrete, and the comfy, slanted backs are made from wood salvaged from the tub. **DESIGN:** Steve Siegrist Design.

STONE·SCAPING

WITH ALL OF ITS GEOLOGIC FAULTS, volcanoes, and glacial features, the West is full of rocks. But because they seldom occur naturally in urban landscapes, we bring them into our yards to use as accents among plants, to create rock gardens, and to build walls, paths, and benches.

Quarries and rock yards can supply many kinds of decorative rock, from small stones to huge boulders and columns. Before you buy, consider your site (put a 2-ton rock in the wrong place and you're stuck); it's wise to work with a landscape architect, designer, or contractor with plenty of experience installing rock. And if you live on a sloping lot, you may need to consult a landscape contractor or architect to check the slope's ability to hold rocks securely.

Most rock is sold by the ton, although some is also sold by shape (slabs and columns, for example). If you want stones covered with moss or lichen, expect to pay more. But beware: Moss doesn't always survive the move from mountain to backyard patio. You can also tuck ornamental grasses between stones or tuck succulents around them, as shown above. Or light them from below for dramatic effects at night.

BOULDER BASICS

GO LOCAL. Try to work with rock that's naturally available in your region—Sonoma fieldstone in Northern California or Arizona sandstone in Phoenix, for example. It's relatively inexpensive and more likely to suit your landscape.

PLAN AHEAD. At the rock yard, flag the stones that you want with colored ribbon. Figure out where each one will go in your garden and which side will face up. Snap photos of the rocks to help you place them at delivery time.

ALLOW FOR SETTLING AND AGING. For large rocks, the amount of settling can be significant. Rocks look better with time; scars from transport and handling disappear, and lichen grows where the air is relatively unpolluted.

Mounds *(above)* Boulders look best when placed as they might appear in a natural landscape—partially buried rather than sitting fully atop the ground. Woven together with a low-growing groundcover, this group looks like a natural outcropping and creates a subtle focal point in the lawn. **DESIGN:** Roger Warner.

Bridge *(right)* Rough flagstones build a bridge across this dry creekbed in a Washington garden. River pebbles are a natural choice for the creekbed. **DESIGN:** Susan Calhoun, Plantswoman Design.

Focal point *(opposite page)* Beyond the stretches of decomposed granite (½ inch minus Madison Gold)—dotted with bluish *Euphorbia rigida* and golden Mexican feather grass—large boulders rise like desert outcrop. Dropped in place by crane, they embrace the shimmery feather grass. **DESIGN:** Troy Bankord Design.

Play Areas

KIDS LOVE A PLACE IN THE BACKYARD that they can call their own. It can be as simple as a sandbox or rope swing, or as elaborate as a climbing structure or even a treehouse. Whatever your child's play setting, the first requirement to consider is safety.

Preschoolers will feel safer—and can be more easily supervised—if their play area is close to the house. When choosing the location, also take into account sun, wind, and shade. Hot sun increases the risk of sunburn and can make metals and concrete burning-hot, so install such surfaces in the shade or facing north. In very damp areas, however, too much shade can encourage the growth of slippery moss or mold.

For tykes on bikes, skates, or scooters, a smooth concrete surface at least 24 inches wide is best. Along boundaries, the need for fencing is obvious. Securely protect the play area from the driveway, as well as from any pool, spa, or other body of water. Finally, you'll want to create a secure place to keep sharp and heavy tools, garden supplies, and other equipment.

Climbing corner *(above)* With its sky blue panels and brightly colored holds, this climbing wall in Oakland, California, invites exploring. Its spongy checkerboard floor squares (called SofTiles) cushion any falls. Made of recycled rubber, they're set atop an inch-thick layer of decomposed granite. **DESIGN:** Shades of Green Landscape Architecture.

Stylish hopscotch *(right)* Just see how long you can stay seated when faced with this fun feature set into a backyard lawn. The concrete is flush with the lawn, which makes mowing around it a breeze.

Circle of sand *(opposite page)* The "sandcircle" is the main attraction here, but playful discs of color dot the concrete retaining wall and keep the mood light. A swirl of synthetic turf grass guarantees low maintenance. **DESIGN:** Kathleen Shaeffer Design.

Ponds and Fountains

IT DOESN'T TAKE A LOT OF WATER to soothe the soul. Even a small pond can have a cooling effect—both physically and psychologically. Locate your pond where it will be protected from strong winds and sited away from messy trees. Don't choose a low-lying area that will constantly overflow in wet weather. Children find ponds irresistible, so use a protective barrier if children are around. Check with your local building department about any requirements for such barriers, as well as for setbacks from property lines, electrical circuits for pumps and lights, and pond depth. Generally, ponds less than 24 inches deep do not need a building permit.

To bring the welcome sound of splashing water to the garden, install a recirculating fountain. You can make a simple pond with a watertight liner and a small recirculating pump.

Light steps *(above)* Bluestone pavers traverse this water feature in Alamo, California. Attached to a concrete pillar built into the bottom, each paver is cantilevered 4 inches out from its pillar. These dark-hued pillars, along with dark Mexican pebbles, make the water more reflective. The round fountain in the foreground is an old millstone polished smooth on top. **DESIGN:** Stefan Thuilot, Thuilot Associates.

PRIMITIVE CHIC In hot and dry Arizona gardens, a water feature is always welcome. But this artful composition goes the extra mile with an abstract fountain, a single bold stream, and a blue pedestal set against a red-wall backdrop. DESIGN: Steve Martino Landscape Architect.

WATER VIEW A geometric pool makes a bold statement in this San Francisco garden, especially when viewed from the upper level. DESIGN: Arterra Landscape Architects.

NATURAL POND FILTERS

Keeping even the smallest ponds clear and free of algae can be challenging. Biological filters, which combine mechanical and bacterial filtration, help. But introducing water plants and scavengers such as water snails and tadpoles into a pond is easier and less expensive.

Water plants shade ponds, protecting them from heat buildup that stimulates algae growth. They also consume carbon dioxide, which helps keep the water clear. Snails and tadpoles are nature's garbage disposals, feeding on decaying plant material and fish waste.

Choices include oxygenating grasses to supply the water with oxygen; dwarf papyrus; and water lilies *(Nymphaea)*. Some aquatic plants, such as duckweed, frogbit, parrot's feather, and water hyacinth are available, but they are highly invasive; keep them away from natural waters nearby.

Spiller *(top right)* Fountains don't need lots of room to make a bold statement. This slim-lined steel wall fountain, tucked up against a bold, cobalt blue wall in a Central California garden, adds angular contrast as it trickles softly behind orange cannas. **DESIGN:** Roy Burch (fountain); Jeffrey Gordon Smith Landscape Architecture (garden).

Bubbler *(bottom right)* This polished stone water feature reflects the sky and surrounding plants, enhancing the tranquil scene. **DESIGN:** Megan Van Linda Design.

Pools

SWIMMING POOLS NO LONGER OCCUPY CENTER STAGE in Western gardens; they've slimmed down to fit into landscapes rather than dominate them. Your garden's sun and wind patterns should help you determine the pool's location. And even if you aren't able to make your pool completely private, you can maximize its seclusion from passersby and neighbors by screening the area with plantings. Since pools can be harsh on nearby plants—thanks to the combination of pool chemicals, strong sunlight, hot concrete, and humidity—refer to the *Sunset Western Garden Book* for the best choices.

For pool construction, concrete is the most durable. But vinyl-lined pools are usually much less expensive, because the liner is prefabricated and the pool can be installed in as little as a few days. One-piece fiberglass shells are also fairly quick to install.

Plan for a nonskid paved area or deck surrounding or adjoining the pool, and make it large enough to accommodate poolside furniture. And remember that nothing adds to the allure of a pool more than good lighting.

Glamorous *(above)* Lightening the mood as they light the pool, these fixtures appear to float like Champagne bubbles above the water's surface in a Pasadena, California, garden. **DESIGN:** Anthony Exter Landscape Design.

Athletic *(right)* Even the smallest garden has room for a counter-current lap pool like this one. A concealed motor creates a powerful, adjustable flow against which the user swims. **DESIGN:** Blasen Landscape Architecture.

Serene *(opposite page)* The plants in this Phoenix garden need very little water, but the homeowners can take a cooling soak whenever they like on waterproof chaise lounges attached to the shallow ledge (foreground). **DESIGN:** Rick Jones and Kristina Floor, JJR Floor.

Water view *(above)* Ferry slip or swimming pool? A 16-by-66-foot lap pool ends in an infinity edge that seems to dissolve into Washington's Puget Sound. At the flip of a switch, 14 dockside spouts turn the pool into a night-lighted fountain. DESIGN: Eric Gedney (pool); Patrick Leuner, Leuner Landscape Design (landscape).

Desert view *(left)* All the elements in this garden, from the infinity pool and perfectly sited spa to the low retaining wall, curve gently toward Camelback Mountain in Paradise Valley, Arizona. A simple sweep of uninterrupted travertine paving complements rather than competes with the stunning view, while two pillars—one housing a gas firepit—frame it. DESIGN: Chad Robert.

PRIVATE "RESORT"
Against a backdrop of tall hedges, this azure pool in Pacific Palisades, California, looks every bit the backyard vacation spot. Vibrant pillows on built-in benches, along with shaded lounge chairs, a small firepit, and blue glass tiles on pool's fountain wall, add to the "getaway" ambience. DESIGN: Russ Cletta Design Studio.

Lap pool *(above)* This pool is the perfect width for long workouts, with a built-in spa located conveniently near the house. Low-growing plants alongside the pool add drama but don't drop leaves in the water. **DESIGN:** Chris Jacobson, GardenArt Group.

Wade-in pool *(left)* The concrete edge of this Tiburon, California, pool curves gracefully to a point at the shallow end, where a gentle slope brings you into the wind-rippled water. **DESIGN:** Bradanini & Associates.

Swimming hole *(opposite page)* A natural-looking pool appears at home against views of California's rugged Santa Monica Mountains. The shallow depression is 3 feet deep in the center and nearly 40 feet wide. It's lined with sturdy vinyl covered with coarse sand and uses the same type of filter and skimmer as traditional pools. **DESIGN:** Nick Williams Designs.

SAFE SWIMMING

For safety, every pool area should have the following:

- A barrier—either a fence or a wall—at least 4 feet high should completely surround the pool, with no gap between the ground and the bottom of the barrier.
- Gates need to be self-closing and self-latching, and should close in the direction of the pool.
- Safety covers for both swimming pools and spas should meet the weight-bearing standards of the American Society for Testing and Materials (ASTM) and have no gaps along the perimeter through which a small child could crawl.
- Rescue equipment, such as ring buoys and a shepherd's crook (a long pole with a hook).

Raised Beds

WHAT'S SO GREAT ABOUT RAISED BEDS? Even one or two overflowing with plants give a garden a beautiful focal point. Raised beds are also practical. Filled with organically rich soil, they warm up quickly in spring, provide perfect drainage, and often yield heavier crops of vegetables and blooming flowers. They also make it possible to garden over heavy clay soil or rock-solid caliche. And they can be underlined with hardware cloth to foil gophers and moles.

When gardening in a raised bed, you'll need to access all plants from the edge. That means the reach to the center should be no more than an arm's length, which totals about 4 feet for the full width. A good length is 8 to 10 feet, and the height should be at least 10 inches.

Most raised beds are framed with wood. Because untreated wood rots fairly quickly where it contacts soil, use rot-resistant cedar or redwood, composite lumber, or pressure-treated lumber (see page 172). Interlocking concrete blocks and dry-stacked rocks and flagstones are also commonly used to form beds. Fill the bed with amended native soil or topsoil purchased at a garden center. Since soil settles over time and organic matter decomposes, you will need to replenish the soil every spring before planting.

On the grid *(opposite page)* The black concrete raised beds and matching firepit in this garden are designed to evoke the patchwork patterns of California's Central Coast farmland just downslope. 'Afterglow' echeveria grows in the bed at left; its vivid hue echoes the red tumbled glass mulch in the firepit nearby. Yellow 'Moonshine' yarrow and blond Mexican feather grass fringe beyond the deck. **DESIGN:** Jeffrey Gordon Smith Landscape Architecture.

Front-yard berries *(right)* A two-railed "fence" tops a low concrete wall that edges landscape architect Calvin Abe's sunny front-yard strawberry patch in the Westchester neighborhood of Los Angeles. To fill the 15-by-30-foot patch, Abe started with 225 plants. He makes jam from his 'Chandler' and 'Ozark Beauty' berries.

Striking steel boxes *(below)* Contrasting dramatically with the white gravel, these boxes are made of rusted Cor-Ten steel. Large and strong, they help keep the veggie garden looking neat. **DESIGN:** Lutsko Associates.

GREAT IDEA

When Max Gill heads to his garden to pick strawberries for nibbling, he also picks a few fruiting stems to arrange in mini bouquets. He displays his "foraged finds" in simple white vases, where he can enjoy seeing the different stages of the developing fruit—from small white flowers to shiny red berries among the emerald green leaves.

> "Broken concrete is durable and attractive; it also retains heat, and helps warm the soil."
> —ROB STEINER, *landscape designer*

PRESSURE-TREATED WOOD

To produce lumber that resists decay—even when in contact with soil—pressure-treated wood is impregnated with a preservative. Traditionally, this preservative contained chromium, copper, and arsenic. These chemicals, determined to be unsafe for residential use, have been phased out and replaced by less toxic alternatives. The new products are safer, but some gardeners, concerned that chemicals may leach into the soil, avoid using pressure-treated wood in raised beds for growing vegetables. To get the look of wood, consider eco-friendly composite lumber made of recycled wood and plastic.

Super-easy raised beds *(above)* These ingenious brackets, fashioned from recycled metal, make building a raised bed almost effortless. Simply set the corner brackets in place and slide in the boards.

Recycled concrete *(left)* When the homeowners replaced their driveway, they used the broken concrete pieces for these stylish beds. The more irregular edges face inside, and thick-set mortar guarantees stability. The trellises are made from architectural wire mesh and rebar. **DESIGN:** Rob Steiner, Rob Steiner Gardens.

Rusted metal *(opposite page)* Bands of steel were gently bent to make this raised bed, their rusty color echoing the tones of the tree trunk and the gabion wall in the distance. Architectural aloes bloom in the foreground. **DESIGN:** Christy Ten Ecyk, Ten Ecyk Landscape Architects.

Sheds

EVERY GARDEN CAN BENEFIT FROM a spacious, well-organized, safe shed in which to store garden tools, supplies, and equipment. But with a few modifications, that simple outbuilding can turn into a garden getaway—a potting shed, a craft studio, a children's playhouse, or just a place to read, tinker, and relax.

Before starting to build such a structure, make sure that it will comply with local regulations. Most small garden sheds can be built without a permit, but there are exceptions. In many municipalities, any shed larger than about 120 square feet requires a building permit. In some places, the issue is whether the structure is considered permanent—that is, does it have a poured foundation? Certainly if you are planning to bring electricity to the shed from your house panel, you'll need an electrical permit. Don't get too attached to a particular spot in the garden before checking on any zoning restrictions, setback requirements, or easements. Finally, be sure to integrate your shed into your landscape design.

A room of her own *(opposite page)* With an aged-brick path, an outdoor potting bench, and a surround of lushly planted beds, this repurposed tool shed is garden writer and designer Rebecca Sweet's "sweet spot"—an office and a "girlfriend's getaway." **DESIGN:** Rebecca Sweet, Harmony in the Garden.

Bottom-hinged windows *(top left)* Since they open outward from the top, the shed's recycled windows invite inside the garden's soft breezes, birdsong, and floral fragrances.

Cozy furnishings *(top right)* Inside Sweet's retreat, a rattan love seat, rustic wood furniture, and a wall hanging made from twigs combine to create an ideal spot for curling up with a good book—or seed catalog.

Eye candy *(bottom)* The shed's generous windowsills make space to grow houseplants or root cuttings inside, and to display Sweet's treasures, collected on trips or gifted from family or friends. A glass egg refracts and adds color to the sun's rays.

Fairy-tale charm *(above)* Cedar rounds set in mortar give this 12-by-12-foot timber-framed shed a rustic air. Built by the owners of recycled materials near their vegetable garden in Washington's San Juan Islands, it's the perfect place to dry freshly harvested onions, arrange flowers, and repot plants.

Multipurpose interior *(left)* An attached greenhouse with translucent roof is for tender plants such as potted tomatoes. Clear glass bottles tucked into the interior wall let light in from the greenhouse; marbles and other collectibles fill in around them. The floor consists of brick set atop filter fabric, for easy drainage.

Handsomely sturdy *(opposite page)* This compact garden structure is built to last. Set on a concrete slab, it is edged in brick and has a vented metal roof that can stand up to the elements.

For 20 favorite garden cottages and sheds, see sunset.com/sheds-cottages

Studio-to-go *(above)* The structure, a tool shed from Home Depot, was styled inside by its owner, garden designer Di Zock. Tucked in the back of her tiny garden in Venice, California, it contains everything she needs to work outdoors—desk, chair, bulletin boards. It feels cozy even when the jumbo door is opened to the garden. **DESIGN:** Di Zock Gardens.

Fabulous prefab *(left)* This modern-looking art studio is a 10-by-12-foot customizable structure that was ordered online from *studio-shed.com*. It doubles as a bar for poolside parties.

Bed shed *(opposite page)* On a hillside property near the Mendocino, California, coast, this little getaway used the classic walled tent cabin as a template for a stand-alone guest room. A secondhand chandelier hangs over the bed.

"A backyard haven, wrapped in tall trees and diffused light, can take you as far away, in your mind, as any airplane."
—BRUCE ANDERSON,
travel editor, Sunset

Showers

OUTDOOR SHOWERS ARE A PRACTICAL necessity at beach homes, but you can indulge in the pleasures of outdoor bathing wherever you can create a bit of privacy and run some plumbing lines.

The typical method for supplying the showerhead with water is to extend both hot and cold water lines through the wall of the house or an outbuilding. Components made specifically for outdoor showers are more expensive than for indoor types, but they prohibit rust, which is a problem for both fixtures and faucets.

You'll also need a way for water to drain away. Keep in mind that if you plan to regularly use soap, shampoo, and cleaning products in the shower, the runoff is considered wastewater. Check with your local building department to see if a connection to your home's main drainage system is required.

Locate towel racks or hooks beyond the reach of shower spray, and don't forget ledges for soap and shampoo. Finally, be sure that the floor surface is nonskid and the area around the shower has adequate lighting.

GREAT IDEA

Pops of color make this side-yard shower both inviting and stylish. An oversize glazed urn, which doubles as a spill fountain, defines the space and contrasts with brick-colored tiles behind. The smooth gray concrete box bench and warm brown slatted wooden floor add contrasting textures. DESIGN: Russ Cletta Design Studio.

Hidden shower *(above)* A panel of corrugated metal conceals the plumbing for this contemporary shower, tucked behind a wall in a Venice, California, garden. **DESIGN:** Jay Griffith.

Wall shower *(right)* Indoor plumbing fixtures and a curtain rod from a metal fabricator created this shower in Del Mar, California. The curtain is made of Sunbrella weatherproof fabric. The wooden mat placed on flagstone guarantees sure footing.

Poolside shower *(opposite page)* A soothing spray, backed by yuccas, cycads, and other lush plants, is within easy reach of the pool. Slotted teak boards mask the plumbing and allow water to drain into a hidden shower pan. **DESIGN:** Greg Sanchez, GDS Designs.

If you don't mind a cold shower, this DIY shower is easy to make; it hooks up to the same lines your garden hose uses.

Jungle wall *(top left)* Water-loving plants like papyrus (in the foreground pot), *Ligularia* (at ground level), and pitcher plants (in the wall) thrive in the moist conditions around this shower.

Shower-by-the-beach *(top right)* This side-yard shower near the beach in Pacific Palisades, California, is right by the laundry room door. That's good, because the owner and his three sons, all surfers, can wash off before entering the house (a splash guard of laminated glass channels the water). Flooring is of Mexican pebbles. **DESIGN:** Mark Tessier Landscape Architecture.

Desert simplicity *(bottom)* Turn on the water, which spills from a copper canopy overhead, and this corner of a Phoenix home becomes a cooling oasis. **DESIGN:** Woolsey Studio.

DIY shower *(opposite page)* Two wood-framed, corrugated metal panels and a center pole with plumbing attached make up this simple shower. It uses only cold water lines from a garden hose; water flows into the gravel underfoot. Go to *sunset.com/diyshower* for step-by-step guidelines.

Spas

WHETHER THE FOCAL POINT OF A GARDEN or a private retreat, a spa or hot tub has understandable appeal: a fresh-air bath enlivened with jets of water in a tub large enough to accommodate both social and solitary soaks. Spas can double as decorative water features, with waterfalls, fountain jets, or exit streams that meander to a swimming pool.

To some extent, spa siting is governed by plumbing and the spa's support equipment, which must stand a short distance away. Heaters, pumps, and filters are compact, but they must be connected to electrical and gas lines. No doubt you'll feel more comfortable if your spa is hidden from any passersby, so consider building an arbor or a gazebo around the spa, or screen it with live plantings or an arrangement of fences and walls.

For safety, spas should be inaccessible to young children and should be protected by a secure cover approved by the American Society for Testing and Materials (ASTM). Be sure to light steps, deck edges, and other potentially hazardous places. See page 169 for more information on poolside safety.

Focal-point spa *(top left)* A ribbon of water spills softly through a low privacy wall and into this spa, built into one side of a raised stone patio. On the other side, an L-shaped bench is a great place to warm up after a long, slow soak. **DESIGN:** Huettl Landscape Architecture.

View spa *(top right)* Edged with rugged stone that blends with boulders nearby, this spa in Jackson, Wyoming, is perfectly positioned to take in views of the Grand Tetons. The landscape around it, a mix of grasses and wildflowers, blends neatly into the meadow beyond. **DESIGN:** Design Workshop.

Blue retreat for two *(bottom)* A small hot tub off the bathroom of a Santa Monica, California, residence gains privacy from surrounding neighbors with periwinkle blue stucco walls. Benches are of redwood. **DESIGN:** PaysonDenney Architects.

Steps

IN ADDITION TO THEIR OBVIOUS practical function, steps can be accents that set the mood for an entire landscaping scheme. For example, stairs can double as a retaining wall, a base for raised planters, or garden seating.

Scale is important. Main entries need steps that are inviting, and wide enough (at least 5 feet) for two people to walk side by side. Simple utility steps can be scaled down to as narrow as 2 feet, though 4 feet is more typical, to fit their more limited use.

To create a formal look, construct steps from poured concrete, masonry blocks, unglazed tiles, or concrete pavers. Natural materials such as stone and wood fit well in less structured landscapes. Matching the building material used in a patio, paths, or walls can unite the garden's overall design.

Stairway to heaven *(above)* Decomposed granite steps edged with concrete nudge this path upslope in a Portola Valley, California, garden. Because the steps taper from 8 feet wide at the bottom to 3 feet wide at the top, they appear to cover more ground than they do. A Cor-Ten steel wall enhances the effect; from a $4\frac{1}{2}$-foot base, it shrinks to 2 feet high at the top. DESIGN: Stefan Thuilot, Thuilot Associates.

RUSTIC STEPS Boulders provide accents beside these simple wooden steps—but the real show comes from the red and yellow kangaroo paws and the soft-looking Mexican feather grass in this Tiburon, California, garden. DESIGN: Arterra Landscape Architects.

"Enhance steps with graceful curves and aromatic plants."

—LAUREN DUNEC, *garden design assistant, Sunset*

Boulder lines *(top left)* Flat-topped boulders create the risers for these naturalistic steps topped with gravel.

Planted steps *(top right)* Cut-stone stairs are practically obscured by a colorful mixture of plants that thrive in the well-drained slope. Many—like the blue-green euphorbias and coral twinspur *(Diascia)*—reseed and spread casually. **DESIGN:** Gary Ratway Landscape Designer.

Stone steps *(bottom)* This attractive lantern emits plenty of light to illuminate the small set of steps at night, and it makes an appealing focal point during the day. **DESIGN:** Lane Goodkind Landscape Architect.

SAFE STEPPING

- When choosing materials, be sure that steps give secure footing in wet weather.
- All the risers in any one flight of steps should be the same height; treads may have to vary to accommodate a curve.
- Steps should be adequately lit at night with unobtrusive, nonglare path lights or fixtures built into risers or adjacent walls.
- Building codes usually require a railing for steps leading directly from the main entrance to public-access areas. Railings are always a good idea where children or elderly visitors will be using the stairs.
- On very steep slopes, a zigzag design makes the climb easier.
- When planting alongside steps, use edging plants that spill over but do not present tripping hazards.

Mixed materials *(above)* Who says all steps have to look the same? Here, the lower concrete steps in a San Francisco garden give way to a curved landing made of gravel, and then to steps made from natural stone strips and decomposed granite. The steps ascend along a painted stucco wall, ultimately reaching a deck. DESIGN: Surfacedesign.

Steps or seating? *(left)* The owner of this Avila Beach, California, garden, chose these extra-large stones for steps, which can double as seating. Fragrant thyme lines the seams. DESIGN: Ryan Fortini Design Group.

Walls

WALLS BRING AN UNMATCHED SENSE of solidity and permanence to a garden. They define space, provide privacy and security, edit views, screen out wind and noise, and hold the earth at bay.

Among the most typical materials for garden walls are masonry units: brick, concrete block, or adobe. Poured concrete walls offer more design possibilities because the surface texture and shape are established by wooden forms into which the concrete is poured.

In the hands of a mason, stone forms walls that seem integral to their landscape. Stone that is prominent in your region will look the most natural in your garden. Visit a stone yard or building materials supplier to check your options.

Whatever the wall material, it must be supported with a solid foundation, or footing. Poured concrete provides the best footing because it can be smoothed and leveled. For very low walls—those under 1 foot—you can lay the base of the wall directly on tamped soil or in a leveled trench.

Layers *(above)* A deep rose stucco wall gives way to steel panels allowed to rust naturally. Agaves enhance the drama. **DESIGN:** Steve Martino Landscape Architect.

Illusion *(right)* Panels of frosted glass mark an entry at the end of a driveway, without blocking light or views of the plants beyond. **DESIGN:** Lutsko Associates.

Colors *(opposite page)* Bathed in soft light, this wall is a work of modern art, in an American Society of Land-scape Architects award–winning "garden of water and light" in Palm Springs, California. Painted bluish gray and red, it makes a striking backdrop for slender cactus *(Pachycereus marginatus)* and lacy *Gaura lindheimeri* 'Whirling Butter-flies'. A blue palo verde dangles yellow flowers overhead. **DESIGN:** Steve Martino Landscape Architect.

GABION BASICS

A gabion—from an Italian word for "big cage"—is simply a large wire basket filled to the top with stones or other materials. Line up or stack a few of these modular units, and you have a wall. Huge versions have long been used in large-scale construction projects to create retaining walls, and they can play that role in home gardens as well. But gabions also make striking freestanding walls with a modern, industrial-chic look. Buy the baskets online at sites such as *gabionsupply.com* or *gabion baskets.net*.

Planted wall *(above)* Planting spaces between the rugged limestone blocks make it easy to tuck in compact plants such as campanula and balloon flower. Creepers like ground ivy *(Glechoma)* climb from below. **DESIGN:** Scott Colombo Designs.

Panel of pebbles *(left)* Most gabion walls are sized for large stones, but this contemporary version in Palo Alto, California, uses a small-grid screen to hold small pebbles. Evenly spaced bolts provide additional strength. **DESIGN:** Joseph Bellomo Architects.

Framing a view *(opposite page)* Beyond the vibrant yellow *Verbascum bombyciferum* spikes in the foreground in Linda Ernst's Portland garden, a long, low opening in the stucco wall frames views of blooming shrubs. **DESIGN:** Laura Crockett, Garden Diva Designs.

Partial veneer *(above)* Flat stones embellish a cocoa-colored concrete wall, echoing the stone used in the lower front wall. Spikey cordylines add drama between the two walls. **DESIGN:** Sage Ecological Landscapes.

Patina of age *(left)* This low seat wall, which pairs smooth stucco with pseudo-stone insets, creates the illusion of age—as though time has weathered away the stucco to reveal the stone beneath. **DESIGN:** Gabriela Yariv Landscape Design.

Dramatic opening *(opposite page)* A thick plank of rough concrete straddles the gap between two wall sections in this Phoenix garden. The effect is amplified by the unconventional placement of the low-voltage lighting fixtures. **DESIGN:** Steve Martino Landscape Architect.

PLANTS

Plants are a garden's softeners, but they play other roles as well. Trees provide shade, privacy, and protection from wind. Shrubs give shape and textures to borders, or perfume the air with fragrant flowers. Perennials with colorful flowers brighten beds and borders; groundcovers settle hardscape. Plants can set a garden's mood, whether tropical (palms and plumerias) or sunny Mediterranean (olive trees and lavender). The right plants can also feed and shelter birds, bees, and butterflies. Choose kinds that flourish in your region's climate; plant them where their unique qualities show off best and their colors and textures play off one another; give them the conditions they need; and allow them to fill the roles they're meant to play. Then stand back and watch them flourish.

BLAZING ORANGE
Pheasant's-tail grass *(Anemanthele lessoniana)* edged with green *Carex flacca* helps warm up this patio on a cool day in San Luis Obispo, California. Pheasant's-tail grass is short-lived (less than 3 years) and temperamental; replace it as needed. DESIGN: Jeffrey Gordon Smith Landscape Architecture.

Trees

TREES ARE THE NOBLE GIANTS of the landscape. They set the tone of a garden, providing shade and shelter, framing views, or blocking eyesores. They also establish perspective, make dramatic sculptural statements, and form relatively permanent focal points.

Choose trees based first on your needs. To block the sun, for example, select a species with a good-size canopy. For fruits, look for attractive foliage, interesting bark, or a striking silhouette. When planting near paving, pick a tree with well-behaved roots.

Crimson accent *(above)* Japanese maples are among the most colorful small trees. This one adds vibrant color to a slope in the Pacific Northwest, along with blue-flowered ceanothus and red nandina berries.

Living umbrella *(opposite page)* Fast-growing, with a lacy, wide-spreading canopy, mimosa *(Albizia julibrissin)* is perfect for shading a dining area. Its fluffy pink blooms appear in summer. **DESIGN:** Jacque Authier Landscape Design.

Mimosa trees can spread as much as twice their height. They thrive with summer heat, especially in Southern California's inland valleys.

Light it up *(above)* Changing a grade around a tree is usually a bad idea, as it can cause root problems that can eventually kill the tree. But when a raised terrace was built in this San Francisco garden, a strong retaining wall set back from the canopy and curved around it maintained the integrity of the owners' beloved madrone *(Arbutus menziesii)*. Lighting it from below adds night-time drama. **DESIGN:** Katharine Webster Landscape Design.

Weeping evergreens *(left)* Weeping false cypress trees such as these, which frame a view of Washington's Puget Sound, have long, drooping branches that create a rain-forest effect, like pounding sheets of green rain.

Ginkgo grouping *(above)* Three young ginkgo trees occupy a gravel rectangle flanked by deep green hedges and lavender. In autumn, the trees' bright golden leaves look spectacular lying on the blue-gray gravel. **DESIGN:** Andrea Cochran Landscape Architecture.

Coral bark *(left)* A leafless coral bark maple (*Acer palmatum* 'Sango Kaku') adds winter interest to this mostly green border near Seattle. **DESIGN:** Stacie Crooks, Crooks Garden Design.

Sculpture *(top)* Tucked into a niche, a slow-growing 'Uncle Fogy' jack pine *(Pinus banksiana)* shows off its curves against gray walls, in Santa Fe. **DESIGN:** Richard Wilder, Wilder Landscaping.

Spillers *(bottom)* A venerable weeping blue atlas cedar *(Cedrus atlantica)* drapes itself over a fence and gate, against a backdrop of brilliant fall-colored maples.

Framers *(opposite page)* These pear trees (*Pyrus calleryana* 'Aristocrat'), arranged in parallel rows, frame the patio view. **DESIGN:** Andrea Cochran Landscape Architecture.

BEAUTIFUL BARK

Beauty may be only skin deep, but in the case of tree trunks, it's enough. Bark can influence the look of a landscape as much as foliage. It comes in colors, patterns, and textures you won't find anywhere else in nature. In the desert, blue palo verde trees are greened up by chlorophyll that in other trees is reserved for leaves. In colder climates, trees with beautiful bark include paperbark cherry *(Prunus serrula)*, with bands of copper-colored bark; paperbark maple *(Acer griseum)*, pictured above; and quaking aspen *(Populus tremuloides)*, with pristine white bark.

CALLING A PRO

Arborists do more than prune trees. These professionals, certified by the International Society of Arboriculture (ISA), can evaluate a tree's health, age, present and future size, and any hazards it may pose. If you plan some construction near a tree, it's a good idea to ask an arborist to consult with the contractor to ensure the tree's preservation. In a garden with large trees, annual checkups by an arborist can spot potential problems before they develop into structural failure and property damage.

Tree experts agree that most storm damage to trees is preventable. Arborists can thin a top-heavy canopy of foliage that could catch wind and cause a tree to blow over or limbs to break. They can also shorten horizontal limbs that might break under wind or snow, or install cables for structural integrity. All trees benefit from the regular removal of dead or weakened wood; if the wood is too high for you to reach or too bulky to handle, hire a professional.

Shades of pink *(above)* The spectacular, fragrant blooms of saucer magnolia *(Magnolia × soulangeana)* make their appearance in late winter or early spring, just as the leaves emerge. Choose a late-blooming variety in frost-prone areas.

Open grove *(left)* With its graceful upright form and curious peeling bark, paperbark maple *(Acer griseum)* is an ideal candidate for planting in groves. Its leaves turn scarlet before dropping in autumn. DESIGN: Karen Ford Landscape Architect.

Golden accent *(opposite page)* The golden tones of variegated angelica tree (*Aralia elata* 'Aureovariegata') are echoed in the shrubs below and contrast with a powdery blue hosta.

Palms

THE REAL SYMBOL of Southern California—and the low desert and Hawaiian Islands—is a crown of palm fronds rustling against a blue sky, as they edge swimming pools and create jungle canopies over patios.

Inherently exotic-looking, palms are also eminently practical. Because they have compact root systems, many are easy to transplant even when mature—useful for creating instant landscaping. Palms can be squeezed into narrow parkways or planted close to homes, since their roots won't break up sidewalks or foundations. Palms produce minimal litter, making them perfect beside swimming pools, where their tropical silhouettes are reflected in still water. And they're generally low-maintenance and pest-free.

Tall, stately palms can be spectacular focal points along streets and beaches. But the best kinds for smaller gardens are not seven-story overachievers; they grow slowly and stay compact. Consider Chinese fountain palm *(Livistona chinensis)*; foxtail palm *(Wodyetia bifurcata),* with plumelike leaves; Mediterranean fan palm *(Chamaerops humilis)*; pygmy date palm *(Phoenix roebelenii)*; and triangle palm *(Dypsis decaryi).*

Reflections *(top left)* Mexican blue palms *(Brahea armata)* pair with blue-gray senecio in a Southern California poolside garden. The palms grow slowly to 35 feet, tolerate heat and wind, and are hardy to 18°F. **DESIGN:** Pamela Palmer, ARTECHO Architecture + Landscape Architecture.

Mixed company *(top right)* Tall Mexican fan palms, backed with columnar cactus, may seem unlikely bedfellows in this poolside garden in Southern California. But they take the same conditions and celebrate verticality among lower agaves. **DESIGN:** Gabriela Yariv Landscape Design.

Accents *(bottom)* A trio of queen palms mingle with bronze cordylines, a potted *Furcraea foetida* 'Mediopicta', and blue pansies in this Los Angeles garden. **DESIGN:** Brent Green, GreenArt Landscape Design.

HARDY PALMS

Palms in Idaho? Although it seems unlikely, some palms can survive periods of cold. In fact, three familiar palms are cold-hardy. Mediterranean fan palm *(Chamaerops humilis)* endures temperatures as low as 6°F; it's a clump-forming type, although over time it gradually elevates its tufts of fan-shaped leaves on short trunks. For a hardy, single-trunk type, windmill palm *(Trachycarpus fortunei)* lifts a crown of fanlike leaves on an upright, shaggy trunk eventually to 30 feet; plants survive winter lows to about 10°F. Even the classic desert oasis date palm *(Phoenix dactylifera)* has endured temperatures as low as 4°F, though foliage is severely damaged when the thermometer hits 20°F.

In regions where winter lows typically are below freezing but not truly frigid, the following palms will persist as long as temperatures fall no lower than about 20°F: Mexican blue palm *(Brahea armata)*; Guadalupe palm *(B. edulis)*; Canary Island date palm *(P. canariensis)*; palmettos (*Sabal* species); California fan palm *(Washingtonia filifera)*; and Mexican fan palm *(W. robusta)*.

Cluster *(above)* Sealing wax palms *(Cyrtostachys renda)*, also called lipstick palms, rise like torches near the corner of this home in Hawaii. These slender, multistemmed palms are slow-growing; native to Malaysia, they need moisture and are hardy to 40°F.

Circle *(left)* Slow-growing palms *(Carpoxylon macrospermum)* from the South Pacific archipelago of Vanuatu form an outdoor room on windward Oahu. Planted on a platform of soil and edged with stones, they recall the heiaus (ancient Hawaiian temples) still standing throughout the islands. **DESIGN:** Greg Boyer–Hawaiian Landscapes.

Screen *(opposite page)* King palms *(Archontophoenix cunninghamiana)*, underplanted with ferns *(Blechnum)*, edge this poolside garden in Venice, California. Their trunks stay slender, making them perfect for confined spaces. **DESIGN:** Shortridge Architects.

PALM·SCAPING

FEW PLANTS SAY "TROPICS" better than palms. Even a single small palm can turn a garden into a backyard resort reminiscent of your favorite vacation island. Cluster palms around swimming pools to create the look of a blue lagoon, plant them singly, as accents, beside breezy patios, or mix them in borders with cannas and other tropicals. You can add night lighting to show off their stateliness and spectacular fronds. Or you can backlight them, shine spotlights up on them from below, or direct lights to silhouette them dramatically against a pale wall.

Leafy umbrella *(above)* Well-manicured Mediterranean fan palms *(Chamaerops humilis)* lean like beach umbrellas over a Los Angeles patio. These palms tolerate poor soil and wind; their curving offshoots develop clumps to 20 feet tall. **DESIGN:** Callas Shortridge Architects.

Plumes *(top left)* Feathery fronds of Manila palms *(Veitchia merrillii)* brush the eaves of this beach cottage in Puako, Hawaii. Also called Christmas palms, they bear clusters of red fruits in winter.

Giant centerpiece *(top right)* A Kentia palm *(Howea)* grows through a patio table in Southern California.

Blue lagoon *(bottom)* Luxuriant king palms *(Archontophoenix cunninghamiana)* help set the mood of a South Pacific lagoon in this Southern California backyard. These regal palms grow fast and don't like windy areas.

Shrubs

JUST AS A SOFA AND CHAIRS help fill a room, shrubs add weight and substance to a landscape. Shrubs become permanent fixtures that can define the shape and limits of the garden, alter traffic flow, or divide various areas of large gardens into more intimate spaces. And just as furniture determines a room's character, shrubs help define a garden's style. Closely clipped hedges lend formality; those with dramatic natural shapes set a contemporary tone. Shrubs with cascading branches establish naturalism in a border, while those with loose, flowering branches can help determine a garden's overall color palette.

Shrubs are most often used as hedges, focal points, or members of mixed borders. Like trees, these woody plants are either deciduous or evergreen. They grow—or can be clipped—in a variety of shapes. With showy flowers, fruit, or leaves that turn vibrant shades of orange or yellow in fall, they also offer seasonal appeal. Some serve as a foil for more colorful foreground plants; others have variegated, showy foliage year-round. Finally, some of the garden's most divine fragrances come from flowering shrubs, such as Angel's trumpet, *Daphne odora*, *Choysia ternata*, gardenia, and mock orange *(Philadelphus)*.

Backing a boulder *(top left)* A vibrant pincushion *(Leucospermum)* thrives in a well-drained soil on a Southern California slope. Growing this shrub near a boulder also improves drainage and offers protection for the sensitive roots.

Bright berries *(top right)* Heavenly bamboo *(Nandina domestica)* puts on a winter-to-spring show of vibrant berries in the Albers Vista Gardens *(albersvistagardens.org)* in Bremerton, Washington. Blue-flowered *Ceanothus* grows behind.

Blue hydrangea *(bottom)* For a moist spot in dappled shade or morning sun, it's hard to beat hydrangeas, whose big flower heads in pink, blue, or white appear in summer. These hydrangeas, with fluffy blue flowers, add a cooling touch to a Northern California garden.

PERFECT SYMMETRY
Clipped hedges surround a patio where X marks the center spot. In keeping with the formal theme, the pots are planted with boxwoods trimmed into neat spheres. DESIGN: Mia Lehrer + Associates Landscape Architecture.

SHAPING SHRUBS

Most shrubs, like those above in the shapely planting by Andrea Cochran, need some regular pruning to keep their shape, reduce disease, and produce healthy flowers and fruit. Correct pruning at the proper time of year will lead to bushier plants with more flowers. Most flowering shrubs should be pruned after their blossoms fade, but other deciduous shrubs bring forth long stems each year from the base and benefit from an early-spring removal of some older stems. Evergreens (such as boxwood and many conifers) can be pruned at any time of year; exceptions are bloomers such as camellias, which should be pruned after blooming. To keep hedges neat, give them a light shearing several times a year rather than cutting back severely once a year.

Some of the best flowering shrubs are medium-to-large-size plants that have been trained to a treelike form with a single, upright trunk. These are known as standards. Others are multitrunked and have been pruned up to reveal sculptural trunks and to form a treelike canopy. For more advice on pruning and caring for shrubs, consult a gardening professional or the *Sunset Western Garden Book*.

> "Containers with small trees can be treated as garden art, adding visual interest to shrub borders."
>
> —STACIE CROOKS, *garden designer*

Summer fragrance *(right)* In late spring, a snowy white 'Natchez' mock orange (*Philadelphus* 'Natchez') bears fragrant white flowers.

Medley of leaves *(below)* A potted full-moon maple *(Acer japonicum)* underplanted with black mondo grass (*Ophiopogon planiscapus* 'Nigrescens') rises above *Euonymus obtusa*, with yellow-gold-edged leaves, and evergreen huckleberry *(Vaccinium ovatum)*, with bronze leaf tips. **DESIGN:** Stacie Crooks, Crooks Garden Design.

GREAT IDEA

Although the world's biggest, oldest plants are conifers, the group includes some of the smallest evergreens for the garden; many look and behave more like shrubs than trees. Dwarf varieties spring from conifer groups such as pine, juniper, false cypress, and spruce.

Gardeners in the Pacific Northwest create spectacular effects by tucking golden thread cypress or dwarf blue spruce into borders, or golden green 'Rheingold' arborvitae in a container.

Lilac spires *(above)* Giant flower spikes of Pride of Madeira *(Echium candicans)* emerge from a cloud of artemisia. Cut them back after bloom to prevent rampant reseeding. **DESIGN:** Isabelle Greene & Associates.

Fire-engine foliage *(left)* Red-leaf Japanese barberry *(Berberis thunbergii atropurpurea)* is a tough, adaptable shrub with brilliant red leaves. When the foliage drops in winter, the spiny branches and red berries are clearly visible.

LIVELY SHRUB BORDER
Varying foliage textures, plant shapes, and heights make this Northwest border a standout. A pink-blooming Scotch heather *(Calluna vulgaris)* and a grassy *Carex oshimensis* 'Evergold' embrace the water bowl, while David's viburnum *(Viburnum davidii)* forms an emerald green mound in the center, and a golden-leaf variety of *Euonymus fortunei* on the right adds texture. DESIGN: Stacie Crooks, Crooks Garden Design.

PICK YOUR SCENT

If your backyard paradise lacks seductive perfume, put in fragrant flowering shrubs (and a bulb or two) to enchant your senses. Plant them near decks, paths, patios, and spas.

Lawns

IN MUCH OF THE WEST, even where drought conditions are common, there are times when lawns make sense. Turfgrass is an attractive way to cover bare earth, and it offers a safe and inviting surface for recreation. A lawn need not be large to enhance a property; a patch 20 by 30 feet is enough lawn for most activities. (In drought-prone areas, the city or county may have restrictions on lawn size.)

You can plant a new lawn using seed or sod. A lawn grown from seed is more work to establish, but far less expensive than installing sod. Either way, be sure to select a grass suited to your region and the site; refer to the *Sunset Western Garden Book* for best bets. Most turfgrasses need sun and lots of water water. A simple hose and hose-end sprinkler may serve your irrigation purposes, or you may want to install an automatic sprinkler or drip system. To eliminate tedious edging, install a ribbon of concrete, brick, or flat pavers—just wide enough to accommodate the wheels of a mower—around the perimeter.

For an alternative in less-tailored gardens, grow a meadow of groundcover sedge such as *Carex pansa* to create a framework, then tuck in small perennials. Meadows need just a few mowings a year, with the mower set at 4 inches.

Waves of green *(above)* The long, lax leaves of European meadow sedge *(Carex remota)* give the impression of choppy water in this small garden in Malibu, California, where a substantial boulder doubles as a bench. **DESIGN:** Richard Turner.

Meadow style *(right)* A sea of meadow grass, sprinkled with California poppies and edged with euphorbias and ornamental grasses, gives this garden, in Marin County, California, a planted-by-nature look. **DESIGN:** Mary Scott Design.

Poolside lawn *(opposite page)* As low and tight as a putting green, this lawn of fine fescue is soft and springy underfoot, and in this desert garden, it's a cooler alternative than sun-baked concrete near the swimming pool. Mixed with paving in foreground, it gives the patio a tapestry effect. **DESIGN:** Ten Eyck Landscape Architects.

New Looks for Lawn Grass

What happens when hard (pavement) meets soft (turf) in your yard? You get modern art that you can walk on.

In much of the West, however, drought conditions are common and lawns are a luxury. But by alternating turfgrass and pavers, you can minimize your turf and add a playful touch to a path or patio. The carpetlike patterns underfoot bring a garden alive.

Be sure to select a grass suited to your region and site. A shaded spot beneath a tree may call for a shade-tolerant groundcover. Use sod and cut it to the size you have in mind. The best way to cut grass growing in narrow channels or upright angles? Use a string trimmer—carefully.

Spiral *(above)* TifSport Bermuda grass weaves a double helix through this flagstone walkway in Ojai, California. The builder framed the rectangular space with wood, then laid 4-inch-wide blue foam board as a placeholder for the pattern. After installing the paving, she removed the foam, filled the resulting 4-inch-wide channels with soil, then planted the sod.

Loose squares *(opposite page, top)* Sod squares grow in spaces between pavers in a Los Gatos, California, garden. Plantings behind include blue fescue and bronze phormiums. **DESIGN:** Jarrod Baumann, Zeterre Landscape Architecture.

PLANTS FOR GREEN GRAPHICS

Many other groundcovers can create bold graphics between pavers. In the San Francisco courtyard above, baby's tears grow between cast pavers, creating the bold look of a mod rug. DESIGN: Topher Delaney, SEAM Studio.

FOR PART SHADE TO SHADE:

- Baby's tears *(Soleirolia soleirolii)*
- Blue star creeper *(Pratia pedunculata)*
- *Dymondia margaretae*
- Irish and Scotch mosses *(Sagina subulata)*
- *Sedum rupestre* 'Angelina'
- *Sedum rupestre* 'Blue Spruce'

FOR SUN:

- *Sedum spurium* 'Dragon's Blood'
- Woolly thyme *(Thymus serpyllum)*

Stripes and pyramid *(left)* Narrow bands of fescue point toward a grassy, 8-foot-tall pyramid at this entry in Laguna Beach, California. The pyramid of hard-packed clay soil is covered with plastic mesh and soft fescue, while its base is anchored in concrete. Drip irrigation waters the grass in both areas; the pyramid gets mowed at the base with a reel mower, and near the top with a string trimmer. **DESIGN:** Jana Ruzicka Landscape Architecture.

Groundcovers

IN MANY SITUATIONS, groundcovers are better options than turfgrass—where the ground slopes more than gently, for instance, making mowing difficult, or along paths or between steppingstones.

All groundcovers share a common trait: They grow low to the soil, spreading widely and densely to cover the ground with a solid blanket of foliage.

Among the grab bag of groundcovers are perennials, shrubs, and even vines. Water needs vary; some thrive in shade, while others prefer sun. Some groundcovers even control erosion by making extensive root networks that bind soil. Leaf colors vary from shades of yellow and burgundy to blue and bronze, as do textures, from fine to lush. You can combine them with stunning effects.

Ribbons of green *(opposite page)* Alternating bands of chartreuse Scotch moss and dark green Irish moss create a soft carpet, fringed with purple-flowered *Verbena bonariensis* in a Sonoma, California, garden. **DESIGN:** Roger Warner.

Silver highlights *(top left)* A soft stream of woolly lamb's ears *(Stachys byzantina)* appears to flow between two kinds of thyme—and striking whitish *Dudleya brittonii*—in a Napa, California, garden. **DESIGN:** Roger Warner.

Magic carpet *(top right)* 'Pink Chintz' thyme fills in for lawn in this low-water Albuquerque, New Mexico, garden. To cover the 24-square-foot space, the owners used 256 plants from 2-inch containers, setting them 12 inches apart. Blue catmint and yellow 'Moonshine' yarrow grow along the edges. **DESIGN:** Barb and Vic Bruno.

Soft fringes *(bottom)* Apple green *Thymus × citriodorus* 'Lime' rambles around pavers in a Marin County, California, garden. Dark burgundy cannas grow at left. **DESIGN:** Blasen Landscape Architecture.

PLANTS FOR STEPS

Small plants that grow in joints between paving soften the appearance of steps and add more greenery to the garden.

Tuck succulents such as echeverias and sedums into the seams between stones; they'll quickly reproduce and form interesting patterns. Plants for shady stairs include baby's tears *(Soleirolia soleirolii)* and dwarf sedges. Good for sunny spots: chamomile, corsican mint, *Dymondia margaretae,* and blue star creeper *(Pratia pedunculata)*. Thyme, pictured above, in a garden designed by Richard William Wogisch, is classic for using in nooks and crannies; it releases a delightful scent when stepped on.

"Bubbles" *(above)* Low mounds of moss *(Sagina subulata)* appear to tumble downstream from the stone water bowl, curbed only by boulderlike low-growing *Hebe*, in a Santa Barbara, California, garden. **DESIGN:** Isabelle Greene & Associates.

Notches *(right)* Ajuga spreads into notches that edge this path of staggered horizontal pavers. Lacy white astilbes grow behind. **DESIGN:** Blasen Landscape Architecture.

Grid *(opposite page)* 'Elfin' thyme turns this patio into a giant checkerboard. Growing in 4-inch-wide strips dividing poured-in-place concrete squares, it's irrigated by a subsurface drip system and needs only the occasional light pruning. Sea thrift keeps the grid from looking too controlled. **DESIGN:** Jeffrey Gordon Smith Landscape Architecture.

For 21 inspiring lawn-free ideas, see sunset.com/lawnfree

"Paving brings architecture to the garden. Plants add pattern, yet soften the garden's modern edges."

—JEFFREY GORDON SMITH, *landscape architect*

Squares *(left) Dymondia margaretae* grows between pavers and around low-growing agave, sedums, and aeonium. **DESIGN:** Amelia B Lima & Associates.

Stripes of plenty *(bottom left)* Baby's tears grow in spaces between pavers in the shaded foreground, and 'Elfin' thyme in the sunny back of this Seattle patio, where they echo the trellis patterns overhead. **DESIGN:** Randy Allworth, Allworth Design.

Tessellated thyme *(bottom right)* Creeping thyme *(Thymus polytrichus britannicus)* grows in 2-to-3-inch gaps between sandstone pavers in this garden in Old Snowmass, Colorado. In summer, it is covered with small pink flowers. The stones echo the distant Elk Mountains. **DESIGN:** Richard Shaw, Design Workshop.

PICK YOUR LOOK

The ideal groundcovers to grow between pavers form low, tight mounds. Choose the plants for color and height, to step on, or step around.

Blue star creeper *(Pratia pedunculata)* Tiny flowers dot it in spring. Filtered shade. *Zones 4–9, 14–24.*

Dymondia margaretae Spidery leaves have white undersides. Striking with sandstone; takes light foot traffic. Sun or part shade. *Zones 15–24.*

***Sedum spurium* 'Dragon's Blood'** Reddish brown leaves make a smoldering backdrop for pink and gray echeverias. Sun or part shade. *Zones 1–10, 14–24.*

Woolly thyme *(Thymus serpyllum)* Undulating mat of woolly gray leaves is sometimes covered in midsummer with pinkish flowers. Sun or part shade in hottest climates. *Zones A2, A3, 1–24.*

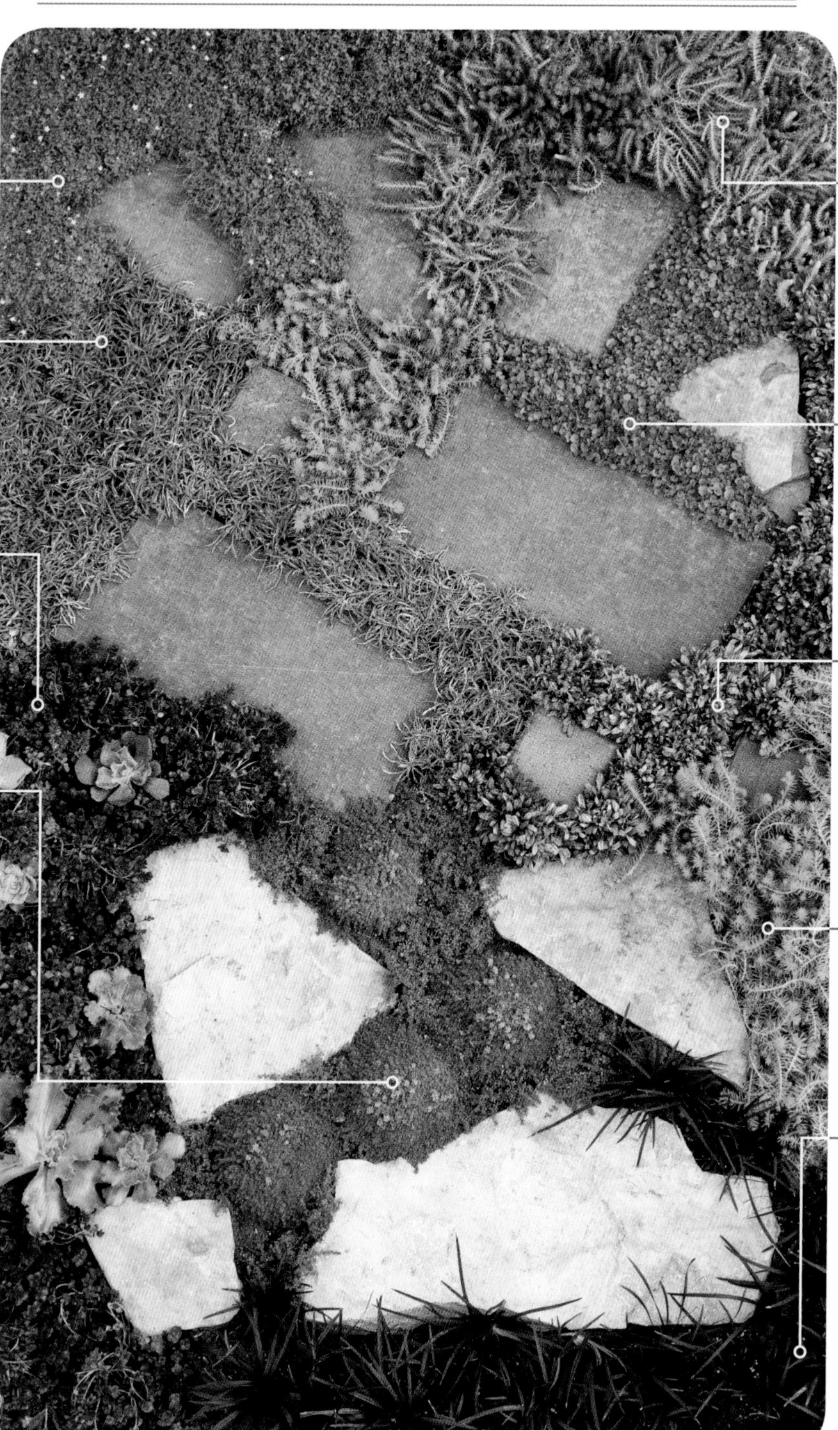

***Sedum rupestre* 'Blue Spruce'** Needlelike foliage resembles blue spruce, except it's soft and succulent. Sun or part shade. *Zones 2–24.*

Baby's tears *(Soleirolia soleirolii)* Cool-looking groundcover with tender leaves you won't want to step on. Part shade, or sun in cool climates. *Zones 4–24; H1, H2.*

Carpet bugle *(Ajuga reptans* 'Dixie Chip') Leaves of green, cream, and rose-purple are topped with violet-blue flower spikes in spring. Sun or part shade. *Zones A2, A3, 1–24.*

***Sedum rupestre* 'Angelina'** A chameleon; yellow-green foliage often turns orange at the tips in fall. Sun to part shade. *Zones 2–24.*

Black mondo grass *(Ophiopogon planiscapus* 'Nigrescens') Leaves emerge green, then turn black. Sun, part shade inland. *Zones 5–9, 14–24.*

"A blue and white color palette is always cool and soothing to the eye, but especially so in a dry climate."

—MARGIE GRACE, *landscape designer*

Perennials

FLOWERING PERENNIALS stage a comeback year after year, but not all behave in the same way. Herbaceous types die down to the ground in fall, then put up new growth the following year. Others are evergreen and remain leafy and virtually unchanged throughout the year. Still others fall between the two extremes—dying back to low tufts of foliage during the winter months. And finally, there are shrubby perennials with woody-based stems.

The perennial border traditionally mixes flowering perennials in a wide bed against a fence or wall; put one on either side of a walk for maximum effect. Combining plants with varied bloom times, plant shapes, foliage textures—and flower colors, sizes, and shapes—is what gives borders their distinctive looks. Perennials also serve well in mixed borders that include shrubs, roses, bulbs, annuals, ornamental grasses, or even small trees.

Arrange perennials along a path for multiple seasons of color, or plant an "island bed" in the lawn, using plants of varying heights and anchoring the bed with the tallest ones in the center.

Tranquility *(left)* A beautiful blend of shrubs and perennials, this serene border mixes low-growing catmint and succulent blue chalk fingers with lavender, spiky Pride of Madeira *(Echium)*, and snowy white roses. The haze of gray along the top is silvery *Centaurea*. **DESIGN:** Grace Design Associates.

Golden abundance *(above)* There's nothing subtle about a big sweep of *Rudbeckia fulgida* 'Goldsturm', which spreads to form good-size colonies. Here, they mingle with purple *Salvia nemerosa* 'Caradonna' and reddish-coral *Phygelius × rectus* 'Passionate' in a Portland garden. **DESIGN:** Laura Crockett, Garden Diva Designs, and Linda Ernst.

Casual pastels *(left)* A soft-looking, naturalistic perennial border features a low-growing yarrow *(Achillea)* backed by purple wallflower (*Erysimum* 'Bowles Mauve'). Both produce loads of flowers.

Globes and grasses *(above)* A sweep of deep purple globe thistle *(Echinops)* looks even more dramatic in the company of grasses like tawny Mexican feather grass *(Stipa tenuissima)* and blue oat grass *(Helictotrichon sempervirens)*.

Spritz of lime *(right)* Chartreuse blooms of *Euphorbia characias wulfenii* add a vivid yet cooling contrast in front of a Japanese maple with smoldering, chocolate-red leaves—a striking color combination in a Northwest border. This euphorbia is a great mixer. It's also pretty beside Spanish lavender or blue 'Wedgewood' Dutch Iris.

Cool border *(above)* In this Seattle border of moisture-loving plants, leaves take the main stage. Featured are a variegated hosta (*Hosta sieboldiana* 'Frances Williams'), a burgundy-leafed *Rodgersia podophylla* 'Rotlaub', and white-flowered Soloman's seal *(Polygonatum biflorum)*. **DESIGN:** Stacie Crooks, Crooks Garden Design.

Winter border *(right)* Pink-flowered hellebores fill a large, ribbed pot, where they accent the sleepy cold-season planting. **DESIGN:** Stacie Crooks, Crooks Garden Design.

PAIRING PERENNIALS

SHAPE. A bed in the shape of a circle or square looks formal, while a free-form bed is casual.

VIEW. Angle the bed for viewing from different parts of the garden and house—from paths, a patio, or indoors through prominent window views.

HEIGHT. One simple way to guarantee variation is to use plants that mature at different heights or add the illusion of height by mounding soil to create a gentle berm.

COLOR AND TEXTURE. Flowering perennials have their individual moments of glory, then retreat from center stage. Intersperse them with permanent foliage plants for visual constants during the growing season. Shrubs with colored or variegated foliage are good candidates.

ACCENTS. A shapely boulder, a well-placed piece of garden art, or a low-growing Japanese maple can make just the needed finishing touch.

EDGING. If you want a bed to look crisp, outline it with pavers like brick or stone. For an informal margin, plant billowy, spreading perennials along the edges.

Sizzling border *(above)* Golden gloriosa daisies, along with red and yellow kangaroo paw *(Anigozanthus)*, brighten this summer border. Orange cannas grow in the foreground. This colorful pathside border is organized around an overflowing fountain made from a large urn. **DESIGN:** Sherry Merciari, Merciari Designs.

All-in-pots border *(left)* Fiery-hued tulips and burnt orange pansies add a vibrant finishing touch to this patio "border" made up of coral bells *(Heuchera)* with foliage in caramel-to-chocolate shades in low, wide bowls. Ferns, heucherella, golden *Acorus gramineus* 'Ogon', and other greens add subtle contrast. **DESIGN:** Stacie Crooks, Crooks Garden Design.

For 20 border designs, see sunset.com/border

LUXURIANT LAYERS
Perennials arranged by height frame the view in this Pacific Northwest garden. Purple-flowered *Verbena bonariensis* rises in the center, along with red *Crocosmia* 'Lucifer', silvery spires of 'Cuprea' Scotch heather, and blue-flowered 'Rozanne' geranium. DESIGN: Stacie Crooks, Crooks Garden Design.

BORDER BASICS

A border looks its best if you build in these elements.

CURVES. Curving borders are more interesting than straight-sided ones. If your border space is tight—as along a driveway or curb strip—soften its edges by clustering low plants there that billow and ramble.

LAYERS. Arrange plants by height, from lowest in front to tallest in back. Space plants close together so their "shoulders" will touch when they're grown. Include backbone plants to give the border some structure in winter—small evergreen shrubs or dwarf conifers, for instance.

COLOR ECHOES. A cohesive border has a primary color theme—pastels, for instance, or sunny yellows and blues, or shades of green foliage with hits of burgundy. These colors repeat throughout the border. Plant in clusters or drifts, by plant type, or by flower color. When choosing your plants, keep in mind the colors of your house, fences, and walls.

ACCENTS. To give a border visual punch, cluster a few plants whose flowers are bigger or of a deeper color than the surrounding plants. Strappy-leafed phormiums, or a colorful glazed urn, are other good choices.

LACE. Small-flowered plants such as asters, coral bells, and yarrow are great fillers. Plant them in drifts between larger-flowered ones. To edge your border, use low, mounding plants such as curly sedge, lime thyme, creeping zinnias, or—in shade—*Lamium maculatum.*

Playground partners *(top)* This kid-friendly garden edging a red jungle gym includes plants that are fun to touch. Kangaroo paws *(Anigozanthus)* have fuzzy blooms; yarrows *(Achillea)* resemble small umbrellas.

Edge softeners *(bottom)* Coral bells *(Heuchera)* and blue fescue *(Festuca)* fill in the narrow crevice at the wall's base, while coral Santa Barbara daisy *(Erigeron karvinskianus)* tops a stucco wall. **DESIGN:** Huettl Landscape Architecture.

Annuals and Bulbs

FOR A QUICK INFUSION OF COLOR, gardeners most often turn to annuals. Cool-season annuals such as snapdragons and pansies brighten mild-winter, low-elevation gardens from late winter through early spring, from early to late spring elsewhere. Warm-season annuals such as cosmos and marigolds take over then, blooming through fall. Nurseries provide a dazzling array every year in cell-packs and pots—or in seed packets for still more choices. Use annuals to punch up a mixed border, make an edibles patch more ornamental, or refresh containers.

Bulbs—a category that may include corms, tubers, rhizomes, and tuberous roots—also add bursts of color. But they go in the ground earlier. Plant spring-flowering bulbs such as daffodils in early fall. Summer bulbs such as dahlias and gladiolus go in the ground in late winter or early spring.

Annuals and bulbs make good companions. Plant low-growing annuals such as sweet alyssum *(Lobularia maritima)* above bulbs as place markers. Intermingle taller annuals, such as snapdragons, with bulbs to hide their yellowing foliage at the end of the season.

Contrast *(top left)* The cheerful orange of California poppies *(Eschscholzia californica)* complements the cool blue of catmint (*Nepeta racemosa* 'Walker's Low'). Since poppies reseed readily, one sowing might keep this show going indefinitely.

Center stage *(top right)* A colony of tall, bearded iris is the yearly star in this spring border at Albers Vista Gardens *(albersvistagardens.org)* in Bremerton, Washington. Lilacs blooming in the background and yellow and purple wallflowers tucked in below echo the colors of the iris.

Mood maker *(bottom)* Dahlias with nearly black foliage, such as 'Bishop of York', bring dark drama to a garden, especially against the backdrop of a red wall.

Edibles

IF YOU HAVE A GARDEN of even modest size, you can grow edibles. A classic produce patch takes less room than you think. If you're growing only for your own table, you don't need dozens of everything. Even a single zucchini plant and a couple of prolific tomatoes should provide a sufficient harvest. No need to hide vegetables in the far corner, either. With a little planning, your edible garden can be worthy of center stage, especially if you mix them with ornamentals.

Begin by creating a strong geometric pattern such as the classic German four-square (shapes of equal size arranged in a grid) or keystone (beds arranged around a T-shaped path). For an even more orderly look, grow your crops in stylish but durable raised beds of stone, recycled concrete, or rusted metal. Create generous paths covered with gravel or bark between beds.

As you set out plants, think of complementary colors and textures—chartreuse Bibb lettuce next to a burgundy romaine, parsley next to sage, for example. Train your vertical edibles along handsome supports like a pyramid-shaped *tuteur*. And tuck in a few flowers for color.

Spillers *(below)* Cherry, grape, and paste tomatoes are easier to grow in pots than full-size tomatoes because you can forgo staking—use determinate varieties—and just let them drape. **DESIGN:** Jack Chandler, Chandler & Chandler Landscape Architects.

Weavers *(above)* Lettuces, mustard greens, spinach, squash, and other leaf crops can be planted in ribbons of contrasting color and texture, just as you would perennial ornamentals. Here, a colony of orange dahlias adds brightness; flowering dill provides height in back.

Tuck-ins *(right)* Cabbages and arugula grow contentedly in a narrow strip of soil between two levels of a terraced garden in Oakland, California. **DESIGN:** Randy Thueme Design.

Shapers *(opposite page)* Handsome raised beds laid out in a simple geometric pattern with ample room for neatly groomed paths in between—it's a formula for a beautiful edible garden that never fails to please. **DESIGN:** Blasen Landscape Architecture.

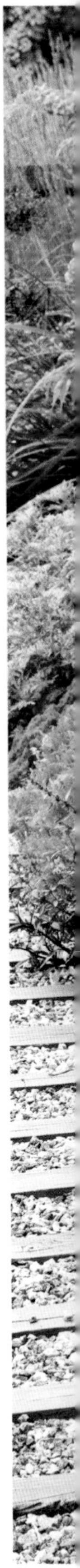

Fillers *(above)* Bibb and leaf lettuces and beet greens fill in between pavers in a Berkeley, California, garden instead of the usual creeping thymes or mosses. DESIGN: Keeyla Meadows Gardens + Art.

Framers *(right)* 'Anna' apple trees, trained to cover the sides of an arbor, will eventually meet at the top to create a green tunnel. Most stone fruit trees—including peach and plum—can be espaliered in the same way.

Edgers *(far right)* 'Bull's Blood' beet foliage alternates with the ferny green marigolds in the front row of a mixed edibles and ornamentals border. Red *Salvia coccinea* and yellow pear tomatoes make up the back row.

EDIBLES IN DISGUISE

Not ready to commit to a full-fledged vegetable bed? Try stealth crops. Pick out the most attractive ones and incorporate them into your landscape wherever they'll look prettiest, just as you would any other ornamental.

- Line paths with low-growing, mounding herbs such as sage, savory, and thyme. They're the perfect height and shape—with aromatic scents as a nice bonus.
- Edge flower beds with leafy lettuces. The rosettes are a pleasant contrast to the shapes of most perennials. Chives and parsley are other good choices.
- Tuck taller leafy crops into mid-border. Chards, kales, and mustard greens all have big, beautiful leaves that make great foils for spring and summer flowers. Purple-leafed basil works the same way.
- Use handsome crops as seasonal color in containers. Lettuces, chards, and kales can all do solo turns. Chile plants look sweet alone too. So can tomatoes if you choose a compact patio variety. Or use herbs—basil, chives, parsley, sage, thyme—as foliage plants with seasonal flowers.
- Treat perennial crops as permanent foliage plants. Put artichokes, bronze fennel, or rosemary in the back of the border. Use blueberry shrubs as a hedge. Shade an arbor with a grape rather than a flowering vine.

Verticals *(above)* Vining crops like tomatoes, green beans, peas, and Malabar spinach look more orderly when trained upright and are easier to harvest as well. They also add a vertical dimension that counterbalances the flat-growing crops. **DESIGN:** Blasen Landscape Architects.

Mixers *(left)* The heart-shaped leaves of winter squash *(Cucurbita maxima)* look striking next to a fine-textured woody perennial, especially one with a contrasting leaf color, such as the *Caryopteris* × *clandonensis* 'Worcester Gold' seen here.

GREAT IDEA

One plant per pot looks as modern and fresh with edibles as it does with ornamentals. Secrets to this trio's success: the three pots are similar in size and shape but not identical; same with the edibles—all are leafy but they are different crops. Left to right: 'Giant Red' mustard, bok choy, and 'Redbor' kale.

Floaters *(above)* With their delicate umbrella-shaped blooms hovering high overhead, dill and fennel give the edible garden a misty quality. Here fuzzy blue forage, spilling onto the path, adds further shimmer.

Downsized *(left)* 'Raspberry Shortcake' is a fraction of the size of most raspberry varieties. It tops out at 3 feet and grows in a moundlike shape rather than in tall erect canes, making it suitable for the tiniest urban garden.

No space is too small to grow good things to eat. Plant blueberries in pots, or rainbow chard with violas in a colorful border.

Focal point *(opposite page)* Pomegranate trees are decorative enough that you can situate them in any sunny spot that would benefit from a small (15 feet tall and as wide) graceful tree. Fruits ripen in late fall.

Ramblers *(top right)* Squash plants like to roam, and their upturned leaves are prettiest when allowed to do so as in this Washington garden.

Pot perfect *(bottom left)* 'Peach Sorbet' blueberry, growing only 2 feet tall, is ideal for containers. The leaves have a peachy pink cast in spring and, where evergreen, an eggplant purple tone in winter, making the shrub decorative year-round.

Color echoes *(bottom right)* The dark veins of Swiss chard are repeated in the foliage of a black-leafed dahlia.

Ornamental Grasses

ORNAMENTAL GRASSES ADD POETRY to the garden in a way no other plants can. With their upright, arching shapes, they seem like living fountains—adding motion to the landscape even when the air is perfectly still and beginning to sway when there's barely a breath of a breeze. Grasses are also superb light catchers, especially when placed where they're backlit by the rising or setting sun. Because of their neutral colors, they are excellent mixers, compatible with most other plants. But some put on quite a show in fall, turning red, yellow, orange, or purple—adding interest to the garden just when most flowers are fading. And ornamental grasses don't require fertilizer, rarely have insect problems, and need only minimal maintenance.

Just one caveat: Because they produce so many seeds, all grasses have the potential to be invasive. To protect native habitats, check websites such as the California Invasive Plant Council *(cal-ipc.org/paf)* before planting, to find out which grasses are problematic in your area.

Learn the difference between good plants and weeds. Then choose grasses that are appropriate for where you live.

GLOWING BACKDROPS

Deciduous trees whose leaves glow like stained glass when backlit by the sun make the perfect backdrop for shimmery golden grasses, especially in fall when both are wearing their autumnal colors. Plant one or more off to the side of a border to make the most of natural backlighting, and watch how the trees and grasses enhance one another. Try Japanese maples, 'Bloodgood' (scarlet) and 'Ever Red' (crimson); Chinese pistache, orange and red to gold; and ginkgo, buttery yellow.

Motion picture *(above)* Breezes off the water keep the grasses in this Bainbridge Island, Washington, garden dancing most of the day. They include *Miscanthus, Nasella, Chasmanthium, Calamagrostis,* and *Helictotrichon. Sedum* 'Matrona' and two varieties of sumac add different textures.

Blue ribbon *(right)* A ribbon of silvery blue *Leymus condensatus* 'Canyon Prince' courses through a field of green like a cool stream. Switch grass *(Panicum virgatum)* grows behind. DESIGN: Lane Goodkind Landscape Architect.

Tropicals

WITH THEIR LUSH FOLIAGE, brilliant flowers, and seductive scents, tropical gardens seem like paradise. If you live in an area of the West where frosts are light or nonexistent, you can re-create the same magic in your own backyard using the huge array of subtropicals that will grow in your climate. To achieve a similar effect in harsher climates, substitute plants that look lush but are actually hardy, such as Japanese banana *(Musa basjoo)* and *Gunnera*.

First, you'll need some plants with leaves as big as umbrellas, such as banana or elephant's ear *(Alocasia)*. Then, add foliage with bright stripes or splotches, such as canna, copperleaf *(Acalypha)*, phormium, and, in summer, caladium and coleus. You'll want exotic shapes too, such as palms, tree ferns, cordylines, and cycads. Of course, there's no paradise without flowers. Make sure they're bright and/or big and that at least one is fragrant enough to make your head swim—angel's trumpet *(Brugmansia)* or gardenia, for instance. Vines are a must, and use groundcovers instead of mulch. Layer after layer, pattern after pattern, is the effect you want.

Layers of green *(above)* Following the pond's curves, a ribbon of baby's tears, with feathery cycads and Kentia *(Howea)*, and Lady *(Rhapis)* palms, create a welcome in a San Diego, California, entry. **DESIGN:** Debora Carl Landscape Design.

STRIKING PALETTE
'Intense Rainbow' remains a popular plumeria thanks to its vivid colors—golden center and ruby edges fading to pink—heavy texture, and sweet fragrance.

GREAT IDEA

For a quick hit of the tropics in the summer garden, bring in some bromeliads. Guzmanias (pictured above) are widely available, and have green leaves and brightly colored flower bracts that last for weeks. Vriesias have wider leaves and vivid, paddle-shaped bracts. Both are easy to grow. Plant several in a wide bowl to display on a lightly shaded patio. Unless you live in the tropics, overwinter these plants indoors.

Native born *(above)* Hapu'u *(Cibotium glaucum)* is a native Hawaiian tree fern much admired for its long, arching, intricately divided fronds. It can grow up to 20 feet tall and spread 15 feet wide.

Splash of color *(right)* Tree ferns and Kentia palms thrive in a sheltered location shaded by an overhead balcony. Bright cushions pick up the colors of the nearby bromeliads. **DESIGN:** Debora Carl Landscape Design.

TROPICALS IN COLD ZONES

If you don't live in a frost-free zone, you can still grow tropicals—at least summer through fall. Start with foliage plants that feel tropical but can survive the winter lows in your area. Possibilities include *Gunnera*, Mediterranean fan palm *(Chamaerops humilis)*, and windmill palm *(Trachycarpus fortunei)*, all frost-tolerant to Zone 4; Japanese banana *(Musa basjoo)*, cold-hardy to Zones 2 and 3 with protection; and plantain lily *(Hosta)*, to Zone 1.

If you want to risk plants that are marginally hardy for your area, place them in the warmest, least exposed areas of your garden—under roof overhangs or near walls where they will benefit from reflected heat. Or grow them in containers and move to a frost-free garage for the winter.

After the danger of frost has passed, add tropical bulbs, especially splashy, fast-growing canna and elephant's ear *(Colocasia esculenta)*. Dig them up in fall and store to replant the following year. As the final touch, plant caladium, coleus, and New Guinea impatiens for summer seasonal color.

Green and black *(above)* Exuberant foliage emerging from black lava rock is quintessentially Hawaiian. This island planting includes a large hala tree *(Pandanus tectorius)*, several Ravenea palms, and akia *(Wikstroemia)*, an endemic Hawaiian groundcover. DESIGN: Janice Palma-Glennie.

Jurassic rhubarb *(right) Gunnera tinctoria*, a South American perennial of prehistoric origin, creates a tropical effect in this Washington garden. It can easily grow 8 feet tall and as wide and produce leaves 4 to 8 feet wide in one season. Begonias bloom below.

For how to plant a living wall, see sunset.com/livingwall

"With tropicals in my backyard, I can pretend I'm on vacation in Hawaii—one of my favorite vacation spots on Earth."

—A *SUNSET* READER

Shell ginger *(top left)* Most gingers can be tricky to get to bloom outside the tropics, but *Alpina zerumbet* 'Variegata' is worth growing for its 2-foot-long, glossy, spectacularly striped leaves alone.

Jungle geranium *(bottom left)* Vibrant red blooms cover *Ixora coccinea*, grown as a showy summer annual in all climates. But in warm climates such as Hawaii, it can sprint into a shrub large enough to stand up to a mature agave.

Pineapple flower *(bottom right)* Tall, thick spikes covered with smoky pink flowers rise from a rosette of large leaves on *Eucomis comosa* 'Sparkling Burgundy'. Silvery *Euphorbia characias* 'Tasmanian Tiger' grows behind.

The Native Tropicals

When you picture a Hawaiian garden, most likely an oasis filled with plumerias and flaming red Chinese hibiscus *(Hibiscus rosa-sinensis)* comes to mind. True, these are among the most iconic plants of the Islands, but in reality they came to Hawaii from somewhere else—plumeria from Mexico and the Caribbean, Chinese hibiscus from Asia.

Less well known are the true native Hawaiian plants, such as otherworldly ahinahina *(Artemisia mauiensis),* shapely olulu *(Brighamia insignis),* and delicate akulikuli *(Sesuvium portulacastrum)*—all breathtakingly beautiful. Hawaii is home to some 1,200 native flora species; 10 percent are indigenous (native to Hawaii), and the rest are endemic (found only in Hawaii). Until recently, these plants weren't easy to find at nurseries because many are endangered in their natural habitats.

But over the past two decades—thanks to efforts by the Kauai-based National Tropical Botanical Garden to locate, identify, and propagate native flora—native Hawaiian plants have become more available to home gardeners, and native-specialty growers and nurseries are cropping up throughout the Islands.

Among the showy natives suitable for Hawaii's home gardens are 'ohi'a lehua *(Metrosideros polymorpha)*, a small-scale tree whose vivid, brushlike blooms entice birds, bees, and butterflies; leafy, thick-stemmed olulu, which in the wild grows on sea cliffs and thrives in borders among lava rock; and the world's only naturally fragrant hibiscus, the pualoalo *(Hibiscus arnottianus),* which makes a beautiful hedge. Sweet-smelling nau *(Gardenia brighamii)* makes a great accent.

"In Hawaii, our culture is based on our surroundings," says Rick Barboza, co-owner of Hui Ku Maoli Ola nursery on Oahu. By planting natives, you're "preserving Hawaii's cultural identity." Also, many native plants require little additional water.

Find details at *nativeplants.hawaii.edu, ntbg.org,* or *hawaiiannativeplants.com.* For a list of nurseries that sell Hawaiian native plants, check out *nativeplants.hawaii.edu/nursery.*

Hawaiian hibiscus *(right) Hibiscus arnottianus*, endemic to the Hawaiian Islands (Molokai and Oahu), produces papery, slightly fragrant white flowers.

Succulents

SUCCULENTS ADD DRAMA to the drought-tolerant garden, and they do it without much maintenance on your part. Unlike most drought-tolerant plants—which have small, thin leaves—succulents adopted an alternative survival strategy. They developed big, thick, waxy leaves that soak up and retain water. Some have enlarged stems that do the same. Perhaps even more useful from the standpoint of landscape design, succulents evolved into either precise geometric shapes or, frankly, into bizarre forms. As a result, they seem otherworldly, more like juicy, living sculptures than plants. Yet, for all their drama, succulents are easy to care for. Their only demand is good drainage. Lighten heavy soil with decomposed granite or pumice, and they'll be happy.

Gardeners in almost all climates can grow a few of these striking characters, but the warmer your winters, the more varieties you can enjoy. Use them to add structure to a wildflower bed, provide novel textures in a drought-tolerant mixed border, accent a rock garden, or fill in difficult shallow planting pockets.

Succulents are also ideal candidates for vertical gardens and containers. Because they tolerate low humidity, some even thrive indoors, especially small species like *Haworthia*.

Good partners *(opposite page)* The gray-green leaves of fan aloe *(A. plicatilis)* look twice as smooth when paired with the stiff, dark green, fiber-fringed leaves of *Agave filamentosa*. **DESIGN:** Bernard Trainor + Associates.

Sea world *(top left)* A mauve echeveria and apple green aeonium look like underwater creatures when combined with kelplike *Lomandra* and small succulents. **DESIGN:** Flora Grubb Gardens.

Dr. Seuss tree *(top right)* A mature *Aloe barberae* in a Berkeley, California, garden is festooned with tree-scale-size prayer beads made by Marsha Donahue, adding to its naturally dramatic appearance. Pig's ear succulents *(Cotyledon orbiculata)* pay homage at its feet. **DESIGN:** Brandon Tyson.

Gentle giants *(bottom)* Unlike most agaves, the leaves of *A. attenuata* are soft and spineless, but give this plant plenty of room. Situate it where its stout trunks and wide rosettes can be fully appreciated.

Reliable performer *(right)* Spider aloe *(Aloe × spinosissima)* is loved for its manageable size and controlled habit almost as much as for its months-long flower display. Crème brulée agave *(A. guiengola)* is its ghostly companion. **DESIGN:** Bernard Trainor + Associates.

Great mixer *(top left)* The very dark purple leaves of 'Zwartkop' aeonium make it a good foil for the gray-green and blue-green foliage of most drought-tolerant plants. Its mustard-colored summer flowers are a pretty bonus.

Wall art *(top right)* Various colors of *Sempervivum* are arranged in a pleasing composition. *Sedum* 'Angelina', spilling from the frame, adds amusement. **DESIGN:** Robin Stockwell.

Cocktail hour planter *(bottom)* Tiny rosettes of *Sempervivum* cover this tray-top table except for the spaces left for pots of *Kalanchoe luciae* and the tiles set in to hold wine or cocktail glasses. **DESIGN:** Harte Brownlee & Associates.

SUCCULENTS IN COLD CLIMATES

Though the majority of succulents are frost-tender, a fair number can tolerate temperatures in the 20s or high teens, and a handful can handle even lower. The most frost-tolerant groups are ice plant *(Delosperma)*, sedum, *Sempervivum*, and yucca. A few euphorbia fall into this category, such as *E. griffithii*, *E. myrsinites*, and *E. polychroma*, and so do a few agave, notably *A. palmeri* and *A. parryi*.

If you want to push the envelope and try growing succulents marginal for your area, keep your soil as dry as possible in the winter. The combination of wet soil and cold does more damage to them than low temperatures alone. Here are other steps you can take to help succulents survive the winter.

- Amend your soil so it drains quickly.
- Plant on mounds or in crevices between boulders.
- Mulch with gravel so the crowns of plants stay dry.
- Cover plants with frost covers or bushel baskets when low temperatures are predicted.
- Consider growing plants in containers, so you can move them under eaves or beneath a porch to keep them dry during winter rains.

For more on using succulents, see sunset.com/succulents

> "Everything I ever imagined for succulents, and more, is now in play. People are using them everywhere—on walls, roofs, even on dining tables."
>
> —ROBIN STOCKWELL, *specialty grower, SG Succulents*

Tabletop decor *(top left)* A trio of small succulents—*Sempervivum*, echeveria, and sedum—planted in a chicken feed trough make a charming, offbeat centerpiece for a patio table. **DESIGN:** Molly Wood Garden Design.

Solo turn *(bottom left)* *Aloe ferox* is always showy. Its shiny gray-green leaves sport a contrasting red edge. When in bloom in late fall, each branched inflorescence holds hundreds of red-orange flowers.

Pastel beauty *(bottom right)* The pale green, cream, and pink leaves of a 'Kiwi' aeonium add a feminine contrast to succulents of bolder shape and darker color.

PICK YOUR SHAPE

Succulents are among the most enthralling plants on the planet, with jewel-toned leaves, bold forms, and obliging natures. Put them together with imagination, and you've got art.

IF YOU WANT A LILY PAD EFFECT…
Aeonium tabuliforme
Topping unbranched stems, these rosettes are nearly as flat as lily pads. Because they grow 10 to 18 inches across, they're sometimes referred to as saucer or dinner-plate aeoniums. Perfectly symmetrical, each one is a work of art by itself. Sun in cooler climates; light shade elsewhere. *Zones 15–17, 20–24.*

IF YOU LIKE BLOWSY BLOOMS…
Hen and chicks
(Echeveria secunda × 'Glauca') Planted closely together, these silver-blue rosettes add pointy tips and a soft raspberry blush to the composition. *Zones 8, 9, 14–24.*

IF YOU LIKE TIGHT LITTLE ROSEBUDS…
Hen and chicks
(Echeveria elegans)
Tight grayish rosettes with an icy tinge grow to 4 inches across and spread freely by offsets. Clusters of pinkish flowers are a bonus. Can burn in hot sun. *Zones 8, 9, 12–24.*

IF YOU WANT FRILLS…
***Sedum rupestre* 'Angelina'** This creeping stonecrop creates a lacy but temporary fringe between the larger succulents pictured here. As it spreads, its tidy tracery will disappear. Foliage is chartreuse in light shade, yellow in sun. *Zones 2–24.*

Cactus

MANY SUCCULENTS have smooth, firm stems and leaves that invite touching. But the fascinating succulents known as cactus are better viewed than handled, as they have clusters of spines. These unusual features—great at catching light—and the incredible variety of overall plant shapes make cactus a natural as the focal point in a dry garden. Cactus are like living sculptures to highlight against colored walls, and many even have colorful, fragrant blooms.

Cactus look splendid in containers, which also provide the well-drained conditions these plants prefer. And they easily tolerate lapses in watering or feeding that would be disastrous to other plants.

To create a desert feature, fashion a low raised bed out of stones in a sunny part of the garden. Fill it with cactus potting mix and add your favorite cactus. Instead of using organic mulch, surround the plant with gravel to prevent the buildup of moisture around the base, which often leads to rot. When planting or potting a cactus, use wadded newspaper to make a thick bundle around the plant, creating a barrier between your hands and the spines.

SAVING SAGUAROS

Native to the Southwest deserts, saguaros can grow 60 feet tall or more in the wild, and live for 150 to 200 years. They don't develop arms or flowers until at least 60 years old. For this reason, majestic specimens have fallen victim to rustling. It is illegal to harm or dig up a wild saguaro, but you can buy nursery-grown plants from reputable suppliers (learn more at *dbg.org* or *desertmuseum.org*).

Circles of blue *(above)* The blue-green pads of this Santa Rita prickly pear *(Opuntia macrocentra santa-rita)*, are perfectly round and blushed with purple. A blue agave grows in back.

Sculptural spires *(left)* Thick upright stems of *Cereus peruvianus* stand out against a plain stucco wall painted soft sage green, with a gravel mulch around the base. **DESIGN:** Steve Martino Landscape Architect.

Dryland entry *(opposite page)* Drought-loving *Yucca rostrata* and various cactus, including the striking golden barrel cactus *(Echinocactus grusonii)* fill this front yard in San Diego, California. Tucked among boulders, they thrive on rainwater alone.

Natives

TO CREATE A SUSTAINABLE GARDEN, just replicate the native species growing in the wild areas nearest you. No matter what the challenges of your particular climate—soggy winters, sizzling summers, acid or alkaline soil, lots of fog, heavy winds—there are plants that have adapted perfectly to these conditions. Use them in your garden, and you will need little or no soil amendments, supplemental water, fertilizer, or pesticides. Your carbon imprint will be minimal, and so will your labor.

If you want a habitat garden, regional natives are excellent choices. They've evolved with the local wildlife, so the flora and fauna support each other. Plant these natives, and your garden will be alive with birds, butterflies, beneficial insects, and other creatures. Or plant natives just to celebrate your own particular niche of the West.

Though general nurseries usually carry some natives, for a wider selection, shop native plant specialty nurseries; botanical gardens that feature native plants, such as California's Theodore Payne Foundation *(theodorepayne.org);* or sales sponsored by native plant societies. The Native Plant Conservation Campaign *(plantsocieties.org)* can help you find the society nearest you.

Heaven scent *(opposite page)* Cleveland sage *(Salvia clevelandii)* is the most deliciously scented plant in the California chaparral. Both foliage and flowers are intensely fragrant. 'Allen Chickering', seen here, is an especially abundant bloomer. **DESIGN:** Pamela Burton & Company Landscape Architecture.

Choice ceanothus *(right)* As ceanothus go, 'Skylark' is petite—3 to 6 feet wide, 3 to 4 feet high—with a tidy mounding habit, making it an ideal candidate for smaller gardens. Other virtues: a later, longer bloom cycle and a tolerance of summer irrigation.

Year-round interest *(below)* California buckeye *(Aesculus californica)* has apple green spring foliage, bottlebrush-like white flowers in summer, pear-shaped fruit in fall, and a beautiful silvery gray bark, exposed when the leaves drop, in winter. **DESIGN:** Donald Tarahonich and Leslie Zander.

"Native plants are in perfect sync with our weather, our soils, and our wildlife species. Choose the right ones, and they'll outperform any exotic."

—MIKE EVANS, *founder, Tree of Life, wholesale native plant nursery*

Borrowed wildland *(opposite page)* Coffeeberry, manzanita, mimulus, and a carpet of yarrow make this green rooftop in Northern California feel like an extension of the native oak woodland behind it. **DESIGN:** Karen Ford Landscape Architect.

Matchless mimulus *(right)* Sticky monkey flower *(Mimulus aurantiacus)* has a short but colorful life. All mimulus bloom over a long period initially, but hybrids, especially, often rebloom in the fall.

Hawaiian chameleon *(below)* 'Ohi'a Lehua *(Metrosideros polymorpha)* never looks the same twice. It can take the form of a prostrate shrub or a 100-foot-tall tree or anything in between. Red flowers are most common, but you also see yellow, orange, pink, and white. Leaf color and shape can vary as well.

GREAT IDEA

During their famous overland expedition to the West, Meriwether Lewis and William Clark collected more than 200 plant specimens, many new to botanists. Some of these native "heritage" plants are worth growing in gardens, especially in the Northwest and intermountain areas. They include bearberry *(Arctostaphylos uva-ursi)*; redtwig dogwood *(Cornus sericea)*; common snowberry *(Symphoricarpos albus)*, pictured above; and wild mock orange *(Philadelphus lewisii)*, a fragrant shrub named for Lewis.

Mini ecosystems *(above)* To create this garden near Carnation, Washington, the owners, Jim and Paula Umbeck, took their design cues from nature, saving existing native vegetation, then adding more of those same plants. Here, rhododendron tops the slope, while deer ferns and sword ferns cluster beside a rock-lined recirculating stream, made to step downslope in a series of cascades to Lake Marcel.

Forest combo *(left)* In the wild, *Trillium ovatum* grows in lightly shaded areas with some moisture. Usually surrounded with deep forest duff or groundcover, it's the perfect companion for low-growing ferns.

On the grid *(above)* Neat rows of deer grass *(Muhlenbergia rigens)*, edged with steel headers, grow on a broad terrace of decomposed granite outside this modern, desert-edge house in Paradise Valley, Arizona. **DESIGN:** Ten Eyck Landscape Design.

Geometry *(left)* Tall ocotillo and golden barrel cactus create a desert tableau in a raised bed edged with steel and mulched with black Mexican pebbles.

Local color *(above)* Rocky Mountain columbine *(Aquilegia coerulea)*, Colorado's state flower, thrives under the light shade of quaking aspens *(Populus tremuloides)*. **DESIGN:** Design Workshop.

Scene-stealers *(left)* Whether mingling with meadow grasses or massed in garden beds, lupines make a spectacular show. Flowers of silverstem lupine *(Lupinus argenteus)*, native to the Rocky Mountains, are usually blue, sometimes lilac or white, and grow 2 feet tall.

For 23 knockout native plants, see sunset.com/natives

PICK YOUR REGION

In the wild, native plants rarely exist alone. They are part of an ecosystem of plants that have evolved together and depend on one another for things like shade. Four of the West's most iconic habitats are pictured here. At nurseries, choose kinds that belong together.

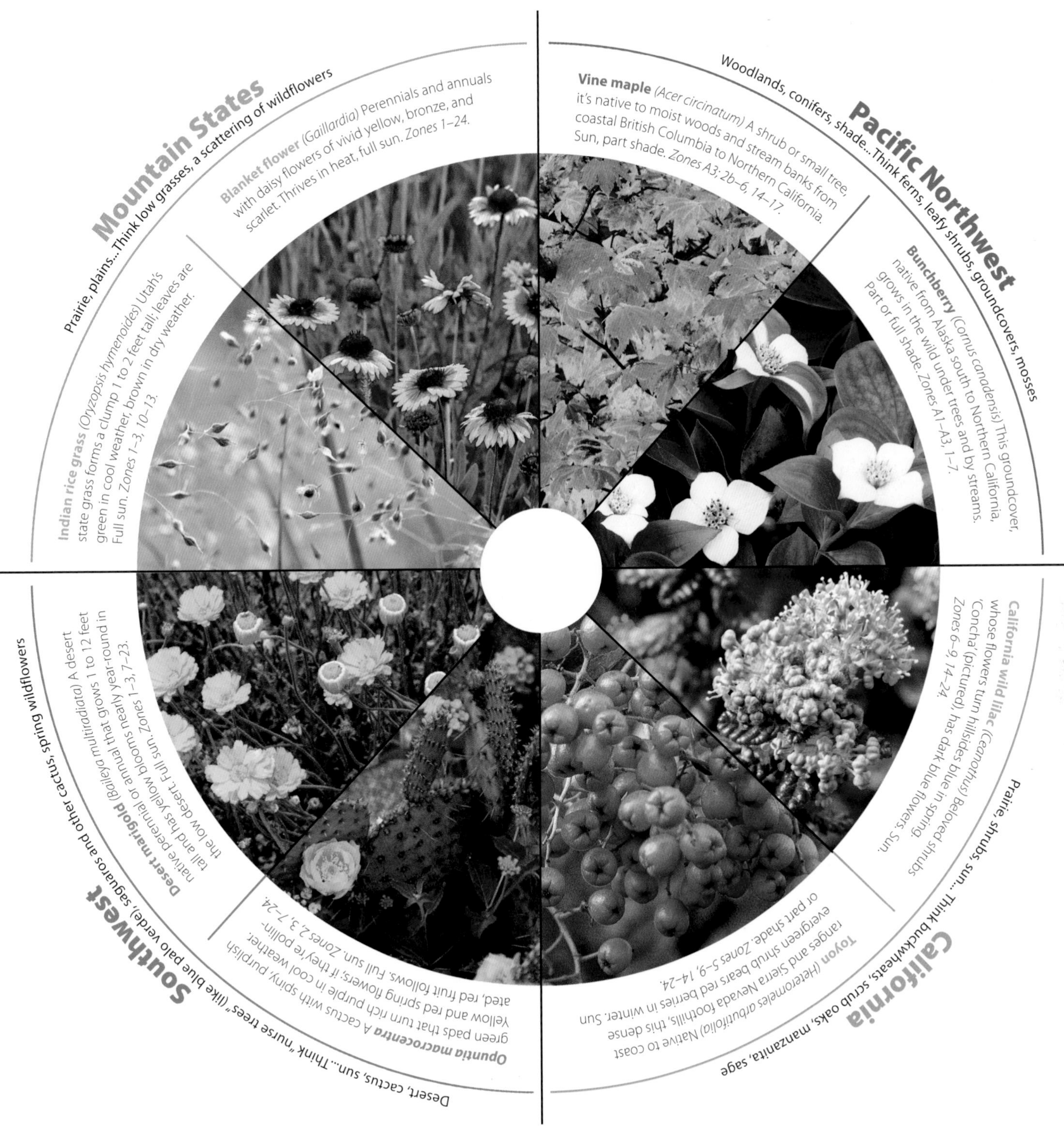

FINISHING TOUCHES

These days, garden art is anything you want it to be. A pricey temple bell from your travels in Bali, perhaps, or a treasured ceramic bowl made by a friend. Maybe it's a much-loved surfboard from your high school days or a vintage flat-bottom boat that you display in a flower bed to recall sweet memories. It might be something you've made of natural materials—stones stacked into a pyramid, for example, or a sculpture made from a saguaro skeleton that adds nighttime drama when lit from below. As you'll discover on the following pages, resourceful gardeners throughout the West are creating spectacular effects with colorfully painted walls, imaginative outdoor lighting, furnishings both cozy and lightweight, and vibrant outdoor fabrics.

COLOR HARMONY Pillow fabrics echo all the garden's colors—the blue tile, orange-red wood, and creamy concrete, even the charcoal-gray of the rocks in the firepit.

COLOR HARMONY Pillow fabrics echo all the garden's colors—the blue tile, orange-red wood, and creamy concrete, even the charcoal-gray of the rocks in the firepit.

> "Art is still somewhat of a surprise outdoors, so its use makes a garden feel more like a room."
> —MOLLY WOOD, *landscape designer*

Art

WHEN THINKING OF ART in the garden, statues typically come to mind. But as lovely as they are, they're hardly your only option. Choose a special place in the garden for any object you love—a treasure from a pottery studio, a handcrafted piece of furniture, a pleasing design straight from nature—and behold how much it adds to the character of your garden.

Handsome empty containers, such as old Greek olive oil jars or sleek and shiny modern ceramic cylinders, find new purpose. Stone columns or other architectural fragments make striking accents. Repurposed ornate metal grilles or advertising signs become wall hangings. Found objects from nature—driftwood, twisted branches, chunks of basalt—function as art too, when displayed creatively.

Eye-catching art can also be integral to the structures and furnishings of the garden. Your gate could be a brightly painted, one-of-a-kind creation straight from the artist instead of one from a manufacturer's template. Opportunities to incorporate art into your outside areas are everywhere: the garden bench, your dining table, even your children's play set.

Eye-catchers *(left)* Three panels of fused glass, created by the homeowner, hang from a sturdy hog fence panel in Linda Ernst's Portland garden. The panels stop your eyes at the flowers instead of letting them travel to the storage shelves in the background. **DESIGN:** Laura Crockett, Garden Diva Designs.

DISPLAY BASICS

SHOW OFF YOUR STARS. Place your important art pieces in front of a solid-colored wall or simple green hedge so they'll stand out. The center of a fountain or pool is another good location.

GO BIG. A few large, dramatic pieces trump a dozen little ones every time—especially in a small garden. This may seem counterintuitive, but they'll make your tiny garden seem bigger than it is.

GO UP. Create more presence for a small piece of art by elevating it on a column, pedestal, or plinth.

VARY THE THEME. If you're a collector, mass all those Bauer pots, Catalina tiles, or vintage birdhouses in one location. They'll have more impact than if scattered around the garden.

HIDE A SURPRISE OR TWO. Tuck a concrete rabbit in your produce patch, hover a dragonfly permanently over your pond, or set up a trio of Japanese tribal masks peeking out from your bamboo grove. Create a few smiles.

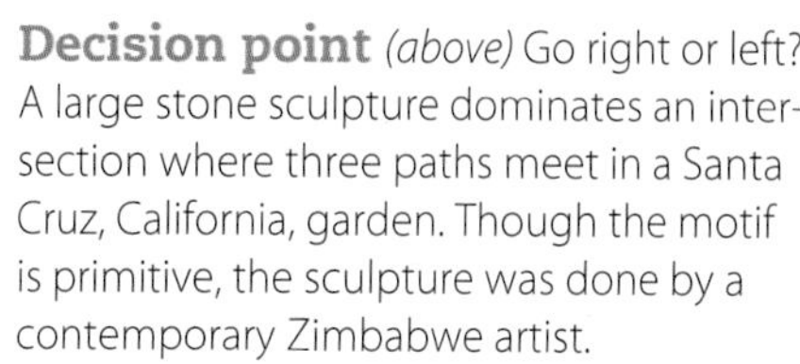

Decision point *(above)* Go right or left? A large stone sculpture dominates an intersection where three paths meet in a Santa Cruz, California, garden. Though the motif is primitive, the sculpture was done by a contemporary Zimbabwe artist.

Sphere of influence *(left)* A rusty metal globe adds structural interest to a floriferous West Linn, Oregon, garden. **DESIGN:** Sherry Sheng.

Mood maker *(far left)* An obelisk of dark blue glass rods adds intensity to the paler blues of penstemon and globe thistle *(Echinops)* in a Portland garden. The glass also catches the sun, contributing a bit of sparkle. **DESIGN:** Laura Crockett, Garden Diva Designs.

"I keep an open mind (and wandering eye) for everyday items that I can repurpose. Found items can add a dose of personality to a garden."

—REBECCA SWEET, *garden designer*

Salvaged treasure *(left)* A Victorian mantel, found in an alley, adds interest to an ordinary fence in Los Altos, California. The homeowner/garden designer affixed the shells. **DESIGN:** Rebecca Sweet, Harmony in the Garden.

Boardwalk *(bottom left)* Old surfboards turn a wooden fence into an art gallery at a bungalow in Kauai, Hawaii.

Spirit boat *(bottom right)* Artist Jack Chandler transformed a French *parouge* (flat-bottomed marsh-fishing boat) into a sculpture for his Calistoga, California, garden by supporting it with a steel spine anchored to a steel base.

Pyramid *(opposite page)* A pair of sculptural stone pyramids accent a Southern California garden. The straw bale wall behind them is covered with handmade plaster. Subtle paintings in a petroglyph style dance across its surface, suggesting animals that might once have lived here. **DESIGN:** Jana Ruzicka.

Birdbaths

NOTHING LURES BIRDS TO YOUR GARDEN as reliably as a birdbath. Thirsty birds refresh with a drink, then remain to bathe. Set a shallow bowl—1 to 2 inches deep—with sloped sides on a post or pedestal and keep it full of clean water. Then watch as resident birds become steady customers. Migratory birds will drop by too, like orioles and tanagers you might not otherwise see. And on an especially hot, dry day, a hawk might even swoop in.

Concrete, terra-cotta, ceramic, and mosaic tiles are the most common materials for birdbaths, but copper, plastic, glass, and resin are also options. Birds aren't choosy. Select a material and style compatible with your garden so you'll be as happy with the birdbath as your avian visitors are.

To help draw birds to your garden, add a device to the birdbath that makes it drip or burble. Birds follow these signs to find fresh water. Some birdbaths come with built-in fountains; otherwise, you can add a dripper or mister.

Glass *(above)* A fused glass bowl rests on a steel base in a densely planted Portland border. Electrical wiring threaded through the base illuminates the bath at night. **DESIGN:** Laura Crockett, Garden Diva Designs.

BIRDBATH BASICS

KEEP IT CLEAN. Dirty, contaminated water can make birds sick. Hose out your birdbath daily to remove stagnant water, and then refill it. Every few days, empty the bowl and scrub away algae and other deposits with a stiff brush. In addition, two or more times a season, sterilize the bowl by scrubbing with a solution of 1 part bleach to 10 parts water. Rinse out thoroughly before refilling.

KEEP IT SAFE. Place a birdbath on a pedestal near shrubs or trees to provide birds with cover and escape routes. A shaded location will also slow down algae growth. For ground-level baths, however, site the birdbath where it has a minimum of 10 feet of space all around so that damp birds can be alert to the approach of cats or hawks.

KEEP IT FROM FREEZING. If you live in a cold-winter climate and want avian visitors year-round, add a heating element to your birdbath to prevent the water from freezing.

Concrete *(top right)* A hand-hewn concrete bowl, chosen for its eccentricity, brings a touch of whimsy to a Tumwater, Washington, garden. Can the garden gnomes and fairies be far behind?

Acrylic *(bottom right)* A frosty white tray on a simple fir post matches the mood of André Price Jackson's serene Venice, California, garden. Price made the bath, securing the tray pieces together with acrylic glue. A galvanized aluminum rod serves as a perch.

Birdhouses

THERE ARE TWO KINDS OF BIRDHOUSES: the ones that add a touch of beauty to the garden and the ones that birds might actually nest in. The former may resemble your own home—with a front porch, a chimney, a cupola, and other charming details. The latter are considerably plainer. That's because the types of birds willing to live in manmade nest boxes are more accustomed to rustic dwellings such as woodpecker holes or hollow logs. Of course, there's room in the garden for both ornamental and functional birdhouses.

Which cavity-nesters will take up residency in your birdhouse depends largely on the size of the entrance hole. All prefer a tight squeeze so they can get in, but predators are kept out. Wrens and chickadees, for instance, like holes no more than 1¼ inches in diameter; bluebirds and swallows, 1½ inches. Larger birds such as flickers and screech owls will require a wider diameter (2 to 3 inches) and bigger structures overall. They also need their homes to be mounted higher off the ground.

If you do invite in avian tenants, be a responsible landlord. A great website for finding out which birds live in your region and what they need in the way of housing is the Cornell Lab of Ornithology's All About Birds *(allaboutbirds.org)*.

Repeat customers *(opposite page)* A nest box under an old oak tree on *Sunset*'s grounds in Menlo Park, California, has hosted bluebirds for years.

Martin motel *(right)* This chic double-decker on the grounds of Oakwood Gardens in Hillsboro, Oregon, was built to accommodate purple martins and does so successfully year after year. Unlike many songbirds, martins nest in small colonies.

Recycled chic *(below)* A birdhouse made from old siding, with a discarded garden spigot as a perch, attracts nuthatches and wrens in Lisa Albert's Oregon garden.

BIRDHOUSE BASICS

CONSTRUCTION. Wood is the best material, as it provides good insulation. Features should include an overhanging roof for rain protection, holes or slots on each side for cross-ventilation, holes on the bottom for drainage, and a removable top or side for easy cleaning. Avoid a house with an outside perch unless you plan to hang it in a protected area.

INSTALLATION. Mount the birdhouse at least 5 feet off the ground, on a well-secured metal or wood pole. Choose a location away from dense shrubs and the hustle and bustle of bird feeders.

MAINTENANCE. Remove old nests at the end of the season and scrub out the interior. If parasites are present, use water and strong soap to rinse well.

Containers

COLORFULLY PLANTED CONTAINERS are the garden equivalent of throw pillows. They're accessories you add to a garden to give it punch and personality. If your mood or the season changes, just switch them out and replace with something new.

But containers in more permanent roles provide other value. Use them to draw eyes to areas you want noticed. Place a matched pair on either side of an entry, for example, or by the French doors leading to the garden, or at the patio's edge to frame a view. Or select just the right container as the focal point of a garden vignette. Picture a tall ceramic cylinder in chartreuse in the midst of a border of dark green foliage. Planted containers are also problem-solvers—use them to block out unwanted views, create privacy screens, act as safety barriers, or redirect traffic.

Besides the traditional materials for containers, such as terra-cotta, carved stone, and cast iron, you can find plastic and resin/fiberglass versions that are convincing imitations—at a fraction of the weight and cost.

GREAT IDEA

Containers don't always have to hold plants. Instead, they can stand on their own. Try an attractive arrangement like this one, where empty pots, related in shape and palette but varied in size, create a handsome picture, especially against a simple green foliage background. DESIGN: Roger Warner.

Protective screen *(above)* A dense assortment of potted plants on a front patio makes a prettier barrier than barred windows. The thorny plants, including agave and cactus, enhance the home's security. DESIGN: GreenArt Landscape Design.

Color contrast *(right)* A quartet of red pots in various shapes and sizes adds a jolt of color to an area devoted primarily to leafy greens in the garden of edible landscaping pioneer Rosalind Creasy.

Scene maker *(opposite page)* Homeowner Linda Ernst turned an unplantable stretch of gravel in front of a plain wall in her Portland garden into a stage. The players include a terra-cotta urn holding a cape rush, a trio of potted 'Southern Comfort' coral bells, and a stone lion with a mane of moss. DESIGN: Laura Crockett, Garden Diva Designs.

Mini divas *(top left)* Three exotic succulents—*Euphorbia lactea variegata cristata*—housed in identical bright orange pots create a showy but easy-care tabletop centerpiece. **DESIGN:** Gabriela Yariv Landscape Design.

Perfect pair *(bottom left)* Plum-colored foliage is a rich accent against soft greens in these easy-care containers. In the smaller pot, *Echeveria* 'Coral Glow', *Coprosma* 'Evening Glow', and *Kalanchoe* 'Fantastic' add rosy contrast to green *Sedum rupestre* 'Angelina', *Sedum adolphii*, and spiky *Euphorbia* 'Ascot Rainbow'. In the larger pot, tall *Phormium* 'Guardsman', *Echeveria pulvinata*, and *Aeonium leucoblepharum* accent the greens—including bushy *Leucadendron* 'Wilson's Wonder' and pointy *Aloe humilis*. **DESIGN:** Daniel Nolan, Flora Grubb Gardens.

Treasure cache *(bottom right)* A primitive Indonesian figure in Davis Dalbok's garden in Marin County, California, holds shell necklaces and shell-like succulents in his lap.

Fire and ice *(opposite page)* *Begonia boliviensis* 'Bonfire' and *Melianthus major* share a large glazed blue pot in Craig Quirk's Portland garden. Chunks of blue glass and gray-blue succulents tucked into the earth at a whimsical angle add further punch. **DESIGN:** Laura Crockett, Garden Diva Designs.

GREAT IDEA

Moody browns and icy blues make striking pairings in pots. Here's a simple combo to try at home: set a powder-covered, iceberg blue *Echeveria* 'Cante' among chocolate-colored plants—'Cheryl's Shadow' geranium, with sweet pink flowers, and 'Black Adder' phormium. The echeveria is clearly the star in the 16-inch-square charcoal-colored container pictured here, but all these plants are striking in their own ways and need little water to thrive.

Classic *(above)* Geraniums and citrus in terra-cotta pots are a Mediterranean tradition. Here, red-flowered ivy geranium is joined by licorice plant *(Helichrysum petiolare)*. A kumquat tree goes solo in the background. DESIGN: Melissa Thompson.

Stairstep vignette *(left)* In Susan Fries' Portland garden, the pots are as important to the color scheme as the plants. Two match the foliage; the other two provide contrast. A trio of silver globes adds sparkle.

Sophisticated *(opposite page)* Silver rosettes of *Graptopetalum paraguayense* add contrast between trailing green *Senecio radicans*, narrow-leafed Dyckia 'Burgundy Ice', and *Encephalartos lehmannii*, a silver-gray cycad. *Pedilanthus macrocarpus* on top is a fountainlike finishing touch. DESIGN: Scott Calhoun, Zona Gardens, and Jody McGregor.

For 40 outstanding container gardens, see sunset.com/containers

Fabrics

WHETHER A GARDEN IS LARGE OR SMALL, the desire to create ample outdoor living space means the addition of hardscape. To soften the effect and make these spaces more enticing, you can counterbalance all the hard surfaces with the soft, gentle touch of textiles.

Fortunately, there are now almost as many choices for outdoor upholstery (sun- and water-resistant 100 percent acrylic fabrics such as Sunbrella) as for indoor. Depending on how much sun you want to block, you can curtain your patio or cabana with solids or sheers, or both—just as you would a room indoors. Fabrics provide overhead shade as well, via traditional awnings or contemporary shade sails.

Even though they're not as durable, regular fabrics add variety and whimsy to the mix: a collection of batik throw pillows to recall a tropical vacation, say, or a drape of mosquito netting around a sleeping platform, just for the romance of it.

GREAT IDEA

A tentlike tepee with an air mattress is so comfortable you may decide to spend the night here in summer. Made of bamboo poles and lemony yellow weather-resistant fabric, it's both a napping spot and a favorite hideaway for kids and pets. You just tether five poles at the top with sisal, spread them out over a waterproof tarp, and drape the fabric around them. Go to *sunset.com/garden/backyard-projects* for DIY details.

Beach blocks *(above)* A trio of pillows—a nautical blue-and-white graphic, another that suggests a coral reef, and a third reminiscent of kelp strands—gives this neutral seating a beach resort feel. **DESIGN:** Bonesteel Trout Hall.

Prayer flags *(right)* Nepalese prayer flags suspended between two posts frame an entry to a home in Hana, Maui, Hawaii, and convey goodwill to all who pass through.

Tropical curtains *(opposite page)* Pareus, usually worn as wraparound skirts, provide some sun protection for the lanai of David Easton's rammed earth house in Hana, Maui. They also add charm, billowing with every breeze. That each is just one color on a white background unites them in theme.

Slice of orange *(above)* Interior designer Diane Lam added a continuous line of orange cushions to the seating area of her San Marino, California, garden to emphasize the strong geometry and to contrast with the overall blue-gray tone. A pair of Marimekko pillows picks up the strong graphics in the pool coping. DESIGN: Darren Shirai, Bosque Design.

Shot of blue *(right)* Sometimes one pillow is all it takes—here, an indigo ikat pattern—to turn a bench into a vignette.

Splashes of citrus *(opposite page)* Bright orange accessories, sprinkled lightly but consistently throughout an otherwise all-white color scheme, add a breath of summer to this Newport Beach, California, garden. DESIGN: Craig Schultz, LS Architects.

UMBRELLA BASICS

While freestanding structures that support a fabric roof with perimeter posts, creating an outdoor room, have become more popular, they will never replace the traditional umbrella entirely. Before selecting your umbrella, here are some things to consider.

FABRIC. Look for fabrics that provide high UV protection and can withstand sun, wind, and rain. Acrylic fabrics are the most expensive but also the most durable.

FREESTANDING VS. OFFSET. Freestanding umbrellas are good choices for general shade or if you have a patio table with an umbrella hole. The cantilevered design of offset umbrellas allows you to shade a dining table and the surrounding seating areas without blocking anyone's view. However, offset umbrellas need weighted slabs to secure their base, making them more difficult to move around the garden than freestanding ones.

SIZE. As a general rule, a patio umbrella should be at least 5 feet larger than the area you want to shade. For example, a 48-inch table would require a 9-foot-diameter umbrella.

Desert coverage *(left)* A pair of architectural sails shades a Phoenix patio from the desert's harsh sun as well as adds bold strokes of color. **DESIGN:** Ten Eyck Landscape Architects.

Furnishings

OUTDOOR FURNITURE can be as serious—and as costly—as indoor furniture. But it doesn't have to be. Furnishing the garden offers the perfect opportunity to be more playful and save money while you're at it. Shop garage sales and flea markets for worn but still serviceable patio furniture that can be brought back to life with a little cleaning up, some minor repair, and a fresh coat of varnish or paint.

Besides being economical, these pieces allow you the freedom to take chances. Few would dare spray new wicker furniture lilac or robin's egg blue. But for older pieces you picked up for a song, it doesn't seem like a big risk. Salvaged goods provide more chances to be creative. You can repurpose old doors or window frames as tabletops, turn packing pallets into benches or shutters into shelves, make tractor seats into barstools, or transform an unused surfboard into a coffee table.

To add interest to a deck or patio, mix chairs in various colors or play with fabrics in multiple patterns.

GREAT IDEA

Turn an old window frame with safety glass into a garden table by securing legs cut from a 2-by-2 and attaching them with door hinges as brackets. New brass screws give some sparkle to the rustic look. If your window doesn't have safety glass, add a sheet of sturdy transparent plastic cut to size by a supplier such as *tapplastics.com.*

Retro cool *(top left)* Lightweight and shapely, these modern chairs add a pop of color to a deck outside a San Diego, California, home and its mostly green backdrop.

Big, bold plaid *(bottom left)* Three chairs of woven plastic on steel frames in a surprising pattern make a strong statement in an otherwise understated garden. They also play off the pattern of the pool's tile.

Primary colors *(opposite page)* A vibrant blend of lightweight red chairs and metallic blue stools adds bold accents to a white table on this outdoor dining deck, against a lush foliage backdrop. Like 3-D wallpaper, the mesh pockets covering the wall are filled with bromeliads, ferns, and purple heart.

HOT SEAT A smooth stone bench, called the Helios lounge, provides a sunny stroke of color at Flora Grubb Gardens in San Francisco. A fusion of sculpture and tech, the bench can be heated. Just plug it in, press a button, and set the tempeature. An adjustable sensor regulates the temperature up to 120°F. DESIGN: Aaron Jones, Galanter & Jones.

THE CLASSIC ADIRONDACK CHAIR

Nothing reminds you that it's time to relax quite like an Adirondack chair. Once you settle into one, plan to stay awhile. The original version was designed by Thomas Lee in 1903 for his summer home in the Adirondacks. The Adirondack chair was quickly copied and has retained its popularity ever since—largely because the combination of low-slung seat and broad fanned back remains unmatched for comfort. The wide armrests—broad enough to hold a cup of coffee or a cocktail, a romance novel or an iPad—are convenient too. If these chairs feel a bit traditional for your garden, consider an Adirondack made of recycled plastic in a bright contemporary color or clean white (pictured above), such as the ones from Loll Designs.

Fiberglass *(top right)* Lunar-looking chairs and a matching table appear even more surreal on a fancifully cutout carpet of synthetic turf. **DESIGN:** Grace Design Associates.

Wood *(bottom right)* A pair of sensuous teak chaises on a sandy overlook in Malibu, California, pick up the tawny tones of the dune grasses in the background. **DESIGN:** Pamela Burton & Company Landscape Architecture.

Deck lounge *(above)* These chaises pop straight out of the decking. Each back is hinged at the base. You just lift up the far end and insert the prop to hold it open. If you want to use the deck for another purpose, lower the chaises so they're flush with the deck.

Polyethylene *(right)* The sensuous curves of a fog-gray chaise make it the clear centerpiece of this deck. Charcoal planters and galvanized tin buckets used as containers repeat the gray tones. Foliage and bright pillows provide just enough color; too much would overwhelm this small space. **DESIGN:** Shades of Green Landscape Architecture.

HAMMOCK BASICS

ROPE AND STRING. Classic rope hammocks come in cotton, polyester, or DuraCord. They're soft and breathable, making them a good candidate for hot climates. Lightweight hammocks are created from a mile or more of string. Most come from Mexico, Guatemala, Nicaragua, or El Salvador, and are often called Mayan hammocks.

FABRIC. Choices are cotton, mesh, or quilted fabric. The first is the most comfortable, the second provides the best air circulation, and the last offers the most style options. All are great for cool climates; fabric can feel sticky in warmer regions.

SPREADER BARS. Rope and fabric hammocks come with or without wooden or metal spreader bars at either end. Although many people prefer the look of hammocks with spreaders, the ones without them are more stable and the best option for sleeping. Mayan string hammocks don't have spreaders. A hammock with a spreader bar at only one end is more stable than one with bars at both.

INSTALLATION. The standard 13-foot hammock should be suspended between trees or posts 15 feet apart ideally, 12 feet at a minimum. If you don't have an appropriate setup, buy a hardwood or sturdy, rust-resistant metal frame.

Easy Lighting

JUST BECAUSE THE ELECTRICITY EXTENDS to the outside areas doesn't mean you have to use it. When entertaining outdoors—even if only for yourself—nothing improves the ambience more than lowering the wattage and bringing in the softer light of candles. Spanning the dining table in votives, sheltered in lanterns or wall sconces, or hanging from overhead beams cradled in mason jars, candles add glamour to the garden.

Solar-powered lights provide myriad ways to romance the garden after dark. Enjoy the mysterious glow of shoji paper lanterns dangling from trees. Festoon an overhang with solar string lights, or outline a deck railing with solar tube lights. Use stake lights or steppingstones to gently light a pathway, or faux rock lights to highlight a favorite garden vignette. Set Moroccan lamps or tiki torches across the lawn or near shrubs without worrying about starting a fire—choose an amber LED light that intentionally flickers, and no one will know you haven't used candles. Solar garden lighting is so flexible you can create a different scene for every occasion.

GREAT IDEA

At first glance, this fountain, made of a stainless steel grid holding shards of tumbled glass, seems physically impossible. How does it hold water? Answer: a clear resin basin inside. The fountain is even more dramatic at night, when lights, also inside, make it glow like a gold cube. DESIGN: Mark Rogero.

String of lights *(above)* Adding a festive mood in this Southern California backyard dining patio, clear glass bulbs set aglow clumping 'Alphonse Karr' bamboo. A vintage, seldom-used 1970s wood-burning stove in the corner enhances the patio's cozy feeling. **DESIGN:** Steve Siegrist Design.

Recycled globes *(left)* Tea lights illuminate plastic globes from within, making them look like sunlit bubbles. They brighten a patio built from recycled granite stones. **DESIGN:** Matthew Levesque.

Sconces *(opposite page)* Fitted with small-lipped glass bottles from a craft store, each containing lamp wicks nestled in olive oil, old hacienda tiles add rugged good looks and a soft, warm glow to an exterior house wall. Wires secure the tiles to the wall, passing through holes drilled carefully through the tiles with a masonry bit.

GREAT IDEA

For a little evening glow, create a centerpiece from matching or even mismatched old chandelier lampshades and set a tea light inside each. For a more stable arrangement, you can drill holes sized to fit the lamp bases into a salvaged piece of lumber. Then prime and paint it white, and nestle the lamp bases in the holes.

DIY chandelier *(above)* Creating romantic lighting for an outdoor dinner party, these votives—which use mini recycled-glass tea light lanterns—are suspended at various heights from low-hanging branches. Use clear fishing line and keep the candles safely away from the leaves.

Portable step lighting *(left)* Moroccan-style lanterns illuminate the low steps along this path when evening comes. They also enhance the garden's tropical magic.

Solar lanterns *(opposite page)* These colorful lanterns turn themselves on. Each 10-inch globe of durable nylon is a Soji Solar Lantern that contains a small photovoltaic panel, a rechargeable battery, and two LED lightbulbs. At night, a sensor turns on the light, which glows for up to eight hours. **DESIGN:** Allsop Home & Garden.

A LITTLE NIGHT MAGIC
Streams of water (laminars), lit by energy-efficient LED fixtures in the decking, glow softly as they arch into this swimming pool. Along with the nearby fence made of clear acrylic "bubble rods" (spaced 4 inches apart), they add nighttime magic, and a touch of party-time glam, to a Northern California garden. DESIGN: Randy Thueme Design.

"Clear acrylic bubble rod fences glisten, glow, and sparkle. They're great for pool owners who love glittery things."
—RANDY THUEME, *landscape architect*

LIGHT·SCAPING

A WELL-LIT FRONT YARD not only welcomes guests and leads them safely to the front door, but also accentuates features that might otherwise be lost in the dark. Your garden can become a stage set, with muted lighting to give it form and depth, or with unexpected silhouettes and highlighted shapes to give it drama at night. The right lighting can draw attention to a garden's focal point or cast shadows of shapely trees or metallic sculptures across nearby walls.

Shown here are options that usually require the services of an expert to install. Path lights are the most needed; typically lining front entries, they're meant to be seen, both day and night. But uplighting—whether of a graceful tree or a piece of outdoor art—adds drama, while "fun" lighting brings smiles.

No two gardens are alike. Asking an expert the right questions will help you light plants, hardscape, and features.

Uplights *(above)* To enhance this sculptural fence in San Francisco, the designer added low-voltage lights at the base. At night, the light plays across the fence's undulating, 12-inch strips of perforated copper (supported by cedar slats and steel) and bathes the trunks of three white-barked Himalayan birch trees. **DESIGN:** Randy Thueme Design.

EASY OPTIONS

Here are four other ways to add lighting, mostly without electricity.

SOLAR LIGHTS. Buy these small solar path lights for less than $20 at big box stores. Each is made of a clear plastic bowl atop a tapered stake and has a lid with a small solar panel on top and a tiny bulb inside. Poke the stake into the soil in a sunny spot. The light goes on at dusk.

SOLAR ILLUMINATED PLANTERS. At night, these planters—typically made of molded, recyclable polyethylene with solar battery-powered LED lights within—cast a soft glow.

FLOATING LIGHT GLOBES. These waterproof orbs of frosted acrylic usually come with rechargeable batteries. Cluster a few in the corner of a patio, or set them afloat in the swimming pool like so many moons in water that reflects the stars.

FIBER-OPTIC LIGHTS. Bringing a touch of Hollywood-style glamour to a garden, these cables—filled with thin strands of transparent glass or plastic—guide light from one spot to another. They're sometimes embedded in paving to create a starlight effect underfoot, or tucked under the rim of a low seat wall near a pool.

Focal point light *(top)* A golden bowl of light is the star of this entry courtyard in an Atherton, California, garden. Lit from within, it appears to spill its light into the shallow, rock-lined pool around it. **DESIGN:** Jarrod Baumann, Zeterre Landscape Architecture.

Stairway lights *(bottom)* These small lights, mounted to a low patio wall, bathe the steps in a soft glow. They have shielded fronts to direct the light downward, where it's needed for nighttime safety. **DESIGN:** Arterra Landscape Architects.

"Paint a big splotch—a quart's worth at least—when you try out a new color. And cover an upper corner so you're seeing it against sky and aren't influenced by old paint colors."
—STEVE MARTINO,
landscape architect

Paint

IF YOU WANT COLOR in the garden year-round, don't plant—paint. Imagine how those concrete block or masonry walls that surround your garden would look if instead of neutral they were painted Moroccan red, pumpkin orange, or blue-violet. Suddenly, all of the evergreens in your garden seem more interesting: their foliage colors more intense, their structure more striking.

Maybe you have fences around your garden rather than walls. But do those pickets have to be white or the wrought iron black? Envision them in lilac or chartreuse. Think about how those hues would lift your spirits on a gloomy winter day, then how sweet your pastel spring flowers would look against them when the season changes.

Garden structures needn't be neutral either. A cobalt blue pergola or gazebo may sound daring, but the dark color makes the structure blend in with the rest of the garden more than if it were white. Paint a garden gate sunshine yellow, a garden bench wisteria. Be bold. Paint is easy to change.

Cocoa enclosure *(left)* The richly colored wall around this Phoenix garden connects it with the desert by picking up the deep tones of the rocks. Yet the color is dark enough to provide a satisfying contrast to the overall scene. It is also a great foil for the brightly colored steel sculpture by Fletcher Benton. **DESIGN:** Steve Martino Landscape Architect.

Lavender expanse *(above)* A long wall in a Napa, California, garden, installed to block an unattractive view, becomes an asset when painted a cheerful purple, underplanted with *Equisetum hyemale*, and paired with a perennial morning glory vine. **DESIGN:** Shades of Green Landscape Architecture.

Parade of stripes *(left)* In this Northern California garden, 19 different colors embellish a concrete retaining wall next to a driveway where planting was not possible. Each stripe was custom-blended to match foliage and flowers in the nearby garden. **DESIGN:** Topher Delaney, SEAM Studio.

Green on blue *(opposite page, top)* A bright blue wall delivers drama without taking up an inch of space in a pocket-size Los Angeles garden. The addition of an acid green rectangle draws attention to the soul of the space, its concrete fire table. **DESIGN:** Rob Steiner Gardens.

PAINT BASICS

No matter what surface you're painting, first make sure it is clean and smooth. Scrub or power wash to get rid of dirt and dust. Use a bleach solution to remove mold or mildew. Scrape or sand off loose paint flakes. Treat for rust. Patch cracks. Then watch the weather reports for a stretch of several days of warm, sunny weather—and jump in.

CONCRETE. Unpainted concrete needs a primer coat to fill pores, preferably an acrylic block fill. You can also apply primer to previously painted concrete. The best top coat is elastomeric (masonry) paint; next best, 100 percent acrylic.

PLASTER OR STUCCO. Apply an exterior acrylic primer for best results, then follow with flat or low-sheen exterior acrylic paint.

WOOD. If the wood is new, seal it first with one or more coats of exterior wood primer. Then paint with a low-sheen exterior acrylic paint. Acrylic stains are also an option.

METAL. Apply a rust-inhibiting primer and paint with an exterior enamel.

Cherry *(left)* A rich red wall adds considerable warmth to this shady garden in Studio City, California. The color is also the perfect complement for the magnificently mottled trunk of the shade provider, a mature Chinese elm. The apricot sofa cushions pick up other tones in the bark, and two red containers extend the wall color into the garden. **DESIGN:** Joseph Marek Landscape Architecture.

"All plants with strong, simple shapes look great with an intensely colored wall behind them."

—PATRICK ANDERSON, *horticulturist*

Cobalt backdrop *(opposite page)* A vivid blue wall sets off the orange and yellow blooms of aloes *(A. ferox, A. microstigma,* and *A. mitriformis)* perfectly in Patrick Anderson's Fallbrook, California, garden.

Spark of lemon *(right)* Painting the stucco fireplace and seating wall citrus yellow gives this Studio City, California, outdoor room a strong focal point. Red chairs and flowers add contrast; lush green foliage, coolness. **DESIGN:** Rob Pressman, TGP Landscape Architecture.

Refreshing red *(below)* Warm-colored stucco, replacing the original cold gray concrete, makes this small, enclosed Oakland, California, backyard feel cozy, not claustrophobic. Trailing red trumpet vine adds softness. **DESIGN:** Shades of Green Landscape Architecture.

GREAT IDEA

Not only is this container recycled, but it does double duty. The discarded wooden nursery planter—the kind specimen trees are grown in—was given a coat of turquoise paint and used to hold a large agave. The house number stenciled in contrasting bright orange adds more charm. DESIGN: Di Zock Gardens.

Water Features

EVEN IF IT'S ONLY A TRICKLE, the sound of water is a delight to the ear. Still water, sparkling in the sun or reflecting the moon, is a treat as well. Both of these pleasures are easy to add to the garden; no plumbing required. For a still-water feature, all you need is a vessel that holds water—a carved-out rock will do. Place it, fill it, done. Moving-water features are nearly as easy. Buy a premade fountain, nestle it against a wall or mount it, add water, and plug in. Or make your own fountain. Waterproof the interior of a pot, urn, or trough, and drop in a submersible pump.

For features where the water spills over the edge and disappears, such as millstone or cobblestone fountains, a little digging is required first. Their water reservoirs and pumps are hidden in a catch basin underground topped with a metal grate. One caveat: All electrically powered pumps need a safe power source. Plug into an existing GFCI (ground fault circuit interrupter) outlet or have one installed.

Maybe you like the idea of a water garden but are worried about the amount of upkeep it would require. Try a miniature water garden instead; you'll never need to get out hip waders to maintain it. A mini water garden can be as simple as a bowl filled with water and a few floating plants such as water hyacinth *(Eichornia crassipes)*. For a tabletop, a glass container is especially pretty, allowing you to appreciate the willowy roots as well as floating leaves.

Deeper in the garden, a more lagoonlike effect might be preferable, and a dark ceramic saucer is just the thing. If you want a more complex landscape, add some shoreline plants such as dwarf papyrus *(Cyperus prolifer)*, sweet flag *(Acorus)*, and taro *(Colocasia esculenta)*. Level the bottom of the container with gravel, then add plants, still in their pots, positioning them so the soil level is just below the water. Still too much work? Then treat the container as a vase. Drop in flower heads from your garden—flat blooms like camellias are especially nice—or just see what the wind blows in.

Ponds in pots *(left)* Though small, these Bainbridge Island, Washington, water gardens are big enough to attract frogs. The glazed lime green pots are planted with small water plants such as water lettuce and black taro. **DESIGN:** Tish Treherne, Bliss Garden Design.

Sky garden *(above)* An elegant, shallow half-circle pool, neatly cobbled with black stones, brings the reflection of the sky into this small San Francisco garden. DESIGN: Christine Reed, c.e.reed.studio.

Forest monolith *(right)* A large circular fountain of shiny black granite picks up the tones of the dark live oak trunks in a Healdsburg, California, garden. The trunks' pattern is reflected in the still surface of the water. DESIGN: Blasen Landscape Architecture.

Simple disk *(opposite page)* A small copper bowl bedded in pebbles and surrounded by grasses and reeds creates a peaceful corner in a Napa, California, garden. DESIGN: Topher Delaney, SEAM Studio.

For 32 inspiring garden fountains, see sunset.com/fountains

GREAT IDEA

Here's a quick and easy way to add a cooling touch to a sunny garden corner. Simply set an outdoor water bowl among stones or plantings. This one is just 8 inches across. Made of caramel-colored hypertufa, it's studded with small ceramic nuggets. Just hose out your bowl regularly to keep the water clean.

Water-wise *(above)* A bamboo spout splashes water into a small hand-carved granite basin in a courtyard garden in New Mexico. The plants around it—yarrow, lavender, sedum—are as water-sparing as the fountain. **DESIGN:** Carlotta From Paradise.

Cool oasis *(left)* A highly glazed ceramic pot converted into a gurgling fountain buffers street sounds in an urban Los Angeles backyard. Frosty blue ceramic globes heighten the cooling effect, as does an edge of water iris. **DESIGN:** GreenArt Landscape Design.

Lotusland inspired *(opposite page)* A sleek stainless steel and glass fountain in Los Altos, California, echoes the graceful curves and blue tones of the agaves in front of it and incense cedars behind it. **DESIGN:** Zeterre Landscape Architecture.

For making a DIY fountain, see sunset.com/diyfountain

Retreats

EVERY GARDEN needs the adult equivalent of a treehouse. Just as cooking, dining, and entertaining seem like more fun when done outdoors, so does playing the escape artist. When you have tired of the bustle and bluster of the world and want only your own thoughts for company, how convenient to be able to escape to a hidden retreat in your own garden.

What constitutes a perfect getaway will depend partially on how you would like to use the space. Do you want to curl up with a fat novel, twist into yoga positions, plein air paint, or just drowse and daydream while watching butterflies flit by? Your escape should also reflect your personality. Will you be content with a simple hammock in the shade or do you long for a garden shed dolled up like a Marie Antoinette fantasy? Your retreat can be whatever you like. There are only three requirements: it should be as private as possible, comfortable, and distinctly yours.

Provençal campout *(above)* An antique French army cot in a shady spot makes afternoon napping irresistible in this Sherman Oaks, California, garden. The cozy red throw adds an inviting touch. **DESIGN:** Comfort Zones Garden Design.

Bali daybed *(below)* This *balé*, from Bali, has poles of coconut wood bolted to a sturdy deck; blue rocks dress the concrete that surrounds their bases. Draped with filmy curtains and fitted with downlights that wash the interior at night, the cozy retreat overlooks a sloping tropical garden near the windward coast of Oahu, Hawaii. **DESIGN:** Greg Boyer–Hawaiian Landscapes.

Cozy alcove *(above)* A weathered teak bench filled with plump pillows in a deeply shaded niche of a San Jose, California, garden invites serenity. Temple bells tinkle, and bamboo rustles in the slightest wind. A vine-entwined ladder contributes to the feeling of escape. **DESIGN:** Forristt Landscape Design.

Grassy hideout *(right)* A graceful teak bench nestles between a pair of evergreen miscanthus *(M. transmorrisonensis)* in a Woodside, California, garden. The area is separated from the garden's more active entertainment section by a shrub border. **DESIGN:** GardenArt Group.

Ideas from *Sunset's* Garden

SUNSET'S GARDEN has seen its share of retreats over the years, with new ones built and tried out regularly. Here are two favorites—both easy to re-create in any garden.

Serene shelter *(above)* An appealing space for meditation, yoga, napping, or dining, architect Tony Gwilliam's basic T-house was inspired by pavilions in Bali. The simple structure, consisting of a 6-by-10-foot deck, 8-foot posts, a pop-up table, and a marine fabric roof, took two people less than a day to assemble from a kit. The structure's spareness inspired the quiet, contemplative "Meditation Meadow" around it, designed by landscape designer and grass guru John Greenlee. It's a floating sea of grasses—including silvery *Carex comans* 'Frosted Curls' and meadow flowers.

Personal patio *(opposite page)* Designed for relaxing at day's end with a glass of wine, or on a lazy afternoon with a good book, this small patio has a low, lightweight chair to sink into, and a "pottoman" (made by filling a bowl-shaped container with potting soil, then planting with soft and spongy Scotch moss), for parking bare feet. There's a "pond" of olive green tumbled glass to look at, complete with a single sweet flag (*Acorus gramineus* 'Ogon') to create the illusion of a fountain.

Matthew Levesque designed the pond, along with the patio surface, entirely of materials that would otherwise have wound up in the landfill. The "paving" is an artistic mix of wood squares, tiles, wine corks, and mini metal canisters set on end.

PLANNING

Once you've identified what you want in your garden and how you want the space to look, it's time to get practical. What steps will you need to take before you can remodel, say, a front yard that's all weeds or a backyard that's pretty to look at but has no patio or deck to sit on? How do you create a garden that adapts well to your site's unique conditions—whether hot and dry, shady and moist, foggy, windy, or perched on the side of a rocky canyon? How can you use your garden to protect your home from wildfires if you live in a wildland interface, or create a lush, flower-filled border in an arid landscape where water supplies are limited? And what features will you need to add if you want to invite bees, birds, and butterflies to visit your garden's flowers, or to give your own dogs, cats, or chickens a healthy place to roam? You'll find answers on the following pages.

WATER-WISE A stylish Phoenix garden, edged with spiky blue agaves and ocotillos and paved with permeable decomposed granite, is designed to tolerate the desert's blazing summers on little water. DESIGN: Steve Martino Landscape Architect.

Evaluating the Site

WHETHER YOU'RE FACING AN EMPTY LOT or renovating an established garden, start by taking stock of key elements. The *Sunset Western Garden Book* assigns climate zones to all areas of the West and indicates for each listed plant the zones in which it can thrive, given average conditions found there. These zones take into account not just temperature, but also latitude, elevation, and prevailing winds.

Your garden's soil also helps determine which plants will flourish. Sandy soil drains fast and doesn't hold nutrients well. Clay soil holds nutrients and water, but not air—so it gets hard as a brick when dry. The perfect garden soil is loam—a light, crumbly mixture of equal parts of sand, silt, and clay, with a healthy component of organic matter. All soils benefit from organic matter, which holds water, nutrients, and air—and is loose enough for roots to penetrate easily.

MICROCLIMATE. Within climate zones—and even within gardens—there is some variation in what you can grow where. Hot spots (like the base of a south-facing wall) and cooler areas (beneath trees on the north side of the house, or under the eaves) may allow you to push the zone envelope.

WATER. In most parts of the West, we can count on dry summers, recurring drought, and a limited supply of water for a growing population. Because water conservation should be part of every Westerner's lifestyle, landscapes must be as water-thrifty as possible. See page 350 for more information.

LAY OF THE LAND. Is your property totally flat, or are there low and high points to consider? A steep slope presents special challenges and may call for terraces and plantings that control erosion.

NORTH OR SOUTH? A south-facing exposure will receive more sunlight and will be the hotter part of your garden—perfect for a vegetable garden. Areas facing north, especially those in the shadow of the house or a tree, call for shade-tolerant plants.

WELCOME IN. Is the trip from the street to your home an inviting path or a straight shot on a concrete runway?

SO LONG LAWN. Do you really need a huge expanse of turf? Lawns require a considerable amount of time, effort, and water to keep looking good. Consider unthirsty groundcovers or flower beds as alternatives to traditional lawns.

LOOK BEYOND. Though you may want to enclose the garden for privacy, don't neglect the potential of distant views, such as mountains or a neighbor's ancient oak tree.

SCREEN IT OUT. Can you block an unattractive view or preserve your privacy by building a fence or planting a hedge?

KEEP OR CUT? Decide whether to remove plants, such as an old, diseased tree that obstructs views. Consult with an arborist before tackling any large tree.

Sloping ground *(above)* As cold air flows downhill, it mixes with warm air just above, making the moving air a bit warmer than the hilltop just above and the valleys below. Grapes planted on the south- or west-facing slopes pick up extra heat, which helps sweeten the fruit.

Borrowed views *(opposite page)* This California garden, on a hillside in Paso Robles, echoes the surrounding oak-and-grasses terrain. Large native boulders—which form curved walls and are used as accents—blend the terrace with the wild landscaping beyond. Native grasses, *Salvia clevelandii*, and shapely opuntia cactus add to the nature look. **DESIGN:** Jeffrey Gordon Smith Landscape Architecture.

Setting Goals

CLOSE YOUR EYES and picture your dream garden. Would it include a patio for entertaining and outdoor dining? Would it have a swimming pool, a small pond, or other water feature? Or would it be a simple secluded retreat? Do you want raised beds for a kitchen garden? Planting beds for colorful annuals and perennials? A lawn for kids to play on? A wildlife habitat area? A flower border, edged with winding stone paths? Dream big, then edit—and be realistic about the space required and about your site's potential.

Think about your garden's style. Would you like it to be wild, with native shrubs and rambling vines, or tailored, with a white picket fence around a square lawn? A modern garden style might showcase art and sculptural plants. If you are unsure, look to the architecture of your house for some initial direction.

Finally, be sure to consider how much upkeep you're willing to take on. To reduce the amount of time and effort your garden will require, avoid high-maintenance features such as lawns, sheared hedges, or large trees that drop leaves in autumn. A formal rose garden is lovely, but it can mean a tremendous amount of pruning, tidying, and tending. Also consider installing time-saving devices such as an automatic irrigation system.

Relaxing *(far left)* This tiny but stylish step-down patio in Venice, California, feels cozy and inviting, thanks to its cushioned, built-in benches and warming, gas-fueled firepit. Tall hedges provide privacy. **DESIGN:** Jeff Pervorse, Bent Grass Landscape Architecture.

Dining out *(left)* This easy-care front yard creates outdoor living space where none existed before. On a sloping lot in Greenbrae, California, it now has a dining area, firepit lounge, and play lawn tucked behind a raised planting strip that provides privacy from the street. **DESIGN:** Shades of Green Landscape Architecture.

Playing *(below)* Badminton, hopscotch, and "fetch" are just a few of the games played in this stone courtyard surrounded by a casual arrangement of screening plants. **DESIGN:** Leslie Sachs.

Design Basics

WHEN THINKING ABOUT YOUR GARDEN, keep in mind some basic principles. In a well-designed garden, all the parts work together to read as a whole rather than as a hodgepodge of disparate elements. Each part—whether a deck, planting bed, water feature, or seating area—is in proportion to the rest of the garden and in scale with the house and property. A sense of rhythm is achieved by repetition of plants, colors, and materials—and is enhanced with occasional accents that contrast with their surroundings. Think of a focal point as a major accent; it leads the eye to a particular spot in the garden. Symmetry can give a sense of balance and formality. You can create symmetry with matching or similar elements placed on either side of a path or patio. An asymmetrical arrangement suggests a more modern style.

GREAT IDEA

Living on a small urban lot presents challenges. But by following the "keep-it-simple" strategy, a pair of busy city dwellers turned their San Francisco backyard, above, into a private outdoor room. Concrete pavers lead across the backyard to a square patio; they're set on the diagonal, to make the space appear larger. An arching metal structure creates overhead privacy and shade. The plantings along both sides of the garden are sculptural, easy-care, and unthirsty. DESIGN: Beth Mullins, Growsgreen Landscape Design.

Repetition *(above)* Descending a hillside among clumping grasses, blue agaves are spaced a few feet apart and offset just enough to create the impression of a meandering stream. Nearly identical in size and shape, they work together to enhance the effect. **DESIGN:** Andrea Cochran Landscape Architecture.

Balance *(left)* The rustic urns on either side of this patio were arranged into groups that are irregular but have similar visual weight. **DESIGN:** Lutsko Associates.

Focal point *(opposite page)* Though a focal point is often thought of as an object or plant, it can be a larger garden feature. Here, a sizable opening in the wall—embraced by a bright red section—is sure to draw your eye to the view beyond.

Design Tricks

IN ADDITION TO BASIC DESIGN PRINCIPLES, design professionals employ an assortment of tricks to overcome landscaping challenges or to enhance a garden visually. Three are pictured here. Other techniques involve altering the perception of space by manipulating colors, textures, and materials; by taking advantage of changes in a garden's elevation; or by placing elements to mask the size and shape of a space.

To make a small garden appear larger, for instance, you can set a patio on the diagonal to disguise its actual shape and dimension. Angled walls and hedges help too. You can add a decorative gate near the back fence to suggest a garden beyond, or hire an artist to paint an outdoor mural on a blank wall for the illusion of a garden that continues, or a beach or forest backdrop to suggest a view.

Bring your garden to life by incorporating some of these tricks. They can be particularly helpful if you are renovating or upgrading an existing landscape.

Borrowed scenery *(above)* This pool not only "points" toward the stunning view, but also mirrors in the water's smooth surface the mountains and a blooming palo verde tree. These "tricks" visually expand this desert garden. **DESIGN:** Steve Martino Landscape Architect.

ILLUSION OF SPACE

CONCEAL PARTS OF THE GARDEN. Even the smallest garden can be made to feel larger if you hide part of it from full view. Add mystery and expectation by not revealing the garden all at once; let windows and portals lead your visitors to discover new spaces beyond.

CREATE A GARDEN OF ROOMS. Clever division of space into a few rooms can make a small garden appear larger. Separate them with low hedges, elevation changes (a step-down patio, for instance), or a border made up of variously sized containers spilling with flowers or succulents.

BORROW SCENERY. A garden can seem more spacious if you draw in views of lakes, canyons, or even a neighbor's tree.

COLOR PLAY. When judiciously placed, bold foliage increases the feeling of depth, especially when viewed against a soft green backdrop.

Color contrasts *(above)* A large brownish red smoke tree (*Cotinus coggygria* 'Royal Purple') presides over swaths of orange *Carex tenuiculmis* 'Cappuccino' and a cluster of orange-tinged *Calluna vulgaris* 'Firefly' in this Pacific Northwest garden. The foreground plantings—all in warmish tones—contrast with the conifers behind, enhancing the sense of arrival near the house. **DESIGN:** Stacie Crooks, Crooks Garden Design.

Bold art *(left)* A gently curving cedar panel, with a design made using a Japanese burning technique, dominates this small San Francisco courtyard and draws attention away from the area's small size. The sculpture with oversize letters, by Ray Beldner, similarly plays with scale. **DESIGN:** Surfacedesign.

Getting Started

TRANSFORMING A BARE DIRT LOT or overgrown weed patch into an inviting garden can seem daunting. After you review the preceding sections, use this checklist as you begin planning your garden makeover. You'll find it especially helpful if you haven't tackled such a job before.

1. DETERMINE YOUR CLIMATE ZONE. You'll save a lot of time, money, and frustration by choosing plants that are proven performers in your area.

2. CHECK YOUR SOIL. Is it predominantly sand, clay, or loam? To find out, thoroughly wet a small patch of soil, then squeeze a handful firmly in your fist. If the soil makes a tight ball with a slippery feel, you have clay soil. If it feels gritty and crumbles apart when you open your hand, it's sandy. But if it forms a slightly crumbly ball, it's loam—the ideal soil for planting.

3. LEARN YOUR GARDEN'S SUN EXPOSURE. Is your site open to the sun all day, or is it largely in the shade? Which areas are sunny in the morning and shaded in the afternoon, and vice versa? Where do the house, trees, and other large structures cast shade in winter when the sun is lowest?

4. NOTE ANY SPECIAL CONDITIONS. If your garden is on a steep slope, you might plant shrubs and groundcovers or plan for terraces to mitigate the abrupt grade. If it's in a windy area, you'll want to choose plants that can stand up to winds, and locate outdoor living spaces in protected pockets.

5. CHOOSE YOUR GARDEN STYLE. Consider the architecture of your house and its surroundings. Casual or formal? Tropical or Mediterranean? Traditional or avant-garde? A Spanish-style house lends itself to a Mediterranean garden with lavender, citrus, and a fountain, while a cedar-shingled house in a Northwest forest would look more at home among rhododendrons, vine maples *(Acer circinatum)*, and conifers.

WORKING WITH PROFESSIONALS

Even if you feel you have the time, skill, and energy to do all of the designing, planting, and building yourself, you may need to enlist the help of professionals for your garden makeover.

Major construction might necessitate the services of a licensed *landscape contractor*, who is usually trained in methods of earthmoving, construction, and planting. If you want to add a patio, deck, pool, drainage system, or outdoor kitchen, a *landscape architect* can be a big help. They are licensed to design exterior structures, solve site problems, and give advice on the placement of service lines, entries, driveways, and parking areas. The *landscape designer* and *garden designer* are professionals who may be self-taught or may have the same academic credentials as a landscape architect, but lack a state license. They are more likely to work on smaller, strictly residential projects.

A *horticulturist* is trained in the selection and care of garden plants; an *arborist*, in the care of trees and other woody plants. Local nurseries and garden centers can be another valuable source of information.

Your local cooperative extension service, a government-funded agency, can be especially helpful in identifying plants that do well in your area, as well as for advice on pest and disease control.

Before *(opposite page, top)* A tired front lawn and an entry walk that looked less prominent than the driveway made this front yard, in Costa Mesa, California, uninviting.

After *(left)* Designer Brooke Dietrich painted the fence a plant-framing black, added a front walk of budget-friendly concrete pads (stained a warm sandstone), then planted shrubs and perennials along the driveway to soften it. Bold succulents—agaves, aloes, and aeoniums—give the garden a tropical look without the heavy water requirements. DESIGN: Brooke Dietrich, Green . . . Landscapes to Envy.

6. CHECK LOCAL ZONING LAWS. If you plan to do any major construction, check with the appropriate local agencies (see "Making It Official" on the opposite page). Contact your water and utility companies with any questions about underground cabling or water use.

7. MAKE A WISH LIST. Jot down features you'd like in your garden. A patio for entertaining? A small pond? Raised beds to grow vegetables? A lawn for kids to play on? A hedge to block an unsightly view?

8. DEVISE A PLAN OF ACTION. Determine how much work will be involved, from laying paths and patio pavers to installing sprinklers or a new lawn. Ask yourself whether you have the time, desire, and know-how to do the work yourself, or line up help where you need it. Measure your garden and be ready to plan.

9. INSTALL HARDSCAPE. Paths, patios, decks, fences, and walls are the bones of the garden. They go in first—along with irrigation, lighting, and permanent elements such as large boulders—before you plant anything.

10. GROW A GREEN SCREEN. Instead of replacing an ugly fence, cover it with leafy evergreen vines such as star jasmine *(Trachelospermum jasminoides)*.

11. SHOP AT NURSERIES. Keep in mind your favorite colors, whether soft and romantic (pinks and lavender tones) or strong (purple and orange hues), and work your palette around those. As you shop, consider plants that add motion (ornamental grasses), fragrance (jasmine and roses), and seasonal interest (spring and fall color).

12. PREP THE SOIL, THEN PLANT. Unless you're planting natives, which mostly like their soil "lean" but fast draining, work in generous amounts of compost or other organic amendments. Set out trees and shrubs first, then fill in with perennials, annuals, and bulbs.

13. ADD FINISHING TOUCHES. Containers, a great bench, an outdoor sculpture, portable water features, and birdhouses make a garden look lived in and loved.

MAKING IT OFFICIAL

How can you find out about zoning or other laws that might affect your landscaping?

- Your property deed can give you the exact location of property lines, easements or rights-of-way, building restrictions, or tree-removal restrictions.
- The local building or planning department can confirm setback requirements; height limitations for fences, buildings, or other structures; safety codes for pools and spas; tree or historic preservation ordinances; and building codes and permits.
- Contact your municipal utility company to find out the location and depth of underground utility lines, as well as building or planting limitations under power lines. Your water company may have restrictions on water use or lawn size.
- The neighbors almost certainly have opinions regarding views into and beyond your property and your mutual need for privacy, light, and wind. They may also have concerns about existing trees and other plants, structures, and shared walks and driveways. Homeowners' associations may dictate certain landscaping rules and specific requirements.

Before *(opposite page, top)* Pots crowded the edge of the driveway—and there was no clear path to the front door. The owners wanted a bit more privacy, but without completely blocking off the yard.

After *(left)* A wide path of cut stone in gravel takes you straight to the front door, with grasses softening the edges. Giving just the right amount of privacy are a staggered fence and a couple of shrubby trees. **DESIGN:** Jared Vermeil Landscape Design.

Soil

HEALTHY SOIL is the foundation of a thriving garden, but not every gardener is lucky enough to have it.

Loam is the ideal garden soil. Made up of organic matter (roots, decaying leaves, and stems) along with large and small particles (clay, silt, and sand), it drains well and holds enough air for healthy root growth. Trouble is, many of the West's native soils are less than ideal. Soil problems may be caused by a variety of factors, listed below. Evaluate your soil before planting. Then choose whether to correct the problem or select plants that will grow despite it.

LACK OF TOPSOIL. When the top layer of native soil, which is usually best for plant growth, is redistributed or removed during grading or construction, what's left is often rocky, hard, sandy, or slippery, and low in organic matter and nutrients. Adding organic matter can help if the problem is not severe, but often the best solution is to replace the topsoil that was removed.

POOR DRAINAGE. Soils that drain poorly, such as heavy clay, reduce the availability of air to roots. Without air, roots suffocate and the plant can't absorb water and dies; molds and rots can take over. Hardpan, a layer of hard soil well below the soil's surface, does not allow water to drain through at all. To evaluate drainage, dig a hole 12 to 24 inches deep and fill it with water. If the hole does not drain in 24 hours, drainage is poor. If you discover hardpan in your soil, contact a landscape professional about solutions. Or plant in raised beds or berms.

SALINITY. In the Southwest, where annual rainfall is low, soils are alkaline, and irrigation water is on the saline side, excess salts often accumulate in the soil and damage plants. Heavy watering to leach salts out of the soil is effective only if your soil drains well. To help lower the soil's pH, add organic matter and acidifying fertilizers, such as ammonium sulfate, sulfur, or gypsum.

The most effective way to improve your soil's texture is to add organic amendments such as compost, composted manure or "zoo doo," wood shavings, ground bark, or local agricultural by-products like grape pomace.

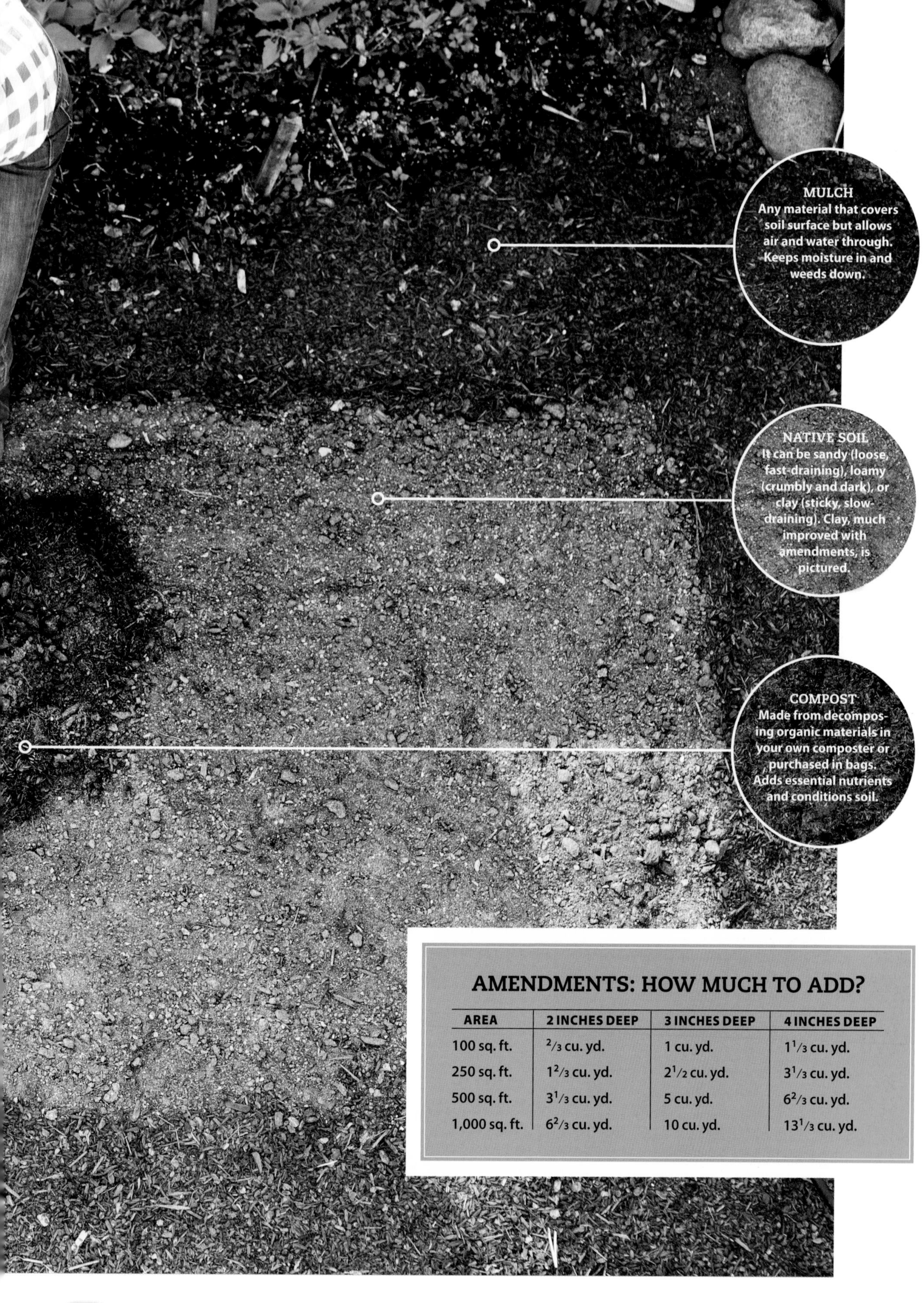

AMENDMENTS: HOW MUCH TO ADD?

AREA	2 INCHES DEEP	3 INCHES DEEP	4 INCHES DEEP
100 sq. ft.	2/3 cu. yd.	1 cu. yd.	1 1/3 cu. yd.
250 sq. ft.	1 2/3 cu. yd.	2 1/2 cu. yd.	3 1/3 cu. yd.
500 sq. ft.	3 1/3 cu. yd.	5 cu. yd.	6 2/3 cu. yd.
1,000 sq. ft.	6 2/3 cu. yd.	10 cu. yd.	13 1/3 cu. yd.

For making perfect compost, see sunset.com/compost

Water

DRY SUMMERS, RECURRING DROUGHT, and a limited water supply for a constantly growing population are just a few reasons why water is the West's most precious resource.

Many Westerners live in a desert or semiarid climate. Aside from a few areas—mainly the narrow coasts of Washington, Oregon, and Northern California and major mountain ranges—the mainland Western states typically receive less than 10 or 11 inches of rain annually. And what nature doesn't supply, irrigation must.

But we're rapidly outgrowing our supplies. In some areas, groundwater supplies are dwindling. Overdrafting (pumping out more water from subterranean aquifers than is replenished) is a chronic problem. The quality of groundwater is also worrisome. Toxic wastes are being detected in well-water supplies all over the West.

That's why water-wise gardening continues to grow in popularity. After an especially wet winter, it may be tempting to revert to endless green lawns and lush gardens. But keeping the big picture in mind can help you make smart landscaping decisions.

Clearly, the responsibility for using water wisely rests with all of us. But smart landscape design and gardening practices can make a difference. The reward is a beautiful landscape that practically takes care of itself.

WATER: HOW MUCH CAN YOU SAVE?

Is it possible to have a lush garden year-round, using 83 percent less water and 68 percent fewer labor hours, with a reduced green waste output (grass clippings and prunings) of 56 percent? Absolutely, says Santa Monica–based landscape designer Susanne Jett *(jettscapes.com)*, who specializes in water-wise landscape design.

To prove that the right garden could result in measurable, significant, long-term resource savings, the City of Santa Monica invited Jett to design two adjacent residential front-yard gardens, each about 1,900 square feet—one with traditional turf and thirsty plants, watered by sprinkler-spray irrigation; the other using low-water California natives such as ceanothus and salvias, water catchment features such as rain chains and dry creekbeds, and drip irrigation.

After nine years of gathering data from these two gardens (comparing actual installation and long-term support costs), Jett found the results were even more dramatic than she expected. Over the nine-year period, the traditional lawn-and-sprinklers garden used 703,813 gallons of water, generated 4,905 pounds of green waste, and took about 528 hours to tend. The natives-and-drip garden, on the other hand, used 130,438 gallons of water (some of it recovered rainwater), generated 2,164 pounds of green waste, and took 167 hours to tend. In total, the natives garden saved 573,375 gallons of water over nine years, kept 2,741 pounds of green waste out of landfills, and freed up 361 hours maintenance time. It also provided habitat for local birds, butterflies, bees, and beneficial insects.

Water-wise, desert *(opposite page)* This colorful, textural collection of cactus, succulents, and dryland grasses and perennials rarely needs water. Boulders and gravel mulch are the perfect accompaniments.

Water-wise, California *(above)* Requiring only moderate water, this backyard features a variegated aeonium and blue chalk fingers *(Senecio)*, with ground-hugging woolly thyme and *Dymondia* between the steps.

For details about the Santa Monica project, visit sustainablesm.org/gardengarden

The source *(above)* Lake Mead, the largest reservoir on the Colorado River, is shown at 46 percent full, down about 110 feet in a nine-year period. Some 30 million Westerners get their water from the Colorado River. Yet average annual rainfall is just 15 inches in Los Angeles, 4 inches in Las Vegas, 7 inches in Phoenix, and 16 inches in Denver. Southern California alone uses 1.3 trillion gallons annually.

A destination *(left)* Careful watering can help prevent waste. Check sprinklers regularly for leaks or clogged heads to prevent loss; avoid overwatering paving.

Drought Strategies

When drought comes—and with it the possibility of local restrictions on lawn watering or punishing hikes in water bills—it's too late to install a water-conserving landscape, since even drought-tolerant plants need water to get established. But you can take steps to save the plants you have. Start with established trees and shrubs, which are costly to replace and have the greatest impact on your landscape. Plants benefit from a thick layer of mulch to help keep moisture in the soil. The best mulches don't compact easily, allowing sufficient air and water to reach plant roots.

TREES. Large landscape trees such as alder, coast redwood, Japanese maple, magnolia, birch, and poplar are often the first specimens to show signs of drought. Water big trees in April and again in June. If the soil is dry at a depth of 10 to 12 inches (check it with a sampling tube), moisten the soil to 18 to 24 inches deep. To increase water penetration, drill 1-inch holes around the drip line and fill them with organic mulch, or use a spade or pitchfork to rough up the soil surface. Coil soaker hoses around the tree at the drip line and halfway between the drip line and the trunk; apply mulch over the root area, then allow hoses to run slowly overnight.

Most stone-fruit trees can survive some drought, but they'll be better off with a deep irrigation in April and again in June. (Citrus may need additional deep watering in summer; watch for wilting, yellowing, or curling leaves.) Apply water slowly and deeply at the drip line with soaker hoses, as just described; or make a basin 4 to 6 inches deep under each tree, extend it to the drip line (3 inches beyond if you can spare more water), and use a hose to fill the basin slowly.

LANDSCAPE PLANTS. Water the plants growing on or near an unwatered lawn. Keep an eye on shallow-rooted shrubs. On azaleas, rhododendrons, and young camellias, watch for wilting or drooping of new growth. Build basins around them (make sure water won't pool around the trunks), and give them a deep soak in April.

LAWNS. To stay green all summer, lawns need 1 to 2 inches of water per week. Turn on the sprinklers for about 10 minutes once a week, turn them off to let moisture soak in, then turn them on again for another few minutes. Or cut back to 1 inch of water every two weeks; under this regime, lawns turn straw-colored but green up again quickly after weather cools in fall.

POOLS. A pool cover can stop 90 percent of water evaporation waste, even allowing for times when the pool is in use.

Low-water color *(top right)* Drought-tolerant aloes bloom alongside this path in Pacific Palisades, California. Along with permeable paving and other water-saving plants and grasses, they keep the garden looking lush on little water. **DESIGN:** Rob Steiner Gardens.

"Drought occurs when supplies are inadequate to meet demand, for whatever reason. It's made worse when there's too little rain or too much heat."

—DR. ANNE STEINEMANN, *Scripps Institution of Oceanography*

STREAM·SCAPING

MEANDERING STREAMS ARE TRANQUIL and beautiful to look at, especially on hot summer days. As they spill through narrow channels, swirl around rocky outcrops, and fan out to form placid pools, they visually cool even the smallest gardens.

You might be lucky enough to have a natural stream running through your property, especially if you live in one of the West's rainy places such as Washington's Olympic Peninsula. But in the many arid regions where water is precious and often costly, creating the illusion of water makes more sense.

You can incorporate a stream of stone into patio paving by setting river rocks of varying sizes end-to-end in mortar, or tucking them between flagstone pavers. As you work, watch the flow take shape, complete with bubbles and eddies. Or put down a dry streambed like one you might find in nature—sinuous and bedded with boulders and gravel.

Dry creek *(above)* A dry streambed brings a sense of water to this landscape, as if, after a cloudburst, it would carry water away. The largest boulders nest in hollows in the center, while smaller, river-washed pebbles are scattered around them. Grasses and red-hot pokers *(Kniphofia)* grow along the edges. **DESIGN:** Richard McPherson Landscape Architecture.

Mountain stream *(left)* A narrow stream of Mexican pebbles widens and spills into a real pond, adding to the sense of flow and distance in this small backyard in Bellevue, Washington. The pebbles are set on edge in black grout and arranged to mimic real currents and eddies. Varying the size, shape, and spacing of the pebbles is key to simulating movement, says the designer. The patio is of colored and textured concrete with Pennsylvania bluestone edging. **DESIGN:** Julian Durant, Hendrikus Group.

Glacial melt *(opposite page)* A rivulet of pale blue Indonesian beach pebbles flows through a flagstone entry walk in this New Mexico garden. Where the flow widens against a wall of chunky boulders, real water dribbles over low rocks into a "lake" of the blue pebbles, set over a grate and reservoir. A pump hidden in the reservoir recirculates the water. **DESIGN:** Mark Licht, Clemens & Associates.

Preventing Runoff

Whether you live on the coast of California or near a stream in the Northwest where salmon run, your goal is the same: prevent runoff. When you fertilize and water your garden, a nearby stream or the ocean a mile down the road may be the last thing on your mind. But when combined with heavy watering or significant rainfall, herbicides, pesticides, fungicides, and fertilizers can run off your property and into storm drains, where they flow, untreated, into lakes, streams, or the sea—polluting once-pristine bodies of water and even causing closure of beaches. These contaminants can also pollute groundwater supplies.

To help prevent such pollution, avoid overwatering after applying pesticides or fertilizers, and don't apply them before rain. If possible, use nontoxic products to control insect pests, weeds, and diseases. If you must use chemicals, spot-treat troubled plants rather than blanket the entire yard, and use the product only as directed on the label. Select slow-release fertilizers that don't wash into streams as easily, or choose organic fertilizers and manage pests with traps and barriers. Never dispose of lawn or garden chemicals in storm drains or the trash. Take any unwanted products to a household hazardous-waste collection center.

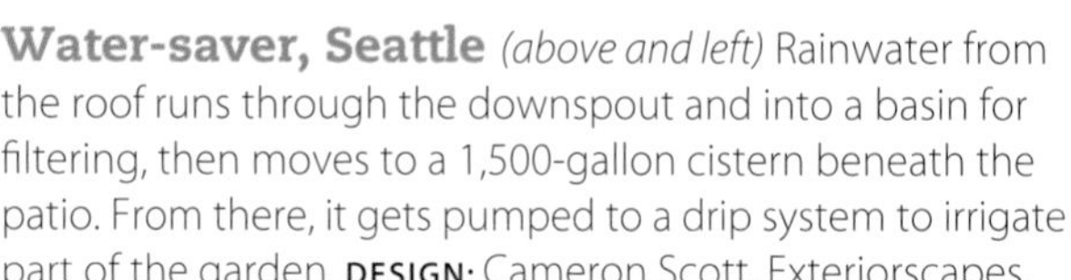

Water-saver, Seattle *(above and left)* Rainwater from the roof runs through the downspout and into a basin for filtering, then moves to a 1,500-gallon cistern beneath the patio. From there, it gets pumped to a drip system to irrigate part of the garden. **DESIGN:** Cameron Scott, Exteriorscapes.

"Ikebana bowl" *(above)* That's what the designer calls this shallow infiltration basin, which collects runoff for a sloping property in Shell Beach, California. French drains in its bottom, backfilled with drain rock, loose soil, and a covering of *Carex divulsa*—which can tolerate fluctuating amounts of moisture—help the basin dissipate as much as 1 to 2 feet of water in a couple of hours. The tall pipes supporting the hammocks double as art forms and light sticks (they have LED lights in the tops). **DESIGN:** Jeffrey Gordon Smith Landscape Architecture.

Harvesting and Storing Water

Water scarcity calls for ingenuity. Harvesting, channeling, and storing rainwater in barrels or cisterns (large tanks or reservoirs) help keep gardens watered in times of drought. For example, an aboveground cistern catches and channels rainwater to a storage reservoir. Easy to install, it uses a simple screen system, set in the reservoir, as a filter. Harvested rainwater is a high-quality "tonic" for houseplants, seedlings, orchids, and other plants that may be sensitive to chemicals and salts found in some water supplies.

In the driest parts of the West, such as the Arizona deserts, you can mimic nature by re-creating desert washes in your garden. Normal rainfall is channeled from roofs through downspouts or along rain chains and along washes to planting areas. When heavy monsoons hit, the washes carry excess rain away from the house.

Natural washes contain various rock sizes: large ones, too heavy to be moved by the flow of water, stay in the center; small ones wash to the sides. Gravel settles in flat areas and bends, and in crevices between rocks. When making your own wash, work with at least three sizes of native rocks that fit the scale of your garden.

Rain barrel *(above)* Even a relatively small container can collect a good amount of rainwater from the downspout, concealed here by a vine. The owners use the attached hose to water patio containers.

Cistern *(left)* In this Tucson garden, a large cistern made of galvanized metal captures rainwater and holds it for use during the dry season. A screening system keeps out leaves and other debris.

Channel *(opposite page)* When rains come to this Las Vegas garden, not a drop goes to waste. The dry creek becomes an actual creek, channeling the water to a lower-lying part of the garden. **DESIGN:** Jack W. Zunino, JW Zunino Landscape Architecture.

"Think of water as sacred. Rather than letting it run off into the street, slow it down. Create places for it to collect."
—CHRISTY TEN EYCK,
landscape architect

RAIN·SCAPING

WHEN RAIN FALLS IN SEATTLE, water that used to run from this garden down to the street now pools in a thickly planted infiltration basin at the garden's edge, where it percolates into the groundwater below. "It's a win-win situation," says landscape designer Malissa Gatton of In Harmony Sustainable Landscapes. "The garden helps reduce this household's environmental footprint. Anybody could do it."

If you have soil that drains well (dig in compost if it doesn't), a rain garden is a great option. You can channel rainwater from the roof, via a downspout or rain chain, into a shallowly buried pipe that empties into an infiltration basin or swale (called a rain garden) at least 10 feet away from your house. Water-tolerant plants such as shrub willows thrive in the basin. Rain gardens filter and cleanse the runoff as they channel it into the ground, and they keep runoff, which is often filled with chemicals and other pollutants, from storm drains, sewers, and, ultimately, nearby lakes, streams, and coastal waters. **DESIGN:** In Harmony Sustainable Landscapes.

Capture the rain *(left)* A copper rain chain, hung from the house eaves, channels water down into a plastic catch basin at the base, hidden beneath river rocks.

Channel it *(opposite page, top)* From the basin, the water moves through a hidden 4-inch-wide flexible plastic pipe, which runs the length of the channel and under a permeable path.

Store it *(opposite page, bottom)* The water then spills from the pipe into the planted infiltration basin, called a rain garden, tucked beside the patio. This shallow depression (typically 12 inches deep with gradually sloping sides) that's filled with fast-draining soil mix collects rainwater like a sponge and allows it to slowly percolate into the ground before it becomes polluted runoff. Water-tolerant plants such as shrub willows thrive in the basin.

RAIN•SCAPING BASICS

CHOOSE THE SITE. Before planting a rain garden, find the lowest point on your property. It should be at least 10 feet from your house, in a naturally low spot of the garden. Observe the site for a day or two to determine the amount of sun or shade it gets, then choose plants accordingly.

PREP THE SOIL. Outline the edge of your rain garden using a hose or string, then remove any existing vegetation. Using a shovel, dig the basin about 12 inches deep, with sloping sides and a level bottom. Work in 3 to 5 inches of soil amendments, including compost.

PLANT. Native plants are ideal choices for rain gardens, since they are adapted to local climates and don't need fertilizer, and many can take wet-to-dry conditions. For sunny spots in the Pacific Northwest, for example, try coastal strawberry *(Fragaria chiloensis)*, Oregon iris *(Iris tenax)*, tufted hairgrass *(Deschampsia cespitosa)*, and Western columbine *(Aquilegia formosa)*. For shade, try creeping oregon grape *(Mahonia nervosa)*, salal *(Gaultheria shallon)*, sword fern *(Polystichum munitum)*, and vine maple. In California, good choices include hummingbird sage *(Salvia spathecea)*, common yarrow *(Achillea millefolium)*, and blue sedge *(Carex glauca)*.

MULCH. Spread a 2- to 3-inch layer of large woodchips (which won't float away) around the plants.

Find additional plants for rain gardens at *12000raingardens.org*.

Elements of a Water-Wise Garden

Spires of Italian cypress jutting into the sky on nearby hills evoke a Tuscan landscape. But the scent of sage wafting up the slope indicates California chaparral. Despite its deep-in-the-country ambience, this Sherman Oaks garden is in the midst of a megalopolis. In addition to creating a peaceful retreat, the garden is very well planned for California—in the plant choices and in such features as permeable paving and living roofs.

Designer Marilee Kuhlmann of Comfort Zones Design combined drought-tolerant California natives such as ceanothus, coffeeberry *(Frangula californica)*, manzanita, salvias, and wild buckwheat *(Eriogonum)* with unthirsty plants from Mediterranean climates. Drifts of carex, fescue, and other small grasses, equally modest in their need for irrigation, help weave together portions of the garden. The plant selections and their abundance, as well as a fountain and birdbath, draw birds, butterflies, and bees.

Permeable paving *(above)* Ribbons of 'Elfin' thyme *(Thymus polytrichus britannicus)* run between the flagstone pavers on the patio. This green "mortar" allows rainfall to percolate into the soil below. Generous planting pockets further blur the distinction between hard and soft, creating the illusion that nature is creeping back into the garden.

Green roof *(opposite page, top)* Mounds of succulents cover the structure containing pool equipment. Their repetition draws the eye into the round shapes of the distant hills.

Unthirsty planting *(opposite page, bottom)* A soft "country" planting takes the place of a fence. Lavender, phormiums ('Jack Spratt' and 'Platt's Black'), santolina, and *Verbena lilacina* 'De La Mina' frame the view and help unite the property with the open space beyond.

LOW- OR NO-COST WAYS TO MAKE EVERY DROP COUNT

- Water young plants thoroughly to encourage deep rooting, which makes them less susceptible to drought.
- Water plants deeply and infrequently—only when needed—and wet the soil only to root depth. (Check moisture in the soil by pushing a soil probe into the ground.) Allow the soil to dry out a bit between waterings.
- Water when temperatures are cool and the air is still, usually at dawn.
- Adjust automatic irrigation systems to put water where it's needed—around plants, not on driveways, fences, house walls, or the street.
- Shrink or replace the lawn with unthirsty groundcovers. Mow remaining lawn higher.
- Control runoff on slopes.
- Don't apply water faster than the soil can absorb it. If necessary, pulse-irrigate: first water plants for 5 minutes, turn off the water for 10 minutes, then water for 5 minutes more.
- Sweep rather than hose down sidewalks.
- If you water with hose-end sprinklers, use a timer so you won't forget to turn the water off.
- Plant in fall, so winter rains will encourage root growth.
- Apply a 2-to-3-inch layer of mulch such as wood chips to garden beds to reduce weeds and moisture loss.
- Remove weeds. They steal water needed by ornamentals.
- In many areas, you can stop watering altogether in winter when days are rainy and cool and plants are growing slowly, if at all.
- If you hire landscape professionals for maintenance chores, let them know water conservation should be a priority.

For 50 water-wise plants, see sunset.com/waterwise

Taming the Sun

THE SUN IS A POWERHOUSE that fuels plant growth. But too much sun can damage plants and make the outdoors unbearable for people. Summer sun also heats up houses, requiring additional air-conditioning, which raises electricity bills and overtaxes the West's supply of power. Fortunately, you can easily protect the most vulnerable plants, and your family and friends, by landscaping wisely to block or filter the hottest sun.

Overhead shelters and leafy canopies cast pools of shade that make gardens livable during the high-heat months of summer. Carefully placed trees and vines can cast shade on the house, sheltering it from intense morning or afternoon sun. You can hang up a stylish woven shadecloth or suspend a dramatic shade sail over a well-used patio. Or surround an outdoor dining area with citrus trees, blue palo verdes, or lacy mimosa trees *(Albizia julibrissin)*.

PROTECT PLANTS

Periods of intense heat in late spring and early summer can hit plants at a vulnerable stage—when they are producing tender new growth and haven't yet become conditioned to hot, dry weather. Take these steps to protect them.

WATER. On warm summer days, plants wilt slightly because their leaves lose water faster than their roots can take it up. During the night, the plants will recover if their roots have water to absorb. Make sure that water is available to the entire root zone (usually the entire area beneath the leaves) so plants can recover after an extremely hot day. Give plants a deep soaking.

MULCH. Applying mulch helps soil retain moisture and cools roots near the surface. For shallow-rooted plants such as azaleas, begonias, and camellias, mulch is essential. Apply a layer of organic material such as compost or ground bark at least 2 to 3 inches deep around the root zones.

Shady spot *(opposite page)* One benefit of a shadecloth is that it can make shade in a very specific area. Here, a stylish cloth protects the dining table but allows plenty of light to reach the sun-loving plantings. **DESIGN:** Steve Martino Landscape Architect.

Portable shade *(above)* A polyethylene canopy *(shadesails.com)* soars above the dining table, providing cooling shade during hot months in this Tucson garden. It's fastened to the house and to steel pipes beyond the free-form patio. For added cooling, the curved wall, painted a sunny Provençal yellow, steps down to an Asian water bowl tucked between the palms. **DESIGN:** Jim Pollack Design.

Natural Cooling from Trees

Planting shade trees is one of the best ways to cool your home and garden. Public utility companies have estimated that properly positioned trees can cut home energy costs for summer cooling by more than 20 percent.

For most houses, the ideal shade tree has a slightly spreading canopy and reaches 25 to 45 feet in height. If the tree is deciduous—such as callery pear *(Pyrus calleryana)*, eastern redbud *(Cercis canadensis)*, or maidenhair tree *(Ginkgo biloba)*—the sun can shine through its leafless canopy in winter, warming the home (and thus reducing heating bills) during the cool months.

The east-facing and west-facing sides of the house are the most important ones to shade. Trees on the east side block the morning sun; those on the west shade your house during the hottest part of the day—afternoon. Trees should be planted no closer than 5 to 10 feet from the house foundation, depending on the size of the tree (larger trees should be even farther away). At that distance, burrowing roots won't damage the foundation, and the canopy can still reach far enough to shade some of the roof. In most cases, you need to plant several trees on each side of the house to provide adequate shading. Direct sun shining through windows can warm the inside of a house in a hurry. Try to position your trees where they'll shade windows but won't block desirable views from inside.

Reflected heat can increase warming of your home during the day; stored heat released from the paving at night can slow the cooling of your house. And shading your air conditioner can reduce its workload and cut energy consumption.

Living umbrella *(above)* A majestic sycamore tree shades this circular, west-facing patio in Alexander Valley, California, from the hot afternoon sun. Ledgestone from Amador County faces the seat wall, and Pacific Gold gravel paves the patio. **DESIGN:** Diana Stratton.

Cooling canopy *(opposite page)* Crowned with a leafy canopy, this spreading tree is the perfect spot for an improv lunch on a summer afternoon.

Natural Cooling with Vines

Fast growth makes vines the ideal plants for temporary screens and permanent structures alike. Freestanding arbors can support hard, woody stems such as grape and wisteria; the stems twirl up the posts, then spread their foliage to shade a patio below. Lightweight wooden or metal trellises can hold delicate climbers such as clematis; use them to cover three wood-framed lath panels, placed side to side where they'll shade a window in summer.

A sturdy, arching arbor with built-in bench seats becomes a haven when used as a support for vines that cast cooling shade. Choose fragrant kinds, such as Japanese honeysuckle, and you double the pleasure of your hideaway.

In wine country gardens, grapevines are classic features; as they dangle their berry clusters through lath or overhead beams, they shade dining patios and spritz the air with fruity fragrance. To shade porches, train annual vines such as morning glory up lengths of twine or garden netting.

Position vines where you need them most as the sun moves across your property, then bask in their delicious cool shade.

SHADE NOMENCLATURE

Not all shade is created equal.

PARTIAL SHADE. As the sun arcs across the sky, different areas of the garden are exposed to direct sun for part of the day and bathed in shade for at least half a day (or three hours during the hottest part of the day).

FILTERED OR DAPPLED SHADE. As sunlight passes through the canopy of a tree, the leaves create a pattern of light and shadow, or dappled sunlight. An overhead lath also provides a filtered effect. In general, filtered shade will support many plants that grow in partial or light shade.

LIGHT OR OPEN SHADE. This bright, fairly even shade is found in gardens that are open to the sky but bathed in shadows cast by surrounding tall trees, walls, or other structures.

FULL OR DEEP SHADE. An area with little or no direct sunlight, such as beneath a dense evergreen tree, is considered full shade. The low level of light restricts the choice of plants.

Overhead shade *(above)* Lush wisteria vines, trained onto an arbor, shade this outdoor dining area in San Leandro, California, on warm summer afternoons. *Pittosporum tenuifolium* 'Silver Sheen' grows at right. **DESIGN:** Patricia Wagner Garden Design.

Poolside arbor *(left)* Four 'Thompson Seedless' grapevines, one at each corner of an arbor (12 feet wide, 8 feet deep, and 8 feet tall), shade this poolside patio in Southern California.

Window shade *(opposite page)* Wisteria shades a window of this New Mexico home during the heat of summer, then sheds its leaves in winter when sun is more welcome. A white form of Jupiter's beard *(Centranthus ruber)* flourishes under its protection. **DESIGN:** Donna Bone, Design with Nature.

Privacy

THE GROWING POPULATION that crowds today's cities and housing developments can make us feel like overexposed goldfish every time we walk into our yard. Fortunately, you can solve most privacy problems through creative landscaping. A well-positioned hedge, fence, or leafy screen can shield your house from the street or from neighbors. A tree or arbor can block the view of your property from a hillside above. Walls and berms, carefully placed, create privacy as well, especially in the front yard.

IDENTIFY INTRUSIONS. Before you can create privacy, determine exactly what you want to block out or be shielded from. As you walk around your property, identify areas that require covers or screens. Also try to evaluate how plantings and additional structures will affect your neighbors, the patterns of sun and shade in your garden, and any views you want to preserve.

KEEP IT DOWN. What can you do to foster quiet in the garden? Plants alone won't deflect noise generated by street traffic or neighbors, although layers of them can help. It takes a solid barrier—a fence or even a thick wall. But keep security concerns in mind. If barriers create shadows near entrances, for example, install outdoor lights for night visibility. The soothing burble of falling water is effective in masking nearby noise. It doesn't so much drown out other sounds as focus attention on a gentler one.

Arrivals lounge *(left)* Nonfruiting olive trees grow along the perimeter of this front patio in Venice, California, providing privacy while letting light through. The slab of raw steel behind the firepit blocks the view of the patio from the street. **DESIGN:** Callas Shortridge Architects.

"You want a garden to unfold in pieces and chapters, and a wall prevents it from being one long haul."

—ROB STEINER, *landscape architect*

Privacy screen *(left)* This rusted wall, which backs a stone bench near the side boundary of a front yard in Portland enhances privacy from the garden next door. **DESIGN:** Rebecca Sams and Buell Steelman, Mosaic Gardens.

Windows and walls *(below)* Freestanding walls create a sense of enclosure for a dining area in this Pacific Palisades, California, garden. The pale yellow is also a great backdrop for red-orange aloe blooms, and the "window" allows visitors in the seating area a peek of the garden beyond. **DESIGN:** Rob Steiner Gardens.

GOOD NEIGHBOR GARDENING

KNOW YOUR BOUNDARIES. Before you begin any landscaping along shared property lines, find out exactly where the boundaries of your property are, so you don't build or plant on your neighbors' land. Also check local ordinances, restrictions, and easements that could affect your plans. Many communities have guidelines that protect solar access or beautiful views.

INVOLVE NEIGHBORS. Any fences or plantings on the property line belong to you and your neighbor as tenants-in-common. So before you begin, talk to your neighbor about what you'd like to do, how it will look, and how it will be maintained. If you can't agree, you may need to install your fence or screen just inside the boundary of your property.

PRUNE CAREFULLY. Under certain circumstances, you can prune branches and roots that extend into your property from a neighbor's tree, but only up to the boundary. You may not trespass on your neighbor's property to prune a tree. If the construction or pruning you do affects the health or shape of your neighbors' plants, you may be liable for damages.

USE COMMON SENSE. When planting, use common sense near property lines. Don't plant trees or shrubs that will eventually outgrow their space or extend too far into neighbors' yards or rob them of sunlight. Avoid planting species that drop a lot of debris.

FRAMED WITH FOLIAGE (ABOVE). Trellis-trained wisteria, set well away from the property line, helps give privacy to this dining patio. Mrs. Robb's bonnet *(Euphorbia amygdaloides robbiae)* grows below. DESIGN: Andrea Cochran Landscape Architecture.

Living wall *(above)* In this front-yard seating area in Pacific Palisades, California, a large hedge of coast-loving *Metrosideros* offers privacy on the left. A second hedge, just getting started on the right, will soon offer screening from the street. **DESIGN:** Rob Steiner Gardens.

Green backdrop *(right)* A low hedge with trees for screening provides privacy behind deck chairs on a narrow gravel strip.

TREES AND SHRUBS FOR SCREENING

If you're opting for fast-growing trees and shrubs to solve a privacy problem, avoid crowding them. They may quickly outgrow the space. Some favorite choices for hedges include clumping bamboo, hopbush *(Dodonaea viscosa)*, and *Pittosporum tenuifolium*; all grow upright and relatively narrow. Here are other choices for privacy hedges and screens.

SHRUBS. Choose among strawberry tree *(Arbutus unedo)*; bottlebrush *(Callistemon)*; pineapple guava *(Feijoa sellowiana)*; toyon *(Heteromeles arbutifolia)*; juniper (upright forms), privet *(Ligustrum)*; and *Osmanthus*.

TREES. Try citrus, Italian cypress *(Cupressus sempervirens)*; tea tree *(Leptospermum)*; fern pine *(Podocarpus gracilior)*; or yew *(Taxus)*.

TALL SCREEN (ABOVE). Established redwoods against the back fence create privacy in this Pleasant Hill, California, garden, while clumping bamboo screens the fence at left. Choose lower-growing conifers for small gardens. DESIGN: Huettl Landscape Architecture.

Fire

BONE-DRY AIR. Drought-stressed vegetation. Add a spark and you have the potential for wildfires in many parts of the West. Compounding the problem, in recent years, fire seasons seem to be arriving earlier than August or September when hot, parching winds typically kick up (the devastating 2013 Camarillo, California, fire, for instance, raged in midspring). Even seasoned firefighters are unnerved. "We've always had large fires," says Del Walters, director of the California Department of Forestry and Fire Protection (aka CalFire), "but not to the degree we've seen in the last few years."

One reason may be climate change. On average, the West—like the rest of the country—is getting warmer. That, says Rick Ochoa of the National Interagency Fire Center in Boise, Idaho, brings a change in the West's fire seasons: "They start earlier and go later. And they're more severe."

On the opposite page are other factors that create the most dangerous fire seasons.

The best protection *(above)* Roofs made of fire-resistant materials, which California now requires for all new houses built in Fire Hazard Severity Zones, help the homes such as these, in Thousand Oaks, California, to survive. The right landscaping also helps keep fires at bay.

RAINFALL. Heavy winter rains encourage abundant grass growth, which increases the hazard of grass fires later in the summer.

DROUGHT. Low rainfall increases the amount of dry, dead foliage, especially if drought occurs over consecutive years.

FREEZE. In open spaces, killing freezes turn plants into crackling-dry fuel.

WIND. Hot, dry winds like California's Sundowners and Santa Anas start in the interior and blow out to the coast, fanning small fires in coastal sage and chaparral.

LIGHTNING. Warm air that cools as it rises into the western mountain ranges creates thunderstorms. As lightning strikes at higher elevations, it can spark fires.

FUEL LOADING. Coastal sage becomes tinder 7 to 10 years after a burn (chaparral 15 to 20 years after a burn). Unless this dry growth is trimmed or burned, it builds up, creating conditions that favor more damaging fires. Ponderosa pine and mixed-conifer forests are vulnerable to catastrophic crown fires due to fuel loading.

POPULATION GROWTH. In the rush for development, some fast-growing communities ignore fire threats, packing new homes among the West's forests and grasslands. More thoughtfully designed, fire-safe subdivisions reduce fire hazards by providing buffers between wildland and houses.

Ironically, the most wildfire-prone areas in the West possess some of the very same characteristics that define the "good life" in this part of the country. As new homes get built on hillsides, surrounded by thick stands of trees and brushy open spaces, or are packed close together in canyons, firefighters can have trouble reaching properties on narrow, curvy, tree-lined roads or on dead-end streets with bridges that can't support fire engines.

How should you protect your home and garden from future threats? As has been seen in recent fires, a good start is to install the right landscaping in the first place.

Water-wise plants *(below)* The plants pictured here, in a Los Angeles front yard, hold moisture in their leaves, which can slow or even stop a fire. They include agaves, tree aloes, and blue *Senecio mandraliscae*. Blue *Dymondia margaretae* grows in the foreground. **DESIGN:** Michael Schneider, Orange Street Studio.

A Fire-Retardant House and Garden

Your house doesn't have to sit in a forest to be vulnerable to wildfire. Windblown embers can fly up to a mile in front of a fire. And if they land on a dried-out juniper in your front yard, you could be in big trouble. That's why, if you live in a fire-prone part of the West, the first thing to do is to create a fire-resistant space around your house.

Think of the first 30 feet from your house as the defensible space. Areas closest to your house (to 5 feet out) should emphasize hardscaping such as paths and patios, along with well-watered plants such as lawn grass and groundcovers. Trees and shrubs should be at least 15 feet from the house. Keep plants in this area well watered and well maintained. From 30 to 100 feet out, plant low-growing fire-resistant types, with trees spaced at least 10 feet apart. Trim them so flames can't spread from one to the next. Selectively thin native vegetation.

Finally, thin, prune, mow, and rake your property regularly so it stays fire-resistant. Avoid highly flammable plants such as California buckwheat *(Eriogonum fasciculatum)*, California sagebrush *(Artemisia californica)*, toyon *(Heteromeles arbutifolia)*, juniper, pines, and rosemary; these plants contain high levels of oil or resin, have foliage with low moisture content, or tend to accumulate large amounts of dead foliage over time.

Defensible landscape *(above)* A watered greenbelt close to the house and a swimming pool that can serve as a reservoir helped firefighters save a rural home near San Diego, California, from a wildfire that scorched the land and native vegetation around it.

Fire-Smart Features

Below are other elements that can help a garden and house survive a wildfire.

HOUSE

SIDING. Nonflammable material such as stucco is preferred. Avoid wooden siding.

EAVES AND VENTS. Eliminate eaves or enclose them with stucco or other nonflammable material. Place vents at the outer edge of the soffit and cover them with ¼-inch wire mesh. If feasible, when fire approaches, block the vents with precut plywood panels.

ROOF. Use noncombustible materials such as tiles.

WINDOWS. Thermal-pane and safety glass are the most resistant to heat damage. If fire threatens, cover the glass outside with shutters, fire curtains, or plywood panels.

GARDEN

A NONFLAMMABLE DECK. Brick, tile, or concrete decking is safest. If you use wood, the recommended 1-hour fire ratings require overscaled decking—at least 1½-inch-thick tongue-and-groove boards over a solid substructure. Decks in wildland areas should be either enclosed with a nonflammable solid skirt—concrete block, gypsum board, stucco, or other exterior sheathing—or built with oversize timbers (6-by-6-inch posts and beams).

WALLS, FENCES, AND RAILINGS. Use nonflammable masonry or wrought iron—particularly adjoining the house. Make wooden arbors or trellises of 4-by-4 or larger lumber.

HOT TUB. A typical hot tub holds about 500 gallons—as much as a tank truck. If possible, make the water source drainable to an accessible hydrant or pumphouse.

PUMP. Have a well-maintained pump (gas, diesel, or propane) of at least 100-gpm capacity, with standard 1½-inch threaded standpipe. Keep a plastic or cotton-jacket fire hose (long enough to reach the far side of the house) and nozzle at hand.

HYDRANT. Near the street, you can install a standpipe for firefighters' use; check the size with your fire department. Make sure it's accessible. If possible, use a gravity feed from a pool.

ACCESS. Keep fire lanes (preferably on both sides of the house) clear enough for firefighters to bring in trucks and other equipment.

FIRE-RESISTANT PLANTS

Given the right conditions or aridity and heat, any plant will burn. But some, like the three pictured here, can slow a fire if they're watered and pruned regularly. For information on fire-resistant plants, go to local websites such as *firefree.org*.

CREEPING MAHONIA *(Mahonia repens)* This is one of the best groundcovers for fall color in mild to cool climates; the dull green leaves turn bronze and pink. Yellow flowers come in late spring. Sun to part shade.

MONKEY FLOWER *(Mimulus)* Many of these narrow-leafed perennials are well adapted to the dry West. Some have orange blooms; others yellow, scarlet, or bicolored. Full sun or part shade.

BEARBERRY *(Arctostaphylos uva-ursi)* These mat-forming groundcovers have small green leaves that turn red in winter, and white to pinkish spring blooms. Sun to light shade.

FIRE•SCAPING

THIS VERDANT GARDEN, which hugs a dry San Diego hillside, looks lush and inviting, but it has all the elements of a fire-wise garden. Trees are widely spaced and do not over-hang the house. Most of the plants, including those nearest the house, are fleshy leafed—blue chalk fingers *(Senecio vitalis)*, century plants *(Agave americana)*, tree aloes. Plants are widely spaced, and the ground is mulched with decomposed granite—not flammable fir bark mulch. Boulders and block walls also help slow the flames. And although the plants are drought tolerant, they still need occasional deep watering to keep them from drying out and becoming potential fuel. **DESIGN:** Todd Pitman, Verde Landscape Design.

Near the house *(top left)* Flanking the concrete steps leading to the patio are fleshy and dramatic plantings, including blue *Senecio mandraliscae*, black aeoniums, a tall tree aloe, and agaves. The floss silk tree *(Chorisia speciosa)* has a muscular trunk that's studded with water-storing prickles.

Farther out *(top right)* Succulents, including barrel cactus *(Echinocactus)*, ribbons of blue *Senecio mandraliscae*, and blue- and green-leafed forms of agave dot the hillside, among boulders arranged as if they'd just tumbled into place. A decomposed granite mulch covers the ground around them.

Poolside *(opposite page)* The swimming pool, a potential reservoir should a fire threaten, is surrounded with permeable paving and well-spaced succulents. Opuntias and agaves grow on the slope in the foreground.

Wind

STRONG WINDS CAN RAISE HAVOC in garden. Irrigation from sprinklers blows everywhere but on plants, foliage dries out, and trees grow irregularly, their limbs subject to breakage. Some parts of the West are regularly affected, such as Southern California by the Santa Anas and the Pacific Coast by onshore breezes and storm winds. If you live in one of the West's many windy areas, you can protect your garden and its plants with these temporary solutions.

STAKES AND TIES. Make sure plants are properly staked and tied, especially newly planted trees. Tie loosely, using flexible materials that don't cut into the trunk or branches.

TEMPORARY WINDBREAKS. When the ground is frozen, cold winter winds can dry out plants, even though the ground contains plenty of moisture. At other times, new plants may need wind protection to help them get established. You can redirect blowing snow or sand with snow fences. For temporary windbreaks, encircle plants with wire or plastic screens and fill in around them with straw. Or you can protect them with burlap, shadecloth, or lath supported on a sturdy frame.

MULCHES. To prevent excess drying of the soil around plants, mulch with organic matter and cover it with chicken wire, landscape fabric, or burlap, pegged at the corners to hold it down securely. Or place a layer of gravel, rocks, or moist soil over the mulch. If you soak the mulch thoroughly before a windy period, it is less likely to blow away.

WATERING. In windy areas, drip irrigation, soaker hoses, and bubbler sprinkler heads are more effective than overhead sprinklers. For lawns, use sprinklers that apply water in heavy streams close to the ground, and, if possible, wait until wind dies down to irrigate.

After a strong wind, irrigate trees and shrubs. Newly planted lawns may need sprinkling several times a day during extremely windy periods. Set container plants in a protected area; soak thoroughly and sprinkle overhead. To prevent moisture from evaporating too quickly from clay pots, set each one in a larger pot, or plunge single pots in the ground.

Sheltered *(top right)* This garden in Gig Harbor, Washington, is exposed to the winds of Puget Sound, but a little nook tucked into the hillside gives just enough shelter for a table and chairs. DESIGN: Scott Junge, Rosedale Gardens.

Buffered *(bottom right)* A sophisticated deck on San Francisco's Telegraph Hill includes an outward-angling deck set with a light-art piece that depicts a redwood forest. The solid structure redirects the wind but doesn't block the view. DESIGN: Hood Studio.

WIND-RESISTANT PLANTS Vibrant red-hot pokers *(Kniphofia)*, low-growing succulents, and Pride of Madeira *(Echium candicans)* stand up to the drying, some-times fog-driven winds off Richardson Bay in Tiburon, California. DESIGN: Shades of Green Landscape Architecture.

Planting in Windy Areas

When strong winds blow, garden plants can experience water stress, as moisture is pulled from foliage faster than roots can draw it from the soil. Really powerful winds can destroy many plants—defoliate or uproot them, or wrench off branches with such force that trunks may split.

Fortunately, if you live in the West's windiest spots, you can protect the plants you already have with careful pruning, windbreaks, and baffles. Choose new plants that can endure high winds without much damage, such as bougainvillea, cistus, olive, junipers, mesquite, madrone, palms, oleander, and rugosa roses. (For lists of wind-resistant plants and plants for seacoast gardens, turn to the *Sunset Western Garden Book*.)

When planting young trees, position the side with the most branches into the wind; when planting bare root trees, place the largest roots toward the wind to improve anchoring. Keep in mind that young trees growing in windy sites can be stunted by as much as 25 percent and usually grow lop-sided, with most of their branches and foliage pointed away from the wind. They need careful pruning to develop a strong structure and a pleasing shape. Consult a certified arborist for help.

LESSONS FROM THE ROCK

Rocky Alcatraz Island, in the heart of the San Francisco Bay, is forever buffeted by strong winds and cloaked with thick fog in summer. That's why Shelagh Fritz, caretaker of these gardens managed by the Garden Conservancy, has advice about best practices for gardening in wind. "Nothing delicate does well here," she explains.

CHOOSE THE RIGHT PLANTS. Among the 200 plants that survive at Alcatraz, the vast majority are from Mediterranean climates around the world. On the slope pictured above, these plants are visible: sturdy aeoniums, bright red *Chasmanthe*, purple Pride of Madeira *(Echium candicans)*, big-leafed bear's breeches *(Acanthus mollis)*, agave (you can see their stalks in bloom), and silver-leafed artichoke.

PLANT WINDBREAKS. In this photo, a New Zealand Christmas tree *(Metrosideros excelsa)*, shaped by the wind, provides shelter for the plants behind it.

WATER CONSISTENTLY. All of that wind dries out soil quickly, so regular irrigation, ideally on a drip system, will help keep moisture even.

Breezy but vivid *(left)* A vibrant bougainvillea tumbles over this cliff in Laguna Beach, California, where it blooms lustily despite sometimes vigorous ocean breezes.

TREES AND WIND: SEVEN DANGER SIGNS

Tall and spreading trees are highly susceptible to wind damage, which can be hazardous to people and property. Tree experts agree that most storm damage to trees is predictable. The following signs indicate trouble.

TOO DENSE A CROWN. A top-heavy canopy of foliage can act like a sail, catching wind and causing the tree to topple or limbs to break. Remove at least half the volume of leaves. (You should be able to see light through the tree canopy.)

DEAD OR WEAKENED WOOD. In winds, these branches often break. Prune them off if they are small and low enough to handle; otherwise, hire a professional.

IVY. Allowed to climb, ivy stems will girdle a tree trunk, interfering with the uptake of nutrients and water. Ivy foliage adds weight and harbors pests. Remove what you can, and keep it cut back.

TOO WIDE A CROTCH. An almost horizontal limb can break under wind, snow, or the weight of rainwater on foliage. Shorten or remove the limb if it isn't too large to handle, or have a professional install a cable.

TOO NARROW A CROTCH. A narrow crotch can split. If the limb isn't too large, prune it off; otherwise, call a professional to install cables.

TRUNK CAVITY. The bigger the cavity, the more it can weaken the tree. Carve out rotted wood and smooth the edges of the bark. If the cavity is collecting water or there are complications involving live wood, seek the advice of a tree professional; the cavity will need a drain or foam filling to keep it dry.

SHALLOW OR WEAK ROOT SYSTEM. A tree can blow over if the root system is weak. Thin foliage if necessary to allow wind to blow through the canopy. Water deeply and infrequently to encourage deep rooting.

Slopes

ROLLING HILLS AND RUGGED MOUNTAINS give the West its beauty and character, but they can also be the source of landscaping challenges. A slope that begins a few feet from the back of the house makes it difficult to find outdoor living space. The slope can also be hard to plant and maintain, and unless it is braced with a sturdy retaining wall, mud can slide down toward the house during rains.

The challenge is matching the landscaping to the slope of your property. There are generally three types—shallow, medium, and steep. For a shallow slope, you can build several terraces, linked by steps, to provide separate levels for a lawn, a play yard, and planting beds. For a medium slope, low retaining walls can create different levels, including a lawn area for easy mowing. Adding a deck is the simplest and least expensive way to provide a level space for a steep slope. Trees planted at deck height lessen the feeling of being perched high above the ground. Before construction on steep slopes, review your plans with a structural engineer.

Shades of blue *(above)* Terraced retaining walls, and the built-in bench on the lowest level, echo the hues of the pool. Blue agaves, trailing rosemary, and California lilac *(Ceanothus)* hold the slope while carrying the color theme through the seasons. **DESIGN:** Russ Cletta Design Studio.

Hill Taming

Building a deck, creating terraces, and planting groundcovers are a few ways that you can tame a slope. Choose fast-growing plants with dense, strong roots that help hold the soil, such as ornamental grasses, prostrate juniper and ceanothus, or low-growing manzanita *(Arctostaphylos)*. Arrange the plants in staggered rows. For steep slopes, install jute erosion-control netting. Unfurl the rolls on the slope across the grade, and secure them to the ground with U-shaped galvanized or plastic-coated pins (usually sold with the jute). Cut small, X-shaped holes in the jute for your plants.

Play slope *(right)* Adults can take the steps to the lower level in this San Francisco garden. But kids can use the smooth slide at right, then pull themselves back up the lawn at left, with help from a sturdy black rope. **DESIGN:** Blasen Landscape Architecture.

View slope *(below)* A well-designed series of concrete walls steps down to the pool level, with each terrace planted in a sweep of a single species. Blue and green grasses and dark-leafed New Zealand flax *(Phormium)* each take their turn. **DESIGN:** Shades of Green Landscape Architecture.

Modern art *(above)* This very steep backyard slope required a tall gray concrete retaining wall, which the designer turned stylish with a coat of mauve paint, framed succulent pictures, and a low fountain. **DESIGN:** Brent Green, GreenArt Landscape Design.

Terraces *(right)* Planted with turf grass, the terraces stair-step up the gentle slope from a cut-stone patio, alongside the steps. Kids love them. **DESIGN:** Martha Angus.

Gentle curves *(opposite page)* Wide stone steps are fitted gracefully to the contours of this moderate slope, and they double as casual seating areas. A lush lawn helps prevent erosion. **DESIGN:** Blasen Landscape Architecture.

Soilborne Diseases

DISEASES THAT LIVE IN THE SOIL are especially insidious: by the time the plant shows clear evidence of infection, the root system has been extensively damaged. Five such diseases—oak root fungus, *Phytophthora* and *Pythium* fungus, Texas root rot, and verticillium wilt—can be serious problems in various parts of the West. All of these diseases are encouraged by overwatering in poor-draining soil, especially during warm weather. Adding organic matter like compost can be helpful, as it ensures a diversity of beneficial microorganisms and can even inoculate the soil against some diseases. Avoid heavy doses of high-nitrogen fertilizers, which can make the problem worse, and try not to compact soils with heavy foot traffic, as this reduces oxygen availability. Instead, create pathways between planting areas. Mulch exposed soils with compost or use groundcovers. And try adding commercially available mycorrhizae, which can boost your soil's disease resistance.

While these soil-management techniques can help to some extent, in heavily infested areas your best approach is prevention: grow plants that have known resistance to each disease.

Oak Root Fungus

This fungus *(Armillaria mellea)* is a problem in low-elevation, nondesert California, particularly in housing developments created in former oak woodlands. The fungus lives on buried wood—mostly dead roots—from which it can infect nearby live roots of susceptible plants. Each new infection leads to a new reservoir of dead root tissue that perpetuates the fungus.

The fungus kills its host by gradually decaying the roots and moving into the main stem; the first symptoms aboveground may be dull or yellowed leaves or sparse foliage. Leaves may wilt and entire branches die; eventually, the plant dies. To identify oak root fungus, check the bark of the stem or trunk (or the large roots) at or below ground level; a mat of whitish fungus tissue just beneath the bark is the indicator. In late fall or early winter, clumps of tan mushrooms may appear around infected plants.

You can try to remove all woody tissue from the soil, but in neighborhoods infested with oak root fungus, it is far safer to choose plants that are resistant to the disease, such as the ones listed opposite.

Acer palmatum 'Bonfire'

Ginkgo biloba 'Fairmont'

'Fuyu' persimmon

Wisteria

Cotinus coggygria

Phlomis fruticosa

Brugmansia

PLANTS RESISTANT TO OAK ROOT FUNGUS

TREES

Abies concolor White fir
Acer macrophyllum Bigleaf maple
A. palmatum Japanese maple
Arbutus menziesii Madrone
Calocedrus decurrens Incense cedar
Catalpa
Celtis occidentalis Common hackberry
Crabapple
Cryptomeria japonica Japanese cryptomeria
× *Cupressocyparis leylandii* Leyland cypress
Elaeagnus angustifolia Russian olive
Eucalyptus cinerea Silver dollar tree
Geijera parviflora Australian willow
Ginkgo biloba Maidenhair tree
Gleditsia triacanthos Honey locust
Jacaranda mimosifolia Jacaranda
Koelreuteria paniculata Goldenrain tree
Liquidambar styraciflua American sweet gum
Magnolia grandiflora Southern magnolia
Maytenus boaria Mayten
Melaleuca styphelioides Prickly paperbark
Persimmon
Pinus canariensis Canary Island pine
Pistacia chinensis Chinese pistache
Pittosporum undulatum Victorian box
Quercus lobata Valley oak
Sequoia sempervirens Redwood
Ulmus parvifolia Chinese elm

VINE

Wisteria sinensis Chinese wisteria

SHRUBS

Brugmansia Angel's trumpet
Calycanthus occidentalis Spice bush
Cercis occidentalis Western redbud
Chaenomeles Flowering quince
Cotinus coggygria Smoke tree
Hibiscus syriacus Rose of Sharon
Mahonia
Nandina domestica Heavenly bamboo
Phlomis fruticosa Jerusalem sage
Pittosporum crassifolium Karo
P. eugenioides Lemonwood
P. tenuifolium Kohuhu
Prunus ilicifolia lyonii Catalina cherry
Vitex agnus-castus Chaste tree

Water Molds

Several *Phytophthora* and *Pythium* fungus are common in the West, but all thrive in poorly drained, overmoist soils. Collar, foot, root, and crown rots are some of the names their damage goes by, but "water mold root rots" best describes the way these organisms work. Telltale signs include stunting, yellowing, wilting, and leaf drop; in time, the plant succumbs.

If your garden has poorly drained "heavy" soil, steer clear of plants that require well-drained soil, good aeration, or infrequent but deep watering. These are the plants that are most susceptible to water mold organisms. Azaleas and rhododendrons are classic examples, as are California natives ceanothus and flannel bush *(Fremontodendron)*. You can build raised beds for such plants, but the simplest solution in heavy soil is to grow plants with no special drainage requirements.

Texas Root Rot

You find this soilborne disease *(Phymatotrichum omnivorum)* in the semiarid and arid Southwest at elevations below 3,500 feet—from California's Imperial and Coachella Valleys through Arizona and New Mexico and eastward. This fungus destroys the outer portions of roots, cutting off water to the plant. The first sign of trouble is a sudden wilting of leaves in summer, with the leaves remaining attached to the stems. At this point, at least half the root system has already been damaged.

Texas root rot thrives during periods of high temperatures in highly alkaline soil that's deficient in organic matter; fortunately, you can combat the fungus by improving your soil. Control measures consist of reducing soil alkalinity (adding soil sulfur is one approach) and incorporating rapidly decomposing organic matter. As with other soilborne diseases, though, the best way to avoid the problem is to grow resistant plants such as the ones listed here.

PLANTS RESISTANT TO TEXAS ROOT ROT

Parkinsonia

Nerium oleander 'Rehte Pink'

Fouquieria splendens

Agave 'Blue Flame'

TREES

Acacia farnesiana Sweet acacia
Celtis pallida Desert hackberry
Chilopsis linearis Desert willow
Citrus (on sour orange rootstock)
Eucalyptus
Lagerstroemia indica Crape myrtle
Parkinsonia Palo verde
Platanus Plane tree, sycamore
Prosopis Mesquite

SHRUBS AND VINES

Caragana arborescens Siberian peashrub
Dodonaea viscosa Hop bush
Juniperus Juniper
Larrea tridentata Creosote bush
Nerium oleander Oleander
Punica granatum Flowering pomegranate
Rosmarinus officinalis Rosemary

ACCENT PLANTS

Agave*
Bamboo
Cactus
Fouquieria splendens Ocotillo
Palms
Strelitzia reginae Bird of paradise*

*Plants immune to the disease

Verticillium Wilt

Verticillium species cause widespread damage in the West, especially in California. The fungus invades and plugs the water-conducting tissues in the roots and stems. The first symptom often is a wilting of one side of a plant. Leaves yellow, starting first at their margins and progressing inward, and then turn brown and die—usually upward or outward from the base of the plant or branch. Fungal development is favored by cool, moist soil, but foliage wilting often doesn't occur until warm, sunny days. The fungus persists in the soil, even in the absence of susceptible plants. There is no cure for infected plants; prune out dead branches, and dig up and destroy infected crops. Where the fungus is present, soil solarization may be an effective control, especially for vegetable beds. (Tomatoes are notoriously susceptible; resistant kinds are identified by a "V" next to the plant's name.) But the best solution in heavily infected areas is to grow only resistant plants such as those listed here.

PLANTS RESISTANT TO VERTICILLIUM WILT

Ceanothus 'Dark Star'

Cistus purpureus

Helleborus 'Party Dress'

Viola cornuta 'Skippy XL Plum-Gold'

TREES

Betula Birch
Citrus
Cornus Dogwood
Crataegus Hawthorn
Ficus carica Edible fig
Gleditsia triacanthos Honey locust
Liquidambar styraciflua American sweet gum
Malus Flowering crabapple
Pinus Pine
Platanus Plane tree, sycamore
Pyrus Ornamental pear
Sorbus aucuparia European mountain ash
Tilia Linden

SHRUBS

Arctostaphylos Manzanita
Buxus Boxwood
Ceanothus California wild lilac
Cistus Rockrose
Hebe
Lantana
Pyracantha Firethorn

PERENNIALS AND BULBS

Anemone Windflower
Aquilegia Columbine
Begonia (semperflorens) Wax begonia
Gaillardia × grandiflora
Helleborus Hellebore
Heuchera Coral bells
Mimulus Monkey flower
Penstemon Beard tongue
Primula Primrose
Viola Violet

Pets

A WELL-PLANNED LANDSCAPE can provide both a safe, comfortable environment for various domesticated animals—and an attractive space for plants and people. Dog owners often recommend planting in raised beds or on mounds, and starting with 1-gallon or larger plants.

Dogs

If you plant landscaped areas densely, dogs will stay out. But remember that owning a dog means giving up perfection and learning forgiveness. Here are a few canine needs.

EXERCISE AREA. Paths give dogs a designated space as well as a venue to perform their perceived job—patrolling your property line and keeping out intruders. If your dogs have already created their own paths through your garden, turn their well-worn routes into proper pathways. If you have an escape artist that needs to be kept from tunneling under the fence, consider installing an underground barrier made of rebar, chicken wire, or poured concrete.

SHELTER. Dogs enjoy basking in the sun, but they can overheat easily, so it's important to give them cooling retreats. They'll happily share arbors, pergolas, and other shade structures with their owners, but most dogs also appreciate a shelter of their own, such as a doghouse.

COMFORT STATION. Set aside a corner of your property, and train your dog to eliminate there and nowhere else. Cover the designated area with material the dog will accept and you can easily clean, such as wood chips or mulch. Avoid mulch made from cocoa shells: dogs like the taste, but cocoa is quite toxic to them.

DOG BASICS

To keep Fido happy and healthy: Add a view window in the gate. Grow romp-proof shrubs and perennials. Keep compost piles off limits. Avoid plants with thorns or sharp spines, which can cause eye injuries, and keep weeds picked—especially foxtails, which can get into ears and paws. Dig out and dispose of any mushrooms that appear. Avoid planting *Amaryllis belladonna*, castor bean, foxglove, and other toxic plants; keep rhubarb (foliage) and tomato (immature fruits and foliage) off limits. Find more at *aspca.org/toxicplants*.

Dig preventer *(above)* To keep pooches from digging holes under the fence in order to explore the world beyond, add a river of stones along the fence's base.

Add water *(left)* Make sure your dog has easy access to fresh water. Keep the dish in a shady location, and change the water often. Automatic pet fountains are another option: a motion sensor turns on the fountain when the pooch approaches.

Dog run *(opposite page)* Dogs need fun too. Keep your pooch entertained with a dog run/play structure like this steel "tunnel" with a mulch floor and low stone wall. It also serves as a shady retreat during hot weather. **DESIGN:** Randy Thueme Design.

For creating a dog-friendly garden, see sunset.com/dogfriendly

"A *catio* (enclosed cat patio) lets your feline experience the outdoors without disturbing your garden's wildlife."
—NICHOLE BOUDREAU, *Humane Society Silicon Valley*

Cats

As adorable as cats are to their owners, they have a reputation as marauders that dig up seedlings in freshly tilled raised beds, use children's sandboxes as litter boxes, and chew the tips from lush, lance-shaped leaves. Or they can grow into predators that stalk and kill songbirds. What to do? Consider following the advice of veterinarians everywhere: Cats live longer and healthier lives indoors than they do outside. Restrict your cat's daytime sunbathing to a windowsill, or limit its treks into the garden to times when you're nearby.

If that's not possible, fence off a part of the patio or garden for a "catio," with a small patch of sod lawn for rolling on, a pot of kittygrass for chewing, and a rug-covered perch or other shelving for sunbathing. That way, Fluffy can stay safe and out of trouble, yet enjoy the garden's stimulating sights, sounds, and smells. Here are other measures.

- Cover a sandbox that is not being used, or top it with a small portable deck that can be easily removed.
- Put row covers over newly planted seedlings, or cover the soil around them with mulch such as ground bark or straw. Or plant thickly to deter access to loamy soil.
- Hang bird feeders from house eaves or mount them atop poles to keep them well out of the cat's reach. Raise birdbaths, too, and place them near dense foliage plants so birds have a quick escape to safety—but not so close that a cat could hide there waiting to pounce.

FELINE BASICS

To keep kitty happy: Plant things that many felines love to play in, such as catmint and catnip. Even a small pot can do the trick. Put a low, water-filled bowl on the patio for easy sipping; hose it out daily to keep water clean. Plant a 6- or 8-inch pot of organic "wheatgrass," the kind sold at markets as kittygrass, nearby, and set it on the patio where your cat can munch the fresh stems. Avoid setting out toxic plants in readily accessible areas, especially grasslike kinds such as daylilies and narcissus, which can be attractive to cats. Visit *aspca.org/toxicplants* for a list.

Plant distractions *(above)* To keep cats away from your prized flowers or crops, plant things they are sure to nibble or roll in, such as the pictured catmint *(Nepeta × faassenii)* or catnip *(N. cataria)*. Be aware that not all cats are attracted to such plants.

Protect plants *(left)* Wire mesh serves two purposes in this raised bed. It keeps cats from using the bed as a litter box, and it gives growing crops some additional support.

Plant thickly *(opposite page)* An area of open soil is an invitation for cats to make it their personal restroom. Here, a bed of closely spaced sage and other plants is better for exploring than for scratching in.

Chickens

As the backyard chicken craze spreads, Fidos all over the West have to share their yards with the ladies. Chickens, increasingly treated like cherished pets, are now relishing their own gardens where they can graze on chard, mustard, and other healthy greens; drink from rain-fed watering stations; flap around in shallow dust baths; and bed down for the night in stylish coops. In short, they're getting their very own "chicken-scapes."

Essentials include a secure coop, a fenced run next to the coop with chicken wire on the roof and on all sides to provide a refuge from predators, and—if your chickens free-range occasionally—nontoxic plants to munch on or hide beneath. Extras might include an eco- lawn mixed with forage plants. To mask the sound of the chattering flock, add bamboo or trees that rustle in the wind, or install a small burbling fountain. And to make use of the chicken droppings, keep a compost pile nearby, where you can add in straw, wood shavings, and grass clippings; turn the pile occasionally; and let it age into a nutrient-rich soil amendment.

CHICKEN BASICS

Is raising chickens right for you? Hens lay regularly for up to five years, but can live and lay sporadically for eight years or more. So before you dive in, consider the essentials listed below. For more details, refer to online sources such as *backyardchickens.com*.

CHECK LOCAL CODES. Many cities, but not all, allow homeowners to keep a few hens (not roosters). Before you buy hens, make sure your city allows them. Roosters are not necessary for the hens to lay eggs.

CONSIDER YOUR SPACE. Each chicken should have at least 10 square feet of yard to run around in, plus 4 square feet of secure henhouse. Chickens need a fenced yard too, free of any plants they shouldn't eat.

LOCATE A FEED STORE. This is a reliable source for purchasing female chicks (make sure an experienced chicken handler has confirmed they are female) and the feed and other supplies you'll need.

FIND A CHICKEN-FRIENDLY VET. Before you acquire your flock, determine where you would take an injured or sick chicken.

Grazing garden *(above)* Give free-ranging chickens their own veggies. They are particularly fond of chard, kale, and other greens.

Chicken condo *(left)* Stylish and functional, this modern coop—with a gabled roof, ventilated walls, four nesting boxes, hinged side panels, and predator-resistant latches—was delivered ready to assemble from *themoop.com*.

Protected run *(opposite page)* A simple, colorful coop provides chickens with indoor and open-air zones, and it's easily moved to allow grazing (and fertilizing) in different areas of the garden.

Welcoming Wildlife

BIRDS, BUTTERFLIES, BEES, ladybugs, dragonflies, and other beneficial insects bring beauty and motion to the garden, besides keeping many pests at bay. By choosing plants they favor, you can greatly enhance your garden's attractiveness to these flying friends.

Butterflies and hummingbirds feed on nectar. Fortunately, suitable plants include many popular garden ornamentals such as beard tongue *(Penstemon)*, columbine *(Aquilegia)*, and delphinium. A number of these favorite plants feature flowers in red or blue, so a nectar-rich garden is sure to be colorful. For an extensive list of hummingbird- and butterfly-attracting plants, as well as plants that support beneficial insects, see the *Sunset Western Garden Book*.

Here are other ways to make your garden a welcome refuge for these colorful visitors.

- Avoid using pesticides of any kind.
- Provide a shallow container of water, with pebbles on which butterflies can perch while drinking.
- Create a sunny spot sheltered from strong winds.
- Grow native plants, which have evolved along with native hummingbirds and butterflies.
- Set up a hummingbird feeder.

Birds help control insect pests. Mockingbirds—world champion songsters—can catch grasshoppers in midair, towhees scratch around in dead leaves for sowbugs and earwigs, and house finches relish aphids.

ATTRACTING BIRDS

Birds (other than hummingbirds) separate into seed eaters and fruit eaters. Seed-eating birds usually find a variety of seeds to consume, but you can almost guarantee their presence if you grow plants they especially like—and allow them to go to seed near the end of flowering. For growers of stone fruits (peaches and cherries, for example) and pome fruits (apples and pears), certain fruit-eating birds are a yearly nemesis, zeroing in on ripening fruits. The only way to prevent damage is to cover the tree with bird netting or enclose individual fruits in mesh bags. But in most gardens, these fruit eaters merely provide entertainment if you have ornamental fruiting plants sure to please them. For a comprehensive list of the best plants for attracting birds, see the *Sunset Western Garden Book.*

Streamside haven *(above)* This natural-looking stream in Wyoming, dotted with flat-topped boulders and flanked with aspen trees, is guaranteed to attract butterflies, hummingbirds, dragonflies, and other winged visitors. The water is filtered and recirculated by a concealed pump system, and the stone-lined edges are planted with a variety of locally native species. DESIGN: Carney Logan Burke Architects.

Hummingbird magnets *(opposite page)* Plant Western natives to attract hummingbirds to your garden. Here, a Columbia lily *(Lilium columbium)* hosts an Anna's Hummingbird. Leopard lily *(Lilium pardalinum)* and Humboldt lily *(L. humboldtii)* also have curving orange petals with red spots.

The Benefits of Bees

Before a flower can set seed or form fruit, it needs to be pollinated. Though some plants are pollinated by bats, birds, butterflies, moths, and wasps, most of the work is done by bees. Unlike wasps, hornets, and yellow jackets, bees are gentle creatures that seldom sting unless handled or provoked. Ambitious gardeners may wish to set up backyard hives for European honeybees and collect their honey and wax, but for those who would simply like to promote a bee-friendly environment in their landscape, here are a few tips.

PROVIDE FOOD. Grow plants that bear flowers with plenty of nectar and pollen. Old-fashioned, heirloom-type flowers like bee balm, black-eyed Susan, cleome, sunflower, and zinnia are excellent choices; they have more pollen and nectar than highly developed hybrids. Lavender, rosemary, thyme, and many other herbs have blossoms that bees favor; see the *Sunset Western Garden Book* for a more complete list. Aim to have something in bloom from early spring to late fall.

FURNISH HOUSING. One of the biggest challenges native bees face is finding suitable nesting sites. The majority of our approximately 4,000 species of native bees are solitary—essentially, single mothers raising their young alone. About 70 percent of native bees are ground nesters. A small patch of soft, bare earth in a sunny spot—as little as 1 square foot—is all they need. The remainder are mostly wood nesters. They occupy holes in trees bored by beetles, or they move into nesting blocks (basically, a box with a grid of small holes in front). You can build or buy bee nesting houses to provide shelter for native bees that prefer to nest in narrow cavities (*gardenerssupply.com* is one source). Hang them against south-facing walls protected from wind.

AVOID PESTICIDES. Nonselective pesticides don't just kill insect pests—they kill bees too. But even if you don't use them at home, keep in mind that plants sold at garden centers may have been pretreated with certain pesticides that have been shown to harm or kill bees. Before you buy the plants, ask whether they have been organically grown.

For creating a bee-friendly garden, see sunset.com/nestingblock

LURING BENEFICIALS

They may not be as beautiful as butterflies, but lacewings, ladybird beetles, assassin bugs, and other beneficial insects can go a long way toward keeping your garden free of insect pests. Attract them with common, easy-to-grow plants like dill, fennel, sage, and yarrow.

Bee bar *(above)* Blue mist *(Caryopteris × clandonensis)* is just one of the scores of mint family members that bees find irresistible. It blooms from midsummer to frost, guaranteeing a long season of bee bounty.

Landing pad *(left)* Bees especially like flat-topped flowers or bloom clusters, like this *Sedum* 'Autumn Joy', where they gather to sip nectar and collect pollen. Purple coneflower and yarrow *(Achillea millifolium)* are other good choices.

Bee border *(opposite page)* At the Melissa Garden, a sanctuary for honeybees, native bees, and other pollinators in Healdsburg, California, the extensive gardens—filled with lavender, oregano, cosmos, sedum, and calamint, among many other attractors—are designed to offer nectar and pollen practically year-round. DESIGN: Kate Frey Sustainable and Organic Gardens.

For a planting plan for butterflies and bees, see sunset.com/pollinators

NATURE·SCAPING

FOOD, SHELTER, WATER: Provide these in your garden, and birds and butterflies will come. The garden pictured above has everything that birds need: trees and shrubs for shelter and wind protection; food plants to supply nectar, seeds, and berries; and a shallow pond for drinking and bathing. For butterflies, there are warm rocks for basking, nectar-rich blooms to feed from, even a few food crops to nourish butterfly caterpillars.

If you don't have room for a pond, tuck shallow (1 to 3 inches at the deepest point) birdbaths among greenery around your garden. Also, hang bird feeders, and put out a few birdhouses. Let some duff build up around bushes where possible, and leave small brush piles in out-of-the-way places for nesting. Or—better yet—plant a big robust rose such as 'Cl. Cécile Brünner' over a sturdy arbor, where smaller birds can find shelter.

Habitat *(above)* This garden has everything wild creatures find inviting: water for sipping and bathing, grasses for seed, flowers for nectar, and tall trees for cover.

WILDLIFE PESTS

Many Western gardeners share their land with wild creatures, but whether you consider them pests depends on what you grow. Raccoons are nocturnal bandits that raid koi ponds, dig holes in lawns as they search for grubs, and dine on your ripe fruits and vegetables. Deer eat many plants, but especially love roses and vegetables. Squirrels dig in lawns and garden beds to bury acorns and other nuts. And rabbits are fond of lush greens. Protect low-growing crops with cloches or wire-mesh cages. In deer country, enclose vegetable gardens with fences at least 6 feet tall.

Garden visitors *(clockwise from top left)* A **monarch butterfly** alights atop a zinnia. A **house finch** feeds its fledgling. These birds often nest under house eaves; cracked corn, millet, sunflower seeds, and thistles are favorite foods. A **Western meadowhawk dragonfly** hunts from a branch, scanning for flies, mosquitoes, and termites. Adults live in ponds among submerged vegetation. An **Anna's hummingbird** sits in her nest, woven of plant fibers and spiderwebs. A male **Western tanager** pauses before moving on through the conifer tops. These birds are most common in intermountain areas.

Diversity is key in a backyard habitat, since different species have different needs.

CREDITS

PHOTOGRAPHY

(B = bottom, C = center, L = left, M = middle, R = right, T = top)

Andrea M. Gómez: 338–339; **Andri Beauchamp Photography:** 249 BR; **William Aplin:** 6 TL; **Debra Lee Baldwin:** 268; **Laurence Bartone:** 168 B; **George Bennett:** 7 R; **Ben Bloom/Getty Images:** 249 TR; **Barbara Boissevain:** 314; **Bruce Botnick:** 101T; **Aya Brackett:** 292 T, back cover TR; **Marion Brenner:** front cover main (Bernard Trainor + Associates), 2–3 (Pamela Burton & Co. Landscape Architecture), 8–9, 42 (both), 43, 59 B, 66 –67 (all), 70, 71 T, 71 BL, 92–93 (all), 100, 101 B, 102–103, 103 T, 111 TR, 117 TR, 117 B, 119 BR, 122 (both), 125 B, 127 TR, 127 B, 128 B, 141 B, 144–145, 148 B, 151 TR, 151 BR, 153 TL, 153 TR, 157 T, 163 TL, 163 B, 165 B, 168 T, 171 BL, 188 TR, 189 T, 191 B, 193 TR, 193 B, 200 T, 201 T, 203, 205 B, 212–213, 215, 221 B, 224, 225 TL, 225 B, 227 B, 232 B (Tommy Church Design), 237 T, 239 B (design: Nancy Heckler), 240, 241 TL (design: Nancy Heckler), 241 TR, 244 T, 245 TR (design: Nancy Heckler), 246, 247 T (design: Nancy Heckler), 247 BR (design: Nancy Heckler), 248–249, 250 B, 252 B, 253 B, 262, 263 TR, 263 B, 264 TL, 264–265, 266 BR, 270, 272, 283 T, 284 BR, 291 TR, 292 BR, 309 TL, 319 T, 320–321, 322, 327 (both), 329, 331 B, 341 TR, 341 B, 343 B, 367, 369 TR, 373, 382 B, 384 R, 387 T, 388, 402, 403, back cover BL; **Rob D. Brodman:** 143 TL, 310, 393 BL; **Nicola Browne/GAP Photos:** 140; **Jennifer Cheung:** 32–33 (all), 44–45 (all), 46–47 (all), 48, 49, 50–51 (all), 72–73 (all), 74–75 (all), 86–87 (all), 88, 89, 90–91 (both), 107, 125 T, 151 BL, 154–155, 171 T, 172 B, 194 B, 266 BL, 269 TL, 269 TR, 277 #5, 282 TL (GreenArt Landscape Design), 292 BL, 299 T, 303 B, 309 TR, 346–347, 375, 380–381 (all), 389 T, 391, 399 T; **Russ Cletta:** 386; **Corbis:** 376; **Jack Coyier:** 146; **Grey Crawford:** 210; **Stacie Crooks, Crooks Garden Design:** 40–41 (all), 234 T, 343 T; **Michael Kevin Daly/Fall Creek Farm & Nursery:** 247 BL; **Bruce Damonte:** 389 B; **Darcy Daniels:** 106, 254 L, 295 B; **David De Lossy/Photodisc/Getty Images:** 396; **Eliza Deacon/Getty Images:** 395 B; **Ricardo DeAratanha/*Los Angeles Times*:** 14–15; **Topher Delaney/SEAM Studio:** 223 TR; **Brooke Dietrich, Green...Landscapes to Envy:** 344–345 (all); **Terry Donnelly (hanaleisurfboardhouse.com):** 284 BL; **Douglas Hill Photography:** 305 TR; **Ecocentrix Landscape Architecture:** 132 B; **Education Images/UIG/Getty Images:** 397 TL; **John Ellis:** 10–11 (all), 24–25 (all), 60–61 (both), 298, 339 B; **Ron Evans/Getty Images:** 71 BR; **Fawn Art Photography:** 228 BL; **Richard Felber:** 340; **Richard Felber/Getty Images:** 364; **David Fenton:** 103 B, 183 TL, 302, 303 TR (design: Aaron Jones), 305 TL, 306, 311 TL (design: Aaron Jones); **Ashley Elizabeth Ford:** 68–69 (all); **Tom Fowlks/The Image Bank/Getty Images:** 352 T; **Tria Giovan:** 311 B; **Lane Goodkind:** 188 B; **Thom Gourley/Flatbread Images/Alamy:** 277 #7; **John Granen:** 20–21 (all), 22–23 (all), 82–83 (all), 177 (both), 250 TR, 356 (both), 385; **Art Gray:** 5 T, 26–27, 28–29 (all), 105 T, 119 T, 147 TL, 154, 180, 181 B, 183 TR, 185 B, 296, 297 B, 370–371; **Simon Griffiths/ACP/trunkarchive.com:** 145 TR; **Tara Guertin:** 159 T; **Bret Gum:** front cover bottom #1, 1 (design: Joe Stead), 36–37, 38–39 (all), 52–53 (all), 178 T, 223 B, 287 BR, 323 BR, spine; **Steven A. Gunther:** 105 B, 109 T, 119 BL, 126 B, 132 T, 136 B, 137, 153 B, 159 B, 161, 163 TR, 165 T, 191 T, 206–207, 211 TR, 211 B, 214–215 (design: Mia Lehrer), 256, 258 BR, 269 B, 273 BR, 275 (both), 285, 305 B, 330, 342, 350, 359, 362–363 (all), 369 B, 377, 392 TL; **Jerry Harpur/Harpur Garden Images:** 190, 316–317; **Ive Haugeland:** 383, 387 B; **Emily Heacock:** 148–149; **Jim Henkens:** 374 B; **Fred Hoffman (farmerfred.com):** 397 B; **Saxon Holt/PhotoBotanic:** 94–95 (all), 147 TR, 148 T, 202 B, 221 T, 227 TR, 235 T, 242 T, 242–243, 252 T, 271 B, 273 T (design: Al Kyte), 277 #1, 277 #6 (design: Tom Peace), 291 B, 368, 390 CL, 404, back cover M (Kelly Marshall Garden Design); **D. A. Horchner/Design Workshop:** 185 T, 228 BR, 276 (both); **Joseph Huettl, Huettl Landscape Architecture:** 184–185, 237 B; **Chloe Humphreys:** 334–335; **Elizabeth Jardina:** 403 TR; **Andrea Jones/Garden Exposures Photo Library:** 15 T, 15 B, 16–17 (all), 117 TL (Steve Martino Landscape Architect), 195, 217 TR, 219 #4, 227 TL, 254 BR, 326; **Lauren Hall Knight:** 127 TL; **Erin Kunkel:** 54–55 (all), 56–57 (all), 84–85 (all), 223 TL, back cover TL; **John Lee:** 399 B; **Holly Lepere:** 62–63 (all), 64–65 (all), 139 TL, 230–231; **Chris Leschinsky:** 30–31 (all), 98–99 (all), 110–111, 138, 170, 172 T, 188 TL, 189 B, 194 T, 196–197, 226, 251 #3, 251 #6, 336, 357, 407, back cover BR; **Jason Liske:** 6–7; **Janet Loughrey:** 176; **Richard Maack:** 156; **Maggie MacLaren:** 354 L; **David Madison/Getty Images:** 147 B; **Mitch Maher (mbmaher.com):** 104, 315 T, 341 TL; **Gerald Majumdar/Getty Images:** 254 TR; **Tyler Manchuck:** 323 BL; **Allan Mandell:** 395 TR; **Charles Mann:** 202 T, 225 TR, 233 T (design: Julia Berman), 328 TR; **Jennifer Martiné:** 143 TR; **Matthew Millman Photography:** 394; **Joshua McCullough, PhytoPhoto:** 126 T, 128 T, 143 CR, 150–151, 192, 205 T, 213 B (Oakwood Gardens), 232 T, 243, 244 B, 253 T, 264 B, 274 B, 280–281, 282–283, 286, 289 (both), 290, 293, 400; **Ginny Mellinger:** 346 TL; **Dana Miller:** 12–13 (all); **Karyn R. Millet:** 4 (interior designer: Bonesteel Trout Hall), 297 TL; **MMGI/Marianne Majerus:** 306–307; **Kimberley Navabpour:** 116, 143 BL, 219 #7, 277 #3; **Camille Nordgren:** 360–361 (all); **OGphoto/Getty Images:** 405 TL; **George Olson:** 352 B; **Jerry Pavia:** 228 T, 238–239, 277 #6, 392 TR; **David E. Perry:** 198 (Albers Vista Gardens), 200 B, 201 B, 213 T, 216 B, 217 TL (Albers Vista Gardens), 218, 233 B (Stacie Crooks, Crooks Garden Design), 234 B, 235 B, 236, 239 T, 403 TL; **Linda Lamb Peters:** 251 #5, 328 TL, 379 B, 390 TL, 390 TR, 390 BL, 393 TL, 393 TR, 393 BR; **Norm Plate:** 133, 134–135, 149 R (Susan Calhoun, Plantswoman Design), 157 B, 166 T, 183 B, 203 inset, 220, 259 B, 260 BR, 355, 365, 366, 372 T, 395 TL; **Jody Pritchard:** 312–313; **Proven Winners:** 219 #2, 251 #2; **Randy Thueme Design:** 241 B; **Trina Roberts:** 266 T; **Trina Roberts and Jon Barber:** 18–19 (all), 58, 299 B; **Lisa Romerein:** front cover bottom #2 (Russ Cletta Design Studio), 78–79 (all), 80–81, 120–121, 139 TR, 167, 181 TR, 208 B, 278–279, 331 TR, 353, 372 B, 374 T; **Andrea Gómez Romero:** 124, 193 TL, 207 TR, 222, 264 TR, 267; **Bill Ross:** 109 B; **Jeremy Samuelson:** 318 T; **Susan Seubert:** front cover bottom #5, 145 B; **Pete Starman/Getty Images:** 358 R; **Eric Staudenmaier:** 209; **Thomas J. Story:** front cover bottom #3, front cover bottom #4, 76–77 (both), 108, 111 BR, 112–113 (all), 118, 123, 136 T, 139 B, 142–143, 143 L, 143 CL, 143 BR, 152, 158, 164, 166 B, 169, 171 BR, 173, 174–175 (all), 179, 181 TL, 182, 207 B, 219 #5, 219 #6, 219 #8, 245 TL, 245 B, 251 #1, 258 TR, 263 TL, 274 T, 284 T, 288, 291 TL, 295 TR, 297 TR, 300–301, 303 TL, 304 (design: Aaron Jones), 307 R, 308 (lamp design: Aaron Jones), 309 B, 311 TR, 318–319, 323 T, 328 B, 331 TL, 332, 333, 337, 339 T, 348–349, 382 T, 384 L, 390 CR, 390 BR, 398; **Studio Shed:** 178 B; **Stefan Thuilot, Thuilot Associates:** 130–131, 160, 186; **E. Spencer Toy:** 229, 271 T, 392 BL, 405 BR; **Dominique Vorillon:** 5 B (Johnston Architects); **Roger Wade, courtesy Carney Logan Burke Architects:** 401 L; **Rachel Weill:** 59 T, 295 TL, 351; **Lee Anne White:** 354 R; **Bob Wigand:** 242 B, 277 #4, 287 L, 392 BR, 401 R, 405 L, 405 CL, 405 CR, 405 TR; **Michele Lee Willson:** 34–35 (all), 96–97 (all), 114–115, 141 T, 162, 187, 315 B; **William P. Wright:** 324–325; **Doreen L. Wynja:** 129, 199, 204, 208 T, 211 TL, 216 T, 217 B, 219 #1, 219 #3, 219 #9, 250 TL, 251 #4, 255, 257, 258 TL, 259 T, 260 T, 260 BL, 261, 265 R, 273 BL, 277 #2, 283 B, 287 TR, 294, 301, 358 L, 379 T, 379 C; **David Zaitz:** 378; **zorani/Getty Images:** 397 TR

SPECIAL THANKS

Arterra Landscape Architects, George Bennett, Marion Brenner, Russ Cletta, Stacie Crooks, Topher Delaney, Renée Del Gaudio, Brooke Dietrich, Lauren Dunec, Erika Ehmsen, John Ellis, Margie Grace, Ive Haugeland, Fonda Hitchcock, Joseph Huettl, In Harmony Sustainable Landscapes, Stephanie Johnson, Tracy Sunrize Johnson, Mitch Maher, Steve Martino, Eric and Leslie McKenna, Megan McCrea, Camille Nordgren, Marie Pence, Alan Phinney, Proven Winners, Shades of Green Landscape Architecture, Steven Shortridge, Jeffrey Gordon Smith, Studio Shed, Randy Thueme, Stefan Thuilot, E. Spencer Toy, Molly Wood

GET THE GLOW
Orange-flowered torch lily and a red cordyline catch the sunlight in this California garden. Low, mounding grasses, including *Carex flacca*, surround them. DESIGN: Ryan Fortini, Fortini Design Group.

"Good gardening touches the planet softly. Relaxed plantings are what the West has always been about."

—JOHN GREENLEE, *Greenlee & Associates*

GO EASY A carefree garden climbs this hillside in Tiburon, California, blending into native vegetation nearby. DESIGN: Arterra Landscape Architects.

INDEX

Page numbers in **boldface** indicate primary discussion of topic.

A

B

C

D

E

L

M, N

O, P

Q, R

S

T, U

V–Z

Savor a view *(opposite)* A raised pool and native plant garden faces Arizona's Camelback Mountain, bathed in evening light. **DESIGN:** Kristina Floor, Floor Associates.

At the end of the day, the garden outside your home is all yours—for play, serenity, or connecting with nature. Make it your own.

©2014 by Time Home Entertainment Inc.
135 West 50th Street, New York, NY 10020

All rights reserved. No part of this book may be reproduced in any form or by any means without the prior written permission of the publisher, excepting brief quotations in connection with reviews written specifically for inclusion in magazines or newspapers, or limited excerpts strictly for personal use.

ISBN-10: 0-376-03010-0
ISBN-13: 978-0-376-03010-8
Library of Congress Control Number: 2013939861
Third edition. First printing 2014.
Printed in the United States of America.

OXMOOR HOUSE
EDITORIAL DIRECTOR: Leah McLaughlin
VP, BRAND PUBLISHING: Laura Sappington
CREATIVE DIRECTOR: Felicity Keane
MANAGING EDITOR: Elizabeth Tyler Austin

TIME HOME ENTERTAINMENT INC.
PUBLISHER: Jim Childs
VP, BRAND & DIGITAL STRATEGY: Steven Sandonato
EXECUTIVE DIRECTOR, MARKETING SERVICES: Carol Pittard
EXECUTIVE DIRECTOR, RETAIL & SPECIAL SALES: Tom Mifsud
DIRECTOR, BOOKAZINE DEVELOPMENT & MARKETING: Laura Adam
EXECUTIVE PUBLISHING DIRECTOR: Joy Butts
PUBLISHING DIRECTOR: Megan Pearlman
FINANCE DIRECTOR: Glenn Buonocore
ASSOCIATE GENERAL COUNSEL: Helen Wan

SUNSET PUBLISHING
EDITOR-IN-CHIEF: Peggy Northrop
PUBLISHER: Brian Gruseke
VP, MARKETING & BRAND DEVELOPMENT: Shannon Thompson
CREATIVE DIRECTOR: Maili Holiman

WESTERN GARDEN BOOK OF LANDSCAPING
EDITOR: Kathleen Norris Brenzel
MANAGING EDITOR: Judith Dunham
ART DIRECTOR: Catherine Jacobes
WRITERS: Sharon Cohoon, Tom Wilhite
PRODUCTION MANAGER: Linda M. Bouchard
COPY EDITOR: Denise Griffiths
PHOTO EDITORS: Linda Lamb Peters, Stephanie Rubin
SENIOR IMAGING SPECIALIST: Kimberley Navabpour
PROOFREADER: Lesley Bruynesteyn
INDEXER: Mary Pelletier-Hunyadi
CONTRIBUTING WRITERS: Jim McCausland, Johanna Silver
PROJECT EDITOR: Lacie Pinyan

See page 406 for more acknowledgments.

To order additional publications, call 1-800-765-6400
For more books to enrich your life, visit **oxmoorhouse.com**
Visit Sunset online at **sunset.com**
For the most comprehensive selection of Sunset books, visit **sunsetbooks.com**
For more exciting home and garden ideas, visit **myhomeideas.com**